THE UNIVERSITY SERIES

Elements

of

General Philosophy

By GEORGE CROOM ROBERTSON

LATE GROTE PROFESSOR, UNIVERSITY COLLEGE, LONDON

*EDITED FROM NOTES OF LECTURES DELIVERED
AT THE COLLEGE, 1870-1892*

By C. A. FOLEY RHYS DAVIDS, M.A.

NEW YORK
CHARLES SCRIBNER'S SONS
1896

100
R649e

INTRODUCTORY NOTE

THAT I have been able to compile a second volume of lectures delivered by the late George Croom Robertson is again due, in the first place, to the kindness of Mr. Charles Robertson in placing at my disposal the MS. notes left by the professor, and, in the second place, to the ready help afforded me, through the loan of their note-books, by those students to whom I acknowledged my debt of gratitude in the *Elements of Psychology*, and to whom I here once more express my grateful obligation [1]. Once more, too, I wish to record my sense of the benefit derived from the corrections and suggestions made by Mr. Charles Robertson and

---

[1] I append the names of those who contributed materials that I was able to use for this manual:—George A. Aitken, Esq.; Rev. Martin Anstey, M.A.; Mrs. Archer Hind (Miss Laura Pocock); Mrs. Sophie Bryant, D.Sc.: Herman J. Cohen, Esq.; Professor W. Hall Griffin, B.A.; Rev. Isidore Harris, M.A.; H. Frank Heath, Esq., B.A., Ph.D.; Rev. Alfred Hills, B.A.; Principal J. Viriamu Jones, M.A, F.R.S. (University College S. Wales and Monmouthshire); J. Neville Keynes, Esq., M.A., LL.D.; Benjamin Leverson, Esq., B.A.; Rev. S. Levy, B.A.; J. W. Manning, Esq., M.A.; Miss Dorothy Marshall, B.Sc.; Andrew Ogilvie, Esq., B.A.; Miss Mary Robertson, M.A.; Ernest C. Robinson, Esq., M.A.; G. Armitage Smith, Esq., M.A.; President J. G. Schurman, M.A., D.Sc. (Cornell University); Rev. E. H. Titchmarsh, M.A.; H. J. Tozer, Esq., M.A.

Mr. Thomas Whittaker when going through the proofs. I am also indebted for kind advice and cordial help to Professor Knight.

Excepting the full draft of an Introductory Lecture on the History of Philosophy, which has been collated with students' note-books to form Lectures III–VI, the author's own materials have been wrought up almost wholly in Part II. For instance, in the concluding three lectures on Kant they practically superseded my having recourse to reports of college lectures. It so happened that, although the professor had more than once had occasion to give college lectures on this subject, only one set of notes on Kant had come into my hands.

The first seventeen lectures, presenting a definitely consecutive treatment—an outline-history of Western philosophy (I–VII) and a somewhat closer consideration of the three main problems of that philosophy (VIII–XVII)—constituted the annual elementary course on General Philosophy, or Epistemology, delivered in alternation with a course on Ethics during May and June. I do not mean that the number was always precisely seventeen; it was usually less. The historic outline had sometimes to be dropped or transferred to the special courses, while the consideration of particular problems was prolonged. I have combined both the one and the other in a slightly enlarged course. Finally, in the two lectures on Logic and Ethics, I have borrowed from the annual courses on those subjects, in order that the manual might be enriched by an outline, however brief, of the author's practical philosophy.

Introductory Note. ix

The special lectures are intended to form a course of somewhat more advanced reading, to succeed the study of Part I. They were delivered to an inner circle of students, small in number, candidates for the most part qualifying for the higher London University examinations, assembled during the years of the lecturer's declining health at a round table in his own house at Notting Hill. The special work or works under discussion lay open before each person. The professor's utterances took therefore the form rather of a running commentary, with here and there a more general disquisition, than of a lecture systematically developed. (This remark does not, of course, apply to the last three 'special' lectures.) Of these running commentaries I have given the substance in a more or less condensed form. Thus the lecture on Plato's epistemology is a condensation of a course of eight conversational discourses on the *Theaetetus*, *Timaeus*, and part of the *Republic* (delivered a few months before the professor's death). The lecture on Aristotle's Psychology is condensed from a like number; those on Descartes from fifteen. There were many such advanced courses given during Professor Robertson's long occupancy of the Grote chair. They would have been even more varied had it not been for the limits in the cycle of philosophical works prescribed by the University of London, to which the curriculum of University College adapts itself[1]. Limits of space made

---

[1] No post-Kantian work was prescribed during Robertson's professoriate for the examinations in history of philosophy with one exception—the *Metaphysic* of Lotze. At that time (1887-88) the professor was, alas! too ill to lecture.

it imperative that I should select, and the choice was determined less by the nature of my materials than by what seems to me to have been a salient standpoint in my master's critical philosophy. Holding by an enlightened Experientialism, he was repelled by the Individualism prevailing in experiential doctrine from Locke till the present century. Advance in biology has rendered in philosophy, as he says[1], for ever impossible the older Experientialist position, that knowledge, with its objectivity, its universality, its necessity, can be acquired by every individual for himself, in the course of his own experience, from the beginning. Close and sympathetic study of the great Rationalist thinkers, from Plato to Kant, enabled him to discern what they, burdened by faulty method and the then scanty store of the fruits of scientific research, were groping after in their insistence on the innate furniture of the mind, namely, the predetermination, the collective endowment of the individual by the race, as a *prius* to whatever his own experience can teach him. Adjusting his own philosophy, on the one hand, to take account of every advance in scientific theory, he was careful, on the other, to bring out the continuous evolution of philosophic thought, history of human error though it might be[2]. And he held that the Experientialism even of to-day needed to be widened and deepened, not only by frankly adopting the evolutionary standpoint, but also by being brought face to face at all points with the best teaching of Rationalist thought, including especially the critical standpoints of Kant. Hence it is that I have selected the

[1] See below, p. 152.   [2] See below, p. 19.

Introductory Note. xi

Cartesian school and the *Kritik* rather than lectures on Bacon, Locke, Hume, and others.

I need not here repeat what is written in the *Elements of Psychology* by way of apology to the memory of the dead philosopher for undertaking a task so heavily fraught with responsibility as the editing of these lectures. That responsibility is but slightly alleviated in the present volume by my having had access, in the lectures where it is indicated, to more complete MSS. by the author's own hand. The task was undertaken in the hope of suggesting to the philosophic thought of the generation that has witnessed the untimely close of a life just come to philosophic maturity, with what generous ardour and constructive thought on behalf of the minds he was guiding, that life for a quarter of a century had spent itself, and more than spent itself, in the ungrateful if noble work of the class-room. At the same time, by presenting a part of that work in practically its original form, and in availing myself of the opportunity afforded me of incorporating it in an educational series, I hope no less to serve the interests of the student, standing on the threshold of the precincts of philosophy, by making him partaker in benefits that the living source so richly dispensed.

If such a student should take up this volume without having previously read and re-read the companion manual, *Elements of Psychology*, or some equivalent text-book of modern date on the same subject, he is earnestly recommended to lose no time in making good that omission. Thus only will he be able to read this volume with the maximum of profit. It was a fundamental principle with Professor Robertson—true to the tradition of the British School—that philosophic considerations, from whatever other groundwork they might spring, should not precede, but be complementary to, the study of psychology—that, in his own words, the consideration of *how* we come to know anything should precede that of *what* it is *as known*. The reader, on the other hand, who has mastered the essential data of psychology, and naturally he most of all who has acquainted himself therewith as they are ordered by the same mind that planned the philosophic arguments in the present volume, will have his reward. Especially will he see how rich in philosophic import becomes that central point in George Croom Robertson's psychological analysis—the theory of objective perception, with its vertebral idea of the coefficient, in sense, of consciousness of activity put forth. He will see this point applied, again and again, in the explanation of such ultimate notions as necessity in knowledge, the conception of substance, the idea of causation, and the belief in an external world. And he will find effective in suggestiveness, not to say guidance, a philosophy thus psychologically based. In that philosophy the tradition handed down in this country—the school of British psychological philosophy—attains a distinct development. More than its well-known modern exponents, Robertson had, in his own phrase, 'gone to school under' Leibniz and Kant. And it is with a philosophic grasp and insight worthy of these two, while carrying on the direct line of succession in the psychological tradition, that he seeks to

Introductory Note.

show how it is no mere metaphor to say that the world as we know it is as we mentally construct it:—that we know it not with, as it were, a quasi-detachable intellect only, but with our whole living energy; that we know in so far as we act, nay, that ultimately, only as we will, as we put forth activity, as we act, can we claim fully to be [1].

CAROLINE A. F. RHYS DAVIDS [2].

June, 1896.

---

[1] See below, Lecture XVII.

[2] All footnotes in the lectures, unless the contrary is stated, are parenthetical remarks made by the professor himself. The works, or passages in works, prescribed for the student's special reading were, in nearly every case, those prescribed by the lecturer himself. In a few lectures I have given references to books or subjects discussed, and also to the lecturer's own published writings.

CONTENTS

PART I.

LECTURE		PAGE
I.	THE BOND AND THE DISTINCTION BETWEEN PSYCHOLOGY AND PHILOSOPHY	1
II.	PHILOSOPHY AS EPISTEMOLOGY	10
III.	THE HISTORICAL ASPECT OF PHILOSOPHY AND OF SCIENCE	17
IV.	HISTORICAL SKETCH OF GREEK PHILOSOPHY	24
V.	MEDIÆVAL PHILOSOPHY	37
VI.	SCHOLASTICISM AND THE RISE OF MODERN SCIENCE AND PHILOSOPHY	47
VII.	MODERN PHILOSOPHY	56
VIII.	UNIVERSALS	68
IX.	UNIVERSALS (*continued*). NOMINALISM AND CONCEPTUALISM	77
X.	THE NATURE OF KNOWLEDGE. KNOWLEDGE AND BELIEF	85
XI.	THE NATURE OF KNOWLEDGE. BEFORE LOCKE	97
XII.	THE NATURE OF KNOWLEDGE. AFTER LOCKE	112
XIII.	THE NATURE OF KNOWLEDGE. CRITICAL PHILOSOPHY	124
XIV.	THE NATURE OF KNOWLEDGE. CAUSATION	135
XV.	THE NATURE OF KNOWLEDGE. EVOLUTION	147
XVI.	THE PERCEPTION OF AN EXTERNAL (OR MATERIAL) WORLD	154
XVII.	THE PERCEPTION OF AN EXTERNAL (OR MATERIAL) WORLD (*continued*)	168
XVIII.	REGULATIVE PHILOSOPHICAL DOCTRINE	181
XIX.	THE BASIS AND THE END OF ETHICS	191

PART II.

SPECIAL LECTURES.

LECTURE		PAGE
XX.	ON THE EPISTEMOLOGY OF PLATO	201
XXI.	ON THE PSYCHOLOGY OF ARISTOTLE	214
XXII.	ON THE METHOD OF DESCARTES	231
XXIII.	ON THE PHILOSOPHY OF DESCARTES	244
XXIV.	ON THE PHILOSOPHY OF DESCARTES (*continued*)	258
XXV.	ON CARTESIANISM	270
XXVI.	ON CARTESIANISM (*continued*)	287
XXVII.	ON KANT'S CRITICAL PHILOSOPHY	304
	I. *Kant's importance in the present state of English thought.*	
XXVIII.	ON KANT'S CRITICAL PHILOSOPHY (*continued*)	317
	II. *General view of the* Kritik *and the* Prolegomena.	
	III. *Mathematical Necessity and Muscular Sense.*	
	IV. *On the Nature and Conditions of Intellectual Synthesis.*	
XXIX.	ON KANT'S CRITICAL PHILOSOPHY (*continued*)	339
	V. *The Ideas of Pure Reason.*	

ELEMENTS
OF
GENERAL PHILOSOPHY.

PART I.

LECTURE I.

THE BOND AND THE DISTINCTION BETWEEN PSYCHOLOGY AND PHILOSOPHY.

General Philosophy as based upon and supplementing Psychology.

IN these lectures I wish to supplement the preceding psychological course in two ways. We found that in the process of psychological discussion certain philosophical questions were more or less involved. Into these, which we then passed by, we will now inquire. Again, our former course touched on many purely psychological questions, which from our wider philosophic standpoint we may review, fill in, and add to. We saw that 'Philosophy of Mind' meant Science of Mind, whatever else it might mean. But we have also seen that science of mind or psychology does not contain all that is meant by philosophy of mind. And psychological treatment needs to be supplemented, before we can be fully satisfied, by a philosophical consideration of the problems of mind. I do not go so far as to say that philosophy is nothing more than a review of the problems of psychology from another point of view, but it is from this side that I introduce students to philosophy, and it is this that I mean by 'General Philosophy.' We are going to take up philosophical questions *on a psychological basis*. Not that we can settle such questions so determinately as those of psychology. We can dogmatise in psychology, for we are there treating of phenomena; but we cannot do so in philosophy, where we can no longer distinguish, as we can in psychology, between thinker and thought. But it is most important for the student to separate from psychology proper the philosophical considerations which arise out of that science, all the more so that in this country psychology has been generally mixed up with philosophy. Mill, Hamilton, Professor Bain, Mr. Spencer are apt to confuse both kinds of inquiry, so that I am the more concerned that students should be fully aware when the aspect is shifted.

General Philosophy as Theory of Knowledge.

Ethics, associated with 'General Philosophy,' is itself a department of philosophy. It would be impossible to treat of philosophy in general without treating at the same time of ethics in particular. And ethics is no part of psychology at all. Equally is this true with regard to æsthetics. But my intention, during at least the greater part of this course, is not to refer to any philosophical questions arising out of the psychology of conation or of feeling, but to such as have all more or less bearing on knowledge. We see, therefore, what part of our psychology it is mainly that we shall rehearse, review, and supplement, viz. the psychology of intellection. In practical philosophy, i.e. in Logic, Ethics, and Æsthetics, we need to know what functions of the mind it is that these doctrines regulate. And if General Philosophy is best faced from the point of view of Theory of Knowledge, then does philosophy follow rightly from psychology as leading from that which appears to that which is, from the consideration of *how* we come to know anything to that of *what* it is *as known*.

Kant's followers, including Green, condemn this method as involving the use of fundamental assumptions before these have been sifted. Then must we indeed begin our sifting early, for all use these assumptions with the use of their mother tongue, every two-year old as well as every costermonger, though they do not come to the ultimate expression thereof. Those writers end by never getting on to psychology at all! It is true, on the other hand, that some English philosophers have been so content with their psychology that they have never passed on to philosophy. I see the force of the Kantian position; no scientific basis is ultimate. But a scientific basis is the only sound starting-point, and I will maintain my view till I get new light. Touching intellect, then, we have to make sure of our psychological ground and see if we may draw philosophical conclusions.

Theory of Knowledge distinguishable from Logic.

Logic, no less than ethics and æsthetics, is a department of philosophy and intimately concerned with the psychology of intellection. Nevertheless, I propose to mark off logic also from our philosophical inquiry, at least for the present, and to confine our inquiry to Philosophy as Theory of Knowledge in relation to science in general and Science of Mind in particular. Logic, like ethics and æsthetics, may be called science from a certain point of view; but that is not the point of view I adopt. For me, as I shall show later on, they are regulative doctrines or disciplines, or Nomology. Logic is regulative discipline of thought. Has science in itself anything to do with regulation? No; the business of science is explanation, or phenomenology. Psychology deals with phenomenology of mind, with intellection as it *naturally* proceeds, with the explanation according to natural laws of the intellectual function called thinking. That function logic sets itself to regulate. This notion of regulation is something which science in no wise expresses. It is one of the ways in which we can define the function of philosophy. And because thought is a means of knowledge, logic in its widest sense is already a part of the philosophical Theory of Knowledge. But logic is concerned with *true* thinking or truth. Now, by truth of thought we mean that our thought has a certain *import*, that it is *valid*. Such considerations, namely, as to whether a given intellectual act has any real validity or not, are altogether outside psychology, though not outside logic. Now, if logic be concerned with the validity of *thought*, let us generalise this, and we get a definition of philosophy as theory, not merely of the validity of thought, but of the validity of *all* knowing. We can know otherwise than by thought, viz. by perception.

Ultimate Inquiry—its Nature and its Names.

'How am I intellective of that pillar?' We resolved my act of intellection into certain sensations *plus* mental activity of a definite kind—a complex function termed Perception. And this was a psychological answer to a psychological inquiry —an inquiry which may be thus otherwise worded: 'How comes it to pass in my consciousness that I perceive that pillar?' But if I ask, '*Is* there a pillar—a *real* one?— a real pillar there apart from my perceptive mind?'—*this* is a philosophical question, and whatever answer is made is a philosophical statement, though it may be determined by psychological insight. For we are here asking a question relating to the import of knowledge; I am concerned to know whether my subjective perception implies a corresponding reality or no.

Such questions may be raised concerning any intellectual function; they belong to the ultimate questions which the human mind is able to raise, and for them is still reserved the ancient term Philosophy. If they are raised, as here and now, in connexion with intellection or knowing, the more specific terms are Theory of Knowledge, Epistemology, or Metaphysic. If emphasis is thrown, as it used to be, rather on the question of 'Being' than of 'Being in as far as known,' they are, or rather were, expressed by the term Ontology. Thus we have got four names which are all more or less related to one another, all being the same in respect of extension but differing in intension; all denoting the same, but having different connotation. Let us enter more fully into their meaning and history, and then more clearly differentiate what they collectively amount to from modern science and psychology.

Philosophy.

Philosophy is the oldest term of them all; first to be started, it will probably survive longest. We meet with 'philosophy' and 'philosopher' in Greek history earlier than with the other three. Plato, e.g., uses only these two. Philosophy originally stood for reasoned knowledge *in general*; it was not differentiated from science. Human knowledge was supposed to be a kind of organic whole, and Philosophy was the word for it. But from the time of Plato, and still more in that of Aristotle, another word began to grow up, viz. Epistemology. And Plato was already commencing to speak of 'the sciences,' though the only science which then underwent development was mathematics. It is not till the modern period that an antithesis or opposition is set up between sciences and philosophy. The sciences were at first rather departments of philosophy, but from the beginning of the seventeenth century mathematics and other sciences were pursued in a certain method of their own, and regarded apart from anything that may still be called philosophy. An ancient philosopher had a complete view of the whole field of knowledge. Now, thinkers are mainly specialists, knowing little, or but vaguely, of any department except their own. The opposition since then has so far widened that some modern thinkers have said there is nothing beyond science. Comte, e.g. called philosophy a co-ordination of the sciences[1]. There is a good deal called philosophy beyond that; at all events, whereas philosophy originally meant all reasoned knowledge, it has now come to mean reasoned knowledge no less, but of a kind that stands apart from certain limited bodies of doctrine pursued according to a strictly definite method called that of the sciences, and apart from psychology too, because in respect of method psychology is as much science as chemistry is.

Philosophy as Wisdom.

Again, all ancient knowledge was bent to a practical issue. This is the specific mark of what was originally called philosophy. Philosophy is 'love of wisdom,' and wisdom is a term of practical import, is knowledge with a practical reference; is not mere insight, but conduct guided by insight. And still our concern in ultimate questions has

[1] V. *Positive Philosophy*, Bk. VI, ch. xiii.

a more or less practical object—an object which we call the wise conduct of life. But this aspect of philosophy is not found in modern *science*. Science as such leaves aside practical considerations. It has reached its present development during the last three centuries by such elimination and specialisation. As long as men could and would think about everything they made little advance.

Metaphysic.

The term Metaphysic in this country and in Germany has been loosely used. It is often used as indistinguishable from psychology itself; e. g. in Hamilton's *Lectures on Metaphysics*, five-sixths of which are psychological, the remainder philosophical, and in which he passes without warning from psychology into pure philosophy. Professor Bain speaks of 'mental science' and sometimes of psychology, but there is a goodly amount of philosophy too in his Manual, certain chapters and much in the historical notes being as philosophical as can be.

Metaphysic also, as a name, has an accidental origin. Aristotle did not use the term, and yet the term has grown out of Aristotle's works. He left, in addition to his treatises on life, mind or soul, and the treatise called *Physica*, another work dealing with what he sometimes calls First Philosophy, with the notion of 'fundamental,' and at other times 'being as being' (τὸ ὂν ᾗ ὄν), in fact, Ontology. The precise word *ontologia* is not found there, yet all is there but the word. His editors and commentators placed this treatise *after* the *Physica*, and called it so (τὰ μετὰ τὰ φυσικά), although the author had called it 'first philosophy.' No sooner had the name arisen than it underwent a change of meaning, and stood, not for what followed 'after' the *Physica*, but for a consideration of things μετά, 'beyond,' the physical consideration of them. There was little that was scientific in Aristotle's physical consideration of things, but in time physics came to be handled from a purely scientific standpoint, while metaphysics represented a standpoint reaching beyond this, and thus we get the notion of metaphysic as opposed to science and equal to philosophy. And by those who were impressed by the characteristic difference between Mind and 'Nature,' metaphysic was supposed to be specially concerned with Mind, as physic was with Nature.

Ontology.

Ontology, then, though not used by Aristotle, is at the point of his pen to be written down. We may, as I have said, look upon it as another name for philosophy, when concerned with things 'as being.' Is science concerned with things 'that are'? In one sense, yes. The difference is this, that in opposing ontology to science as concerned with 'being,' the antithesis (which has become perfectly clear to the modern mind) lies in science dealing with things, not so much as they *are*, but as they *appear* or seem to be—with things *qua* 'phenomena.' Psychology, e.g. deals with mind only as phenomenal. In this century some who have pursued the study of mind scientifically have tried to prove that there is no ulterior consideration; e.g. the Mills and Professor Bain. They discount ontology as a doctrine that has only led men astray and has been superseded. Ontological questions may be difficult or impossible to solve, but no human mind that works fairly can exclude ontological any more than phenomenal questions. Some opponents of ontology try to escape the difficulty by making phenomena into realities.

Epistemology.

Epistemology, a term which has come into use within the last few years, expresses what in Germany is called theory or doctrine of knowledge, philosophical theory being understood. The notion was put forward by Kant and his followers in opposition to ontology, and to maintain that the right way to deal with ultimate questions of *being* is to make a prior philosophical inquiry into the import of *knowledge*. How is this, in respect of extension, commensurate with ontology or metaphysic? How can the doctrine which deals with things as they are, be also expressed as epistemology? Anything that *is*, can be, for us, only as it is *known*. If we do not know of any being, it does not exist for us. Therefore he who provides an ultimate theory of knowledge, in that very fact provides an ultimate theory of being. I am not now speaking of a consideration of how knowledge arises and comes to pass, for that is psychology, but of a certain ultimate consideration of *knowledge as such*, and which cannot but be a consideration of *things as known*, and therefore of things as being, or real. And this is the point of view from which philosophy has more and more come to be presented in modern times. Implicitly already in Locke, but explicitly, with full consciousness, in Kant, modern philosophy has come to be epistemology, as in Aristotle it was ontology.

Passages for reading :—

N.B. The lecturer used to urge students not to omit to supplement LECTURE I by reading his essay 'Psychology and Philosophy,' *Mind*, January, 1883 (or *Philosophical Remains*, pp. 250-273).—ED.

LECTURE II.

PHILOSOPHY AS EPISTEMOLOGY.

Aspects of Philosophy and their Opposites.

LAST day I sought to give a first notion of the distinction between science and philosophy, and more especially between psychology and philosophy. But it was only a first distinction, and one that I shall fill up in the ensuing lectures. When we turned to consider philosophy as such, we encountered a series of terms, each having a special connotation, but all pointing to the same, all denoting the same kind of doctrine, but in different ways. And these we have to a certain extent discussed by, in some degree, denoting the opposite in each case. Everything may to a certain extent be defined by denoting what it excludes. In the way of knowing, everything illustrates the principle of relativity (v. *infra*, Lecture XVI). When we know anything we know something that it is and something that it is not. I have not said all that philosophy is when I say what it is not, but I have said something very important when I say, for instance, that philosophy is not science. Philosophy has its meaning in relation to the sciences, but it excludes every science. Metaphysics is not physics, understanding physics in the widest sense as science of nature, or of natural phenomena generally.

Ontology excludes phenomenology. We may tabulate these opposites thus:—

Metaphysics	Physics.
Philosophy	Science.
Ontology	Phenomenology.

Distinction between Epistemology and Psychology.

Now I cannot give an equally sharp antithesis in the case of Epistemology. But we may oppose it to ontology on the one side, and to psychology on the other. Psychology is not theory of knowledge, but theory of mental phenomena, that is, of knowing or intellection, as well as of feeling and conation. Again, ontology is not theory of knowledge, but of being. Epistemology brings forward what ontology does not bring forward, viz. the subjective reference which is always implied in philosophy as opposed to science. There is no subjective reference in science. One ball, e. g. strikes another, and they move. With this and the like physics is concerned, but there is neither overt nor covert, patent nor latent, subjective reference. Even in psychology there is not the subjective reference there is in philosophy. Psychology is subjective, not because you make reference to the mind knowing, but because it is concerned with the subjective phenomena themselves. It investigates the knowing mind not otherwise than as physics investigates the colliding of the balls; it leaves out of account the knowing mind as such, although it is true that psychology, as concerned with subjective phenomena, stands, as we have seen, opposed to all other sciences. As subjective science, we saw that it faces all the other sciences as objective, and even faces itself as objective. But the subjective consideration which philosophy invariably involves is not in the way of psychological science, but is a view of things in relation to, or from the point of view of, mind. Psychology is a scientific consideration of mental phenomena taken as subjectively, and to a certain extent also as objectively, manifested. Philosophy is not a scientific consideration, but is a consideration of anything and everything in relation to mind. And the name which best expresses philosophy in the fact of its mental or subjective reference is Epistemology. Epistemology is just philosophy, deals with things, deals with being, deals with things going beyond bare experience; but it treats of them in relation to the fact of knowing. Thus the epistemologist cannot help being an ontologist, because his theory of knowledge must be about things also as being; he must also be a metaphysician, because he is concerned with a whole range of things beyond the physical; and he must be a philosopher in being other and more than a man of science, or concerned with things in a way in which science is not. Epistemology as theory of knowing is as wide as philosophy, since for us nothing can be that we cannot know. And while it is philosophy and not science, the special science to which it stands in closest relation is psychology, and, within psychology, the psychological theory of intellection. It does not do that work over again which was done in the theory of intellection. It is not concerned, as that is, with the rise, growth, and development of intellectual consciousness. What Epistemology does apart from this is to inquire into the value, import, validity, of knowledge. These notions have no meaning in psychology. We distinguish between desires as good and bad, but not as psychologists. As such we are merely concerned with the fact of desire. To determine between desires as good or bad is a matter for the philosophical doctrine of ethics.

Distinction between Logic and Epistemology[1].

There is indeed, as we saw last day, another philosophical doctrine concerned with the import or validity of our intellectual consciousness, namely, Logic. Some writers use the term Logic as equivalent to Theory of Knowledge, but such a practice is confusing. Hegel, e. g., in his *Logic*, sets out a theory of the validity of knowing of any kind. Professor Adamson's article on 'Logic' in the *Encyclopædia Britannica* includes the whole field of the validity of knowledge. Mill's chapter 'On the Things denoted by Names' (*Logic*, Bk. I, ch. iii.) has nothing to do with logic, but is a discourse on theory of knowledge. But, as I pointed out, epistemology is the wider consideration, and may be viewed as including logic. And the special line of consideration in each is different. Logic is the doctrine regulative of thought. Epistemology is concerned with the validity of any cognition whatever, e. g., with percept, which is not thought. Again, logic is concerned with the import of thought as general, whether the form of thought be inductive (from particular to general) or deductive (from the more to the less general). And logic is concerned with the import of thought only in so far as it is general. I do not know a single part of logical doctrine which is not concerned with generality, with leading up to it by induction, or down from it by deduction. But the generality of thought does not exhaust the import of thought. Thought, though it is general, is thought about something. What is this something that is thought about? So there is plenty left for epistemology in regard to thought. And in putting logic under epistemology, I have not said that logic exhausts the consideration of thought.

[1] This is a point not clearly answered in the books.

Suppose I ask, in regard, e. g. to that pillar, Does my perception of that pillar mean, or not mean, a pillar really apart from me? This is a real question, but, as we have already seen[1], it is not a psychological question. It is a philosophical question that I have asked, a metaphysical, an ontological, and an epistemological question. As with percepts, so with images and concepts. Does my concept 'man' stand for a reality? What, if any, real thing corresponds to my thought 'man'? Such a question is neither psychological nor logical. Logically we can ask, Is 'man' a general name or not? What is the definition of it? Logic, with regard to concepts, culminates in the doctrine of definition. But when I have defined a notion, have I proved anything of its reality? Does my thought of 'centaur' portend or imply a reality as my thought of 'man' does? In this way, then, we can distinguish between what is called logical, and what epistemological, consideration. And thus if logic in one sense falls within epistemology, it is not the epistemology of thought, inasmuch as there are epistemological considerations of thought apart from the logical consideration of thought in its generality.

Knowledge.

We have now committed ourselves to the use of the word 'knowledge,' a term I refrained from bringing forward in psychology. It is used, no doubt, in psychological works; Hamilton, among others, uses it systematically, and so does Professor Bain, 'cognition' being an equivalent term. Both terms, if used in psychology at all, should be used systematically and apart from any consideration of import, or else be

---

[1] *Elements of Psychology*, Lecture XIV.

abstained from. The latter plan to me seems better, and I substitute the term 'intellection.' Intellection is a purely psychological word, meaning merely a kind of conscious experience, just as feeling means another such kind, and conation another. Knowledge, on the other hand, is essentially a word of philosophical, rather than psychological, import. Both it and cognition, as I have already pointed out (*op. cit.*, p. 25), drag in at once the 'known' or *cognitum*, with its implication of import, validity, or reality. Knowledge is always of something, and of something as *being*, as real or not real, as the case may be. At once the philosophical question arises—Does my knowledge really represent such and such an object? Is the object real? And this is not a psychological consideration. In psychology we consider cognition apart from the notion of import; we ask, How does cognition come to pass? not—Does it mean this? Does it import that? It is true that when we are dealing with perception in psychology, perceiving implies something perceived; but we are then only concerned with the function of perceiving. But now we are concerned with the work of the mind *in relation to the thing known*. The moment we look beyond subjective function to the reality with which the function is concerned, we are no longer psychologising, we are not even concerned with the question of import in the narrow sense of logic, but we are concerned with import of knowledge altogether. Knowledge in relation to the thing known, or the thing known in relation to knowledge, belongs to philosophy. In philosophy it is precisely with the object of thought and its validity or import that we have to deal—'object' and 'valid' understood as that which holds for all minds alike and determines action.

Belief.

While knowledge is thus properly to be limited to philosophical use, there is another word, of essentially subjective import, which psychology has to take into account if it is to be complete, but which has also a prominently philosophical bearing. As when I use the word *know* there is always an object of knowledge, so when I *believe* there is an object of belief. Knowledge is subjective function in relation to an object. Belief is subjective function in relation to an object. I can raise the question of reality in belief as much as in knowledge. No alternative term for belief being available according as we are psychologising or philosophising, its difference of signification must in either case be carefully distinguished. Generally it is well to use separate terms for either aspect, as this will tend to break the habit of mixing up the different considerations. The scope of (subjective) psychology is as wide as that of philosophy, but its function is different. The former deals with everything that is—as subjective experience. The latter deals with everything that is—in terms of ultimate consideration. Philosophy, again, is always interpretable as Philosophy of Mind. Whether it is contemplated as a consideration of things as *known* (facts), or *desired* and sought after (aims, ends, ideals), or as science of Being-*as-thought-of*, there is, we see, always ultimately a reference to the human mind. It can only deal with things as we are conscious of them. This is the explanation of their being so much confused together, and why psychology was so late in being separated from philosophy.

LECTURE III.

THE HISTORICAL ASPECT OF PHILOSOPHY AND OF SCIENCE.

Résumé of the Function of Philosophy as compared with Science.

WE have seen that out of psychology arise certain further questions or more ultimate considerations called philosophical. Psychology suggests them more than any other science. They do not admit of objective verification, but have a subjective value, and the historical study of them is important as giving insight into the development of the human mind. In as far as they may be settled at all, they may be settled by psychology, hence the importance of the latter as a basis to precede and introduce the study of philosophy. If philosophy, e.g. seeks to show what the external world *is*, psychology explains how we get to know what we call 'external world.' Science deals not with what is, but only with what appears, with those phenomenal aspects of nature which inevitably *suggest*—I do not commit myself—some ultimate Reality. Theory of Knowledge (to which metaphysic and ontology are now subordinated), or philosophy in its speculative or theoretical aspect, has to afford *insight*, while philosophy in its practical aspect makes for *guidance*.

Philosophical questionings, I repeat, are not of a nature to lead to definitely verifiable results. Nevertheless, philosophising is natural to the human mind, and, as of old, so now, such questions are asked, and will for ever be asked. And there must be a doctrine to cover and deal with these questions—questions concerning notions which science is obliged to assume. Philosophy in modern times, as we have seen, is supplementary to, and in no sense another name for, the sciences. Comte indeed said that the business of philosophy is to make out the relation between the sciences. The sciences are occupied each with certain aspects or departments of nature, or of things as they appear[1]. 'Co-ordinate each science,' said Comte, and give it a practical bearing, a reference to human action, and that is all that you can know or philosophy can do. Comte here brings insight to bear upon action, and so far returns to the original meaning of philosophy. But his opinion of the scope of philosophy is very unsatisfactory in view of the incapacity of the sciences to deal with questions respecting their ultimate data and the ends of conduct. What is the difference between appearance and reality? What is space (does it exist apart from the human mind)? What is motion? What is a cause? What is a quality? and what is a thing? None of the sciences pretends to answer these questions, and yet they are implied in the language both of science and of common life. Philosophy in past ages dealt largely with these questions before the sciences were, and still concerns itself with them. Aristotle saw the necessity for a deeper inquiry just as much as we do. It is the word 'deeper,' 'ultimate,' that gives the special aspect of metaphysic as the name for philosophy in its relation, not to psychology, but to the objective sciences.

[1] Or, we might say, with aspects of nature and with mathematics, for mathematics is not a science of nature.

And the deeper inquiry is not antagonistic to the scientific. It is often brought against philosophy that it presents motion without progress, but this is not correct; there has been progress. History is for the most part the story of the errors through which men have passed in trying to get at the truth, and the history of philosophy, if good for nothing else, would yet be valuable for what it reveals of the growth of the human mind in its deepest thought respecting itself confronted by the universe. For all their many errors the best minds of antiquity struck out philosophical suggestions of great value, arrived at philosophical results of permanent value, even though their positive science was often purely fanciful. On many points we understand more than the ancients, and many of their errors have been exploded beyond chance of revival. There is, and always will be, room for advance in philosophy. In as far as philosophy has the function of co-ordinating the results of the special sciences—and it has become more and more the object of philosophy to do so—there must of course be advance in the former as the latter advance, as Comte held. But if we also take philosophy as theory of human knowledge, we still understand more than the earlier thinkers, although our progress be not of the nature of that in the positive sciences. Philosophy in one sense encircles, extends beyond, comes after the sciences, varying as they vary, but in another sense it comes before them. It was not necessary to know that the sun stands and the earth moves in order to understand the relation of substance and attribute, whole and parts, &c. True, the discovery of those facts had a most important philosophical bearing, as all great discoveries will ever have; namely, with respect to the evidence of sense and man's position in the universe. But there was a region of philosophy not directly touched by scientific discoveries, and we may find a profit in surveying these philosophies, even though Aristotle and Plato had a defective astronomy. It is one function of philosophy to wait on the special sciences, and to be ever ready to pluck up its stakes and widen its boundaries. For philosophical and scientific definitions are always changing; they are a progress towards the expression of what is. But it is also apparent that to a certain extent philosophy has an independent course to pursue, and has often to make advances, and did often arrive at truths about the whole frame of things before men developed those aptitudes and powers from which has sprung all modern science.

History in Philosophy and in Science.

The history of philosophy has an importance in relation to philosophy which the history of science has not to science. However interesting it may be to compare present with past conceptions of geology, ancient with modern physics, these and all the sciences are adequately taught as bodies of established doctrine without necessarily involving any reference to past theories; at any rate, their teaching does not at all depend upon knowledge of their history. False scientific teachings have to be forgotten; inadequate scientific teachings, while leading to better, need not be remembered. Interest in them is mainly antiquarian. Or if it is not felt for the teachings as such, but for them as illustrative of scientific method, this is to have taken them out of the special sciences and to have brought them into the domain of philosophy, which has a property in the older forms, the cast-off garments of the sciences which these no longer possess for themselves. On the other hand, philosophers of all schools are for ever throwing backward glances at past thinkers and the results they elicited. The history of philosophy is a recognised part of philosophic discipline. The reason for this difference from what we find in science lies in the nature of philosophy, in its being always concerned with ultimate, not with immediate, explanation, not with ways of re-expressing the facts of nature, or giving an explanation of them relative to other and more general facts or conceptions—resolving sound, e.g. into a mode of motion—but with the explanation that is demanded with reference to the *mental* nature of man, to man, i.e. as a *thinking* being.

In chemistry, e.g. we analyse water into its elements, study their properties, and re-combine. We have thereby given a scientific account of water in so far as it falls under chemistry. The mechanical properties of water would be the subject of investigation under another science, and so on for every conceivable relation of water as an object among other natural objects. But our intellectual concern in it as thinking beings is not even then exhausted. It is an object, we say, a substance, a property—what are these? What is analysis, and what composition? Empirical science does not settle these questions, and does not even tell us when they cannot be settled. I should say the decision is given by philosophy as the ultimate interpretation of experience, even in cases where the decision is nothing more satisfactory than a *non liquet*.

The answer, whatever it be, should hold good *universally*. The question of substance and attribute, e.g. was raised in regard to water: the settlement, such as it is, applies to the whole of nature. In one aspect, however, this peculiarity of philosophy is merely a difference in degree. All science, worthy of the name, is also general in its character. To make good, therefore, the opposition between philosophy and the special sciences, the extraordinary universality of philosophic dicta must rest on a special ground, and that is that, whereas in the special sciences we consider relations among facts and data *known*, in philosophy we consider facts, data and relations *as known or knowable*. Now whatever be the objects known, though they be taken from sciences the most widely removed, anything that we settle about the knowing of them must stand good for all alike. The principles of knowledge are of constant and universal application; and philosophy is pre-eminently the science of them and all that they involve.

But if such be the character of philosophy, we may now begin to see why it is natural and right that the philosopher should keep strict account of older speculation, and would err if he neglected it.

Procedure.

Now, seeing the importance of the historical method in philosophy, and how greatly the thoughts of men have varied with regard to ultimate questions, it is better that I should glance over the history of such thoughts, and set out the views of the best minds throughout time, than give only my own individual conclusions.

For our practical purposes we discount Eastern thought, and also that of the earliest civilisations generally, confining ourselves to the Western philosophy which began among Greek thinkers on the coast of Asia Minor B.C. 600, but dealing more at length with those philosophical conceptions of the seventeenth century which appeal more deeply to us than those of Plato and Aristotle, as being more akin to our own. When we take a view of the history of philosophy, we find that philosophical thinkers have been occupied in the main with three questions:—

1. The question of Universals—i.e. of the relation of the Universal to the Particular—known also as the doctrine of the One and the Many. This is predominant in the Scholastic period, and was also prominent in the Ancient period.

2. The Relation of Reason to Experience, in explaining the Nature or Import of Knowledge. This dominates all modern philosophy.

3. The Reality of a Material World, or Perception of an External World, and the Nature of Mind in relation to it. This has been raised especially by British philosophers.

Every philosophy deals with each, but with a different degree of emphasis. Hamilton divides philosophers according to their answer to the third question; hence his view of the earlier philosophers is distorted, since they were really concerned with the larger question of the nature, or origin, or, more correctly, import of knowledge, in which the more special third question is involved. This shows that he is so engrossed in that particular question that he thinks every one else must have been so. He derived this standpoint from his master, Reid; and Reid's standpoint was a protest against that of Berkeley. The answer to any one of the questions will determine a man's answer to either of the others.

But we must first take a survey in outline of the growth of Western philosophy during the last 2,500 years.

For LECTURE IV read :—

G. C. Robertson, *Philosophical Remains*, 'Philosophy as a Subject of Study.'

Ueberweg, *History of Philosophy*, vol. i, 'The Philosophy of Antiquity' (large text).

Or the same epoch in Erdmann's or Schwegler's *History of Philosophy*.

LECTURE IV.

HISTORICAL SKETCH OF GREEK PHILOSOPHY.

Main Epochs of Philosophy and Culminating Periods.

WESTERN philosophy may be said to have begun with Thales, B.C. 600. Thus we have to take account of 2,500 years of constant reflective thinking. These are grouped in three main periods—(1) Ancient; (2) Mediæval, Scholastic, or Ecclesiastic; (3) Modern. The first period terminates in the sixth century A.D., and the second in the fourteenth century. Of all these centuries only about seven or eight are really important. The times in which the human race was really *effectively* thinking were not long, and all the effective thought in Western philosophy, all that has yielded permanent results of any value, falls within three epochs, included by those three main periods and comprising some seven hundred years out of the 2,500, to wit, B.C. 450–250, A.D. 1150–1350, and from 1600 onwards. The rest is all of quite subordinate importance. It might be even more accurate to end the first period of florescence at B.C. 300, but I extend it by preference so as to include Stoics and Epicureans. The accompanying diagram shows at once the three main periods and their respective culminating epochs. It will be seen that the former overlap considerably; no sharp divisions in time would accurately represent the different developments of thought. There is the more or less positive break entitled

B.C. 600 500 400 300 200 100 A.D. 100 200 300 400 500 600 700 800 900 1000 1100 1200 1300 1400 1500 1600 1700 1800

(I) Pre-Socratics

Epicureans Stoics

(II) Neo-Platonists.

Patristic Philosophy

Schools closed (529)

Dark Ages

Arabian and Jewish Philosophy

Scholastic Philosophy (III)

(The dotted lines give the extreme duration ascribable to each epoch. The black lines indicate the effective periods of active original thought.)

the Dark Ages; there is the transition period of the fifteenth century; again, there are the two subsidiary movements of the rise of Arabian philosophy (A.D. 800–1100) and, under its influence, of Jewish philosophy. These, however, did not affect modern Europe in general.

First, 'Ancient,' or Greek Period.

Western philosophy did not absolutely begin with Thales. There was a tendency to philosophy among all the early civilisations bordering on the East of which we have remains. But it is principally in Thales and the inquisitive, quick-witted Ionian Greeks, dating from about B.C. 600, that there began in Asia Minor that conscious and disinterested search for an explanation of the All which philosophy implies. For five hundred years this movement, continuous though not always progressive, was Greek. Then into the philosophy of practice Roman legal conceptions, the spiritual fruit of centuries of sturdy Roman action, began to be introduced; Hebrew and Eastern ideas of the universal order and of human destiny also entered; but Greek acuteness and mental restlessness remained always the truly active forces till another five hundred years and more had elapsed. Finally, in A.D. 529, Justinian, a Christian emperor, closed the pagan Greek schools and cast out the professors and commentators with whom remained the tradition of Aristotle and Plato. Within these centuries Greek thinkers had put forward solutions of nearly all the chief questions of philosophy, some necessarily relative to the positive knowledge of the time, which now appeal only to our curiosity, others of enduring value to the end of time. In the history of humanity there is nothing more astounding than the influence exerted by the thought of Plato and Aristotle. Justinian and his advisers fancied they had cast out the evil spirits; but the spirits came back from wandering up and down on the earth and entered with sevenfold power into the Church and the schools, and it was and is vain to think any more of a new exorcism.

Two Stages in Greek Philosophy.

Greek thought was strictly philosophy—a serious attempt to think out a connected view of the All. In those Ionian cities on the shores of Asia Minor arose men who, looking out on nature, i.e. the external world, tried to find a general expression for it. Their philosophy was not properly religion. Some of the chief among them had religious natures, but the central idea of Greek philosophy, as represented by Socrates, Plato, Aristotle, the Stoics, and Epicureans, which is one of morality and conduct, is not found in that Pre-Socratic period. After it all reasoned knowledge came to be viewed by the best Greek philosophers as bearing on the Perfect Life. Philosophy became divorced completely from inquiries into what are now considered the ultimate assumptions of physical science. But prior to the fifth century B.C. there is no explicit reference to the subjective life; till towards the age of Socrates there is no systematic practice of introspection now held fundamental in philosophy.

Greek Philosophy and Positive Science.

In the theories of Democritus, however, a contemporary of Socrates, but whom we know only at second hand through Aristotle, Epicurus and Lucretius, there are expressions with regard to nature of which modern science has made use. He started the theory of Atomism, i.e. that the material world consists of a multiplicity of atoms or indestructible particles. The mechanical philosophy of the seventeenth century has, in some respects, a close affinity to the Atomism of Democritus. It is a great pity that Socrates treated this definite scientific theory with scorn. Democritus and Archimedes (B.C. 287–213) come nearest to modern science of all the ancients. But they had no immediate successors.

The Sophists and Socrates.

At the time of Socrates, Greek civilisation was at its height. The Sophists were then teaching the art of rhetoric and the conduct of public business, as well as professing to teach men conduct in general on a rather superficial basis. They have been much decried, but have found a modern defender in Grote, and the older conception of them as mere charlatans has now passed away.

Contemporary with them lived a man, himself called a Sophist, a citizen of Athens all his life, who there tried to expose them and turn away his fellow-citizens from following their teaching—I mean, of course, Socrates (469–399). Socrates distinctly discountenanced the investigation of the physical universe. He first, in the West, put himself at the subjective point of view, and taught that the proper study of mankind was Man.

Plato and Aristotle.

His pupil Plato (427–347) took up his standpoint, putting himself at the subjective point of view without regard for knowledge of external nature or science. He carried farther than any one after him the method of thinking by way of rational or reasoned speculation, and has ever stood, in consequence, as the typical representative of (Platonic) IDEALISM. His system might be called a depreciation of sense and a glorification of reason.

Aristotle (384-322), pupil of Plato, distinctly philosophises from a subjective point of view, is a mental philosopher. As with Socrates and Plato, his philosophy leads up to conduct of life. But with regard to nature, he is of a different disposition from Plato, being interested just in that matter which Plato despised. Hence his system includes not only a physical philosophy of nature, but also a descriptive, if not explanatory, science of nature; e.g. he wrote long treatises on the animal world. Nevertheless, his views of nature are mainly superficial, and his so-called science of nature is mainly speculative, and takes no account of the necessity for verification. His interest in man and nature is ultimately only with a view to human conduct.

Epicurus and Zeno.

This is also the predominant idea with the Stoics and the Epicureans. In the moral character of their philosophy they are at one with the Socratics, as well as in that they seek to determine human conduct from a view of conformity to (human) 'nature.' They differ from Plato and Aristotle in flying less high in rational speculation. There are beginnings in their works of sober psychological inquiry. They are Materialists of a very extreme type. Yet neither school did anything to advance positive science. Down to B.C. 250, which covers Epicurus and the more important Greek Stoics, there are no new philosophic ideas introduced, but we find an overpowering interest in human conduct. Both the Platonic school (the Academics) and the Aristotelian (the Peripatetics) were for a time overshadowed by them, greatly though the influence of both Plato and Aristotle had worked in Stoicism as in Epicureanism. Zeno and Epicurus both were influenced by Aristotle; Epicurus in his ethical philosophy was largely connected with Plato. By his natural philosophy, Epicurus is also connected with Democritus. The Cynics and Cyrenaics connect Zeno and Epicurus respectively with Socrates. They began their work at a time when the energy of Greek thought had in a manner spent itself, and when, in consequence of political disintegration, men's thoughts began to be turned to individual conduct and quiet life. Hence the relatively greater importance of their ethical theories.

All the effective thinking of Greek philosophy was the work of these few men, and they are the founders of all the Greek schools of thought. We may see this more clearly in diagram.

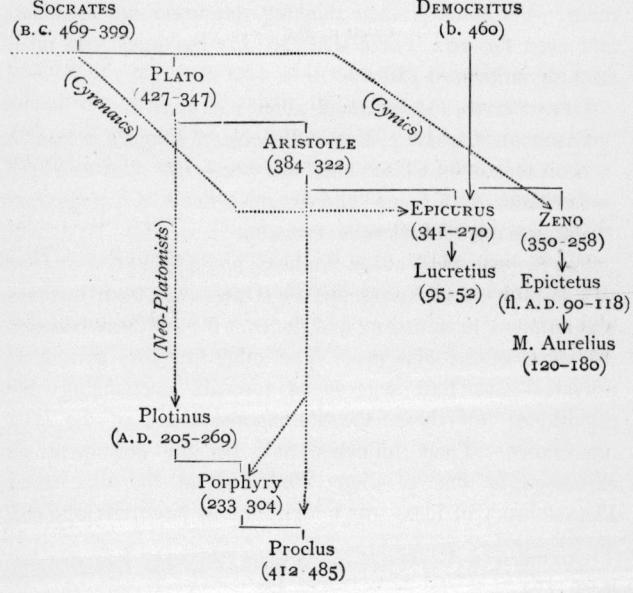

Pre-Socratic and Platonic Thought.

Let us now, before coming to the Christian era, retrace our steps and bring the Pre-Socratic philosophy into some sort of relation with the teachings of Plato and Aristotle.

We see it during those two centuries preceding Socrates active, acute, but slow in development, a movement of great comprehensiveness and variety, and of remarkable philosophic depth. Yet some of what are to us the simplest conceptions were then not attained, and it is only with Socrates and Plato that philosophy begins to be to some extent 'modern.' Scantiness of surviving materials and a general lack of philosophic development justify a somewhat summary treatment. Yet some of their thinking was important for Plato and even for us. There were six Pre-Socratics who most strongly influenced Plato—

HERACLEITUS, the Ionian, *fl.* about B.C. 504.

PARMENIDES, of Elea, Magna Graecia, *fl.* about B.C. 504.[1]

ANAXAGORAS, of Clazomenæ, B.C. 500–428.

PYTHAGORAS, of Samos and Magna Græcia, B.C. 575–500.

DEMOCRITUS, of Abdera, *b.* B.C. 460.

PROTAGORAS, chief of the Sophists, B.C. 480–411.

The problem of knowledge as it presented itself to Plato was an effort to transcend and get over the antithesis between the views of the first two. The other thinkers as well as Socrates gave him suggestions towards overcoming this opposition. Of these, the Pythagoreans are of the least importance. Their influence only became prominent, as expressed by one of them, Philolaus, at the time when Plato's theory of ideas was undergoing its later development.

---

[1] According to Mr. Burnet (*Early Greek Philosophy*, § 70) this date is too early by at least thirty years. ED.

The Pythagorean was the most enduring of the Pre-Socratic schools.

Plato never mentions Democritus by name, but it is probably to this great contemporary he refers as representing Materialism, when setting out in conscious antithesis his own Immaterialism. Democritus, living at Abdera, never came under the influence of Socrates. Anticipated by Leucippus early in the fifth century, he worked out his system from the basis of the earlier thinkers. He is the proper antithesis to Plato. Plato's philosophy is *teleological*—founded on final causes, the ethical element being uppermost. Democritus' philosophy is *mechanical*, and was the first to be developed as such. His importance by the side of Plato was first recognised by Lange (in his *History of Materialism*), who holds him to be the more important thinker of the two, in so far that modern scientific theory joins on to him more than on to Plato, whose views are largely discredited. His very prolific works are mostly lost.

The antithesis between Heracleitus and Parmenides was metaphysical rather than epistemological. Their philosophy, as with all Pre-Socratics, was cosmological, nevertheless it is epistemological also. All tried to find some simpler expression of the complex experience of daily life, but Heracleitus and Parmenides had a novel and deeper insight. Though Heracleitus adduced fire as a fundamental principle, it is the fact of ceaseless Change or Motion in nature that strikes him—πάντα ῥεῖ. Parmenides was struck by Permanence and Fixity in nature. The latter emphasised the One, the former saw chiefly the Many. Thus Heracleitus had to reconcile with his theory the apparent fixity of things; Parmenides had to make the apparent change in things square with his. Heracleitus accounted better for fixity than Parmenides did for change. Both views were of interest to Plato.

Anaxagoras introduced a new principle as determining universal being, viz. νοῦς, or reason. This, as compared with others brought forward by Pre-Socratics, e.g. water, air, fire, was apparently subjective; actually however for him νοῦς is a purely objective moving principle, and he is as cosmological as the rest.

With all of these there is latent the beginning of an epistemological theory. The distinction between experience, as we actually find it, and reflexion on our experience is implicit in all; but no one marked out clearly the difference between experience and reflexion, between sense and thought. They did not ask what the relation is between the two, nor how knowledge arises from both; they all thought of knowing in terms of sense.

But the Sophists and Socrates, with the doctrine of 'Know thyself,' brought the question to the front, causing the theory of knowledge to enter on a new phase. Philosophy, from being cosmological, became anthropological. With Anaxagoras, man is part of the universe. But Protagoras and Socrates view the universe through man. Man is put before the universe—man as *knower* (theoretical aspect of philosophy) and as *doer* (practical aspect). The Pre-Socratics, with their definite theories of being, were ontologists rather than epistemologists, making no definite reference to the subject as such. So far as they are epistemologists they agree, however much they differ metaphysically. They all, namely, are Sensationalists. They take account of sensation only, and of this as something proceeding in us in a material way.

Protagoras, on the other hand, treated the problem of

knowledge so much from the subjective point of view that he never got beyond that standpoint. With him knowledge is impossible. There could of course be no knowledge apart from individual experience, but beyond that individual experience it was impossible to get. Knowledge is sense-perception, infinitely varied and changing; man, the individual percipient, is, through his particular sensations, the 'measure of all things'—for himself. Thus he despaired of physical science, nor did he attempt any other kind of science, but devoted himself to practical life. Thus, in their consideration of the conduct of life, the Sophists employed moral persuasion instead of laying down any principles of moral science. Socrates also despaired of a knowledge of external things, holding that our experience of such is so completely relative to the individual that knowledge proper, i.e. having objective validity, is impossible. Nevertheless he was not content to drop epistemological considerations and go into practical life, but, resigning physical science as a worthy or possible object of search, he declared that a knowledge of man as a moral agent was possible. Though unable to get a knowledge of things, man can attain a knowledge of virtue. Accordingly Socrates set himself to formulate a science of moral conceptions, even to the identification of virtue and knowledge. He attempted to get at a definition of ethical notions by the generalisation of particulars, and thus to form concepts scientifically true. Scientific knowledge for Socrates is generalisation of particulars in the moral sphere, but not outside it. Science for him was general knowledge—to know particulars through the concept. This view of the general notion as embodying science first found expression in the teaching of Socrates. It is Socratic conceptualism.

Plato's 'Theory of Ideas' is a development of the Socratic conceptualism. He inherited both the concept of Socrates and also his high moral purpose. But Plato did not drop the general problem of knowledge; he asks, 'What is knowledge?' and, 'How is knowledge possible?'—questions which he puts into the mouth of Socrates (*Theætetus*, &c.), but which the latter never really asked, since he never conceived the problem of conduct as one to be solved by the problem of knowledge put universally.

End of the First Period.

We shall inquire into Plato's theories and those of Aristotle when dealing more specifically with those main questions referred to at the end of my third lecture. Here we need only briefly notice the conclusion of the period of 'ancient' philosophy.

The Aristotelian and Platonic schools went on, but in the later Greek and Roman period fell, as we have seen, into abeyance before Epicureanism and Stoicism. There was no advance in pure philosophy in Greece beyond Aristotle's time. The strong ethical bent inaugurated by Socrates, but tempered by the universal genius of Plato and Aristotle, prevailed fully by the third century. The full weight of Aristotle's influence did not really tell until the Scholastic period and after that; in the early Mediæval period it was overshadowed by Platonism. The two or three names of importance in Roman philosophy fall under Epicureans, e.g. Lucretius, or Stoics, e.g. Epictetus and Marcus Aurelius Antoninus. Cicero (B.C. 44) was an Eclectic thinker, interesting chiefly for the information he gives of the various movements.

If by the side of these we take thinkers who were not metaphysicians but scientific investigators, we see here and there one working with such success as to influence posterity, and, notably in astronomy, making correct conclusions on false grounds—e.g. predicting eclipses on fallacious conceptions of the relations of sun and earth. When we say the ancients had no science, we make exception of Hippocrates (medicine, B.C. 460-357), Euclid the geometer of Alexandria (fl. B.C. 323-283), Archimedes the physicist, the founder of genuine Positive Science, Hipparchus (fl. B.C. 160-145) and Ptolemy (fl. A.D. 139-161), the astronomers.

An offshoot from Platonic idealism and the so-called Academic philosophy in the Christian era was Neo-Platonism. I have said that Greek philosophy was not religious. Its latest growth however, Neo-Platonism, sought to meet a religious want born of the social conditions of the time, and entered into direct competition with the young Christian faith for mastery over all the thoughts and actions of men, the most important Neo-Platonist being Plotinus. But Greek philosophers had no kind of scruple as to the questions they raised. Socrates had indeed scruples regarding physical inquiry, but these were curiously unlike later and modern scruples, and are to be explained from the state of contemporary knowledge in regard to the subjects more than from anything else. They bore on the limitations of what *could* be settled and how to settle it, and not at all of what *ought*, or ought not, to be discussed. Hence Greek philosophy is the prototype of all earnest and unfettered thought.

For LECTURES V and VI read :—

Ueberweg, op. cit. I, pp. 356, 357, 367, 368 (for the way in which the Scholastic thinkers got Greek thought); pp. 410, 411 (for the way in which Greek works went to the Arabs, and were translated into Syriac and then into Arabic); pp. 417-419 (for the influence of both on Jewish philosophy). Also pp. 430 432.

LECTURE V.

MEDIÆVAL PHILOSOPHY.

Divisions.

OUR second or Mediæval period of Christian or Ecclesiastical Philosophy is divisible into two sections: (1) Patristic Philosophy, (2) Scholastic Philosophy. The former, beginning in the second century, culminated in Augustin (A.D. 354-430), then languished on through the virtually positive break of the Dark Ages, while the break-up of the older Western civilisation was proceeding. The latter (2) dates from the eleventh century, when philosophy was reviving in the monastic schools founded largely by Charlemagne about A.D. 800, when society had assumed somewhat of the form of modern nationalities, and when universities had just been, or were about to be, founded. The doctors of the Church were called *scholastici viri*, and their exposition of Christian dogma according to Greek principles is known as Scholastic Philosophy, still taught to-day in Catholic schools. After William of Ockham (d. 1347) it began to break up, and there intervenes the transitional period of the fifteenth and sixteenth centuries ushering in Modern Philosophy.

Authority and Philosophy.

When Simplicius and his Neo-Platonist companions, the last representatives of Hellenic philosophy, were driven eastwards by the action of Justinian, in A.D. 529, and the Athenian schools, for the first time since the age of Socrates and Plato, were deserted and dumb, there was left the Christian Church, which had grown for five centuries till it was so strong that emperors' edicts stood at its command, and so little unconscious of its future glory and its power, so little indisposed to dominate the thoughts of men, that the crushing out of the philosophical schools was but the last of a long series of blows levelled by it at the authority of human thinking. Unless we form a true conception of the historical relation of the Church to philosophic thought, we cannot comprehend the modern philosophy begun by Descartes.

Greek speculation, though it often had to pick its steps among established faiths (remember the fate of Socrates!) was, as we said, pre-eminently disinterested in its search after reasoned truth. Now too since the last three hundred years it is fully conceded that the human mind may search out anything and everything up to the limit of its powers, in the bare interest of truth and intelligent insight. But between this recurring phase of opinion there was an interval when liberty of thought was not the watchword of most, nor even of the most enlightened, minds. This interval, coincident with the period of supremacy of the Church in all departments of life, dates back to the beginnings of the Christian movement, and covers an interval whose magnitude it takes an effort, not often made, fully to conceive. Even pagan philosophy, viz. in its Neo-Platonist phase, was much affected by the principles and professions of the growing Church. Let us remember that the best Greek thought was excogitated in some four hundred years and less, and that modern philosophy only dates back three centuries.

We have thus 1600 years to account for as against those seven or eight hundred. Reduce this term as we may by the fringes of the dwindling of the first and the earliest growth of the latest periods, still there remains a clear thousand of years during which it was not open to men to think as they liked—and this is a huge slice out of the history of humanity. What the Church did, or permitted to be done for the *enlightenment* of the race took three times as long as the great deeds that are crowded into the something more than three centuries from Bacon and Descartes till the present. Those of course were very different times from ours, and there was plenty of other work, hard and grim, for the Church to do, and the Church did much of it bravely. But we must not forget that the seventh and eighth centuries were as long as the seventeenth and eighteenth. And not to forget this, but to remember and ponder it, in connexion with the intellectual history of mankind, is one of the first things the student of philosophical history is called upon to do.

Greek Philosophy in Harness.

At the beginning of the sixth century the Church finally stamped out the very feeble remnant representing Greek thought. That date is also critical in another way. Not only was it then that the Church grasped the reins, but a turning-point was also reached in her internal development. As in after-ages the Church did not so much *re*press thought as *com*press it within her own limits, so it is not to be supposed that she at this date had stood altogether outside of the philosophical current. The Christian religion, viewed philosophically, rivalled the Stoic and Epicurean schools as a way of thinking towards an ideal of human conduct. The rules of life were given not as rational, but as a revelation from on high. But in time, as the Church grew and brought into her fold more and more men of higher culture, the developed conceptions of pagan philosophy came into contact with the Christian philosophy. Epictetus the Stoic, Marcus Aurelius the Stoic emperor, Plotinus and Proclus, are not the only names of philosophical note in the early centuries of the new era. Origen (185-254), Athanasius (296-373), Tertullian (160-220), and, above all, Augustin (354-430), are not less worthy of notice, for the historian of philosophy as well as for the Churchman. Augustin, a man of developed pagan culture, appearing at the time when Christianity had gained the mastery, first put forth those conceptions, which came to be the accepted philosophy of the Christian Church, with a breadth of thought hitherto unrivalled. He derived his conception of the soul as real and yet as opposed to matter from the Platonists. Metaphysically he was a Dualist, and fixed philosophy from his time onward as a system of Dualism.

In fact the first generation of Christian converts had hardly passed away before philosophic thought began, while three or four centuries of ardent philosophic thinking and dialectical discussion, carried on with Greek subtlety upon principles of Greek philosophy, had been needed before the many-headed dogma of the Church had been settled and the function of the Fathers fulfilled, there being nothing more to create. What one section of Christendom has often bewailed, and another has rejoiced over, may be accepted with some confidence for a fact, viz. that the ecclesiastical doctrine was the result of an incorporation of a few simple tenets with the wisdom of the world, or at least of the interpretation of a small number of practical truths by the refined intelligence of thinkers who had been trained in Greek schools. The fact belongs to the history of philosophy as much as to religion, although the Fathers would for the most part have thrown from them the imputation, so ready as they were to denounce philosophy and all profane wisdom in the interest of faith.

Fathers and Doctors of the Church.

But after a while all the main dogmas were formed by which the Church was henceforth to stand, the edifice being crowned in the fifth century by Augustin, last and greatest of the Fathers. After him philosophising was bent into other than creative channels. This is what happened. Pagan philosophy having been reduced to silence, and the Fathers of the Church East and West having passed away, their dogmatic work accomplished, when next, under the auspices of the consolidated and all-powerful Church, something of the old inquiring and reasoning spirit appeared, it was given the task of interpreting and unfolding, of supporting and upholding, what was there already. To the Fathers of the Church succeeded her Doctors, who in monastic schools and, as time went on, in universities made philosophy conform to dogma, expounding in logical form and sustaining by rational argument the doctrines which no one might any more presume to touch in their substance. This was the second phase or true Scholastic Philosophy.

The Dark Ages.

The transition was not swiftly made. With the final triumph of the Church in the Roman world, about A.D. 600, when the historian comes upon the time of darkness and chaos, when the great world-empire, falling of itself into pieces or broken into fragments by the northern races, was hewn into the rough shapes of modern states and nationalities, the Church held on its way; but it was no longer the Church of Augustin, and not yet the Church of Aquinas. Only perhaps a single obscure name in a century stands out from the time of Augustin to the age of Charlemagne.

The grandiose attempt of the latter, at the close of the eighth century, to organise European society on the basis of a twofold *imperium* of Emperor and Pope gave room for some serious beginnings to be made of provision for intellectual culture in the monastic schools. Half a century later there appeared one of mark—John Scotus Erigena (800–877), a native of either Ireland or Ayrshire, where the darkness had never been so complete as on the continent. He struck the keynote of all that followed in enunciating the perfect unity of religion and philosophy, of faith and reason.

But Charlemagne's construction could not endure, and two centuries more of confusion and anarchy were added to the dismal roll before there arose any prospect of an intellectual succession in Christendom. Erigena was denounced as a heretic for his pains; hence we may not place the beginnings of Scholasticism earlier than the middle of the eleventh century. Thus there was for about five hundred years next to no philosophy among the European races; during that time philosophic activity was confined to Arabians in Bagdad and Moors in Spain. They in the time of greatest darkness carried on disinterested thinking.

Effective Thinking in Christendom confined to the West.

In inquiring into the growth of Scholasticism, let it first be borne in mind, that of the two divisions of the Church it is practically only the Western or Roman Church with which we have to do. The aim of the Fathers was perhaps not less actively promoted in the East than in the West; the development of dogma really took place more at Constantinople and at Alexandria than at Rome. But at the end of the first period, the great consolidation of doctrine made by Augustin for the West, possessed as it was by a force that could survive five centuries, was paralleled by nothing of its kind in the East. And it was for want of this, as much as for any other reasons, that the Eastern Church in the final division of Christendom, although not assaulted by the storms that for centuries beset the West, never to the last did anything for enlightenment to compare with the remarkable if tardy achievements of the Western Schoolmen. The thinkers of Constantinople were men of third or fourth rate power. The authority of Augustin had been the saving of the West. We consider therefore only the Western Church with its Augustinian code.

Philosophic Instruments applied by the Schoolmen.

As to the instruments of the Scholastics for the interpretation of the doctrine handed on to them, the Doctors had some philosophical works of the Greeks which had come across the gulf of centuries. Of course they had, besides, Augustin, but his knowledge of Greek philosophy was gained at second hand only. Of Aristotle they had some minor logical works; they possessed Porphyry's *Introduction to the Categories* (all in the Latin translation of Boethius), and (also in translation) a small piece of Plato's *Timæus*. This was all, excepting one or two inferior works by commentators. Plato's speculations were unknown save as transmitted by Augustin and some of the Neo-Platonists. Even the merely logical doctrines of Aristotle were incompletely apprehended before the middle of the twelfth century, while the full scope of his encyclopaedic work remained unknown till the thirteenth century, when the Schoolmen had in a roundabout way obtained translations of his works. When in A.D. 529 the Greek professors were dispersed, they fled to Bagdad and the East, bearing with them the records of Greek philosophy—the original works of Aristotle, &c. There they were in course of time translated into Syriac and thence into Arabic. The Arabian conquests having established the Mohammedan empire from the East across North Africa into Spain, Greek learning found its way thither in Arabic, and was there again translated by Jews into Hebrew and borne back into Christendom. Then both from Arabic and from Hebrew Latin translations were finally made, and these were received by the Schoolmen as a kind of revelation. But this did not take place till the twelfth century. As it took place, as they became acquainted with Greek philosophy, their view perceptibly widened. And by the time the Schoolmen had learnt their Aristotle as fully as might be in this indirect way, i.e. at the beginning of the thirteenth century, this knowledge began to be supplemented by acquaintance with the original Greek, or by direct translations from the same, the originals being sent or brought by the Greeks of Constantinople.

Limitations of Scholasticism.

Scholasticism was philosophising in support of a limited and foregone conclusion. This is the difference between it and the free movement of Hellenic thought. But still it *was* philosophising. The Doctors did make a step towards the light, in working from blind devotion to more or less rational belief. We can thus distinguish between their greatness and their limitations. If we dwell on the latter, the case against them can be strongly put and maintained. It is easy to abuse Scholasticism. No new or striking conception, like those we find in ancient or in modern philosophy, penetrating to the heart of things, sprang from any one of the Schoolmen. From want of ability or lack of liberty they never carried thought farther than the Greek leaders, and for the most part not so far. Their utter dependence upon Aristotle appears in that, as their knowledge of him widened, their views of philosophy widened and they became able to conceive the full scope of philosophic inquiry. Till the thirteenth century they had no conception of philosophy but as a vague science of dialectic or logic, nor had they made any division of its departments as Aristotle had done. And at the last they incurred discredit through comparison with the Greek philosophy, when the fall of Constantinople revealed this in the original form more fully to the West. They were found to have established no alternative claim to modern respect by taking up any branch of thought which the Greeks had neglected, or in which they had failed. And their very acuteness, through being turned on to a fatally narrow circle of subjects, had led to subtleties that were doomed to be the occasion of some of the bitterest reproaches since heaped upon them.

The Case for Scholasticism.

On the other side it should be noted that the Schoolmen were not responsible for their circumstances, determined by a great and uncontrollable course of events. It was something that, after so great a dissolution, there should have been so considerable an attempt at reconstruction. It was not a little wonderful that they should have applied all the enlightenment handed down to them to rationalise faith, and that they struggled as they did against the conservatism of ecclesiastical authority until official recognition of one newly rationalised doctrine after another was extorted. Theirs became entitled Church philosophy, yet the Church did nothing but accept, did nothing to encourage, their philosophising, witness the case of Scotus Erigena. Often and often was Aristotle solemnly banned before he came to be considered (in the thirteenth century) as 'the forerunner of Christ in the things of Nature as John Baptist was in the things of Grace.' No, we must not speak only of the servility of the Schoolmen; they showed not only wisdom but also courage in their appeal to heathen Aristotle. And it is more becoming at this time of day, and more important besides, that their wisdom and their courage should not remain unacknowledged.

For LECTURE VI :—

The student should not fail to follow up the lecture by reading Croom Robertson's account of British Schoolmen in the essay, 'The English Mind,' *Philosophical Remains*, pp. 34-38.—ED.

LECTURE VI.

SCHOLASTICISM AND THE RISE OF MODERN SCIENCE AND PHILOSOPHY.

Realism in Scholasticism.

INTO the question which chiefly occupied the Schoolmen in their attempt to interpret and rationalise Christian dogma in the light of Greek philosophy—the question of the nature of 'Universals' or General Ideas—we shall enter more fully in a separate lecture. It was not new then any more than it is obsolete now. Before Plato and Aristotle the Greeks had seen its significance; with those two it was a matter of the deepest concern. Plato, with his archetypal ideas as the only Realities, is the great representative of the one extreme view to which the Schoolmen first gave the name of Realism. Aristotle held a modified Realism. The other extreme view, viz. that only particulars are realities, the universal being but subjective, also had its representatives in Greek thought, Epicurus, e.g. approximating to a modern Nominalist, although on different grounds. Of how the question had been discussed by the Greeks the Schoolmen knew nothing. Nevertheless, Porphyry and the fragments in their hands were enough to suggest the problem, and in fact Erigena in the ninth century, in the fervour of his Neo-Platonism, had raised it, and come to a conclusion in the spirit of a thorough Realist. Moreover, as soon as the philosophic interest was aroused within the

Church, the Schoolmen were quick to see the full bearing of the issues. Their philosophy consisting in the intellectual consideration of the mystery of the faith, they discerned at the foundation of how many articles of that faith the problem lay—the Trinity, the Real Presence, the Redemption of the race, the status of the Church as the divinely illumined witness of the Truth. In these and other beliefs they saw how the relation of the Many to the One, the old question of Parmenides and Heracleitus, identical with the later question as to Universals, is implicated.

Now whichever view the Schoolmen took, they made an advance in taking any view at all, and the view held by some from the first, and by the majority at the last, showed more intellect and betokened more independence than is ordinarily ascribed to them. Its promulgation heralded the approach of modern thought.

Divisions of the Scholastic Period.

The whole period falls into three parts:—

Part I. From the eleventh to the end of the twelfth century.
Part II. covers the thirteenth century.
Part III. From the fourteenth century till whenever Scholasticism may be supposed to end; that is, one might say, with the sixteenth century for the active and leading spirits in Europe, with the seventeenth for the universities in the advanced countries, but not even to the present day in the seminaries of the Catholic Church, where Aquinas is still the great philosophical authority.

The first period is the Platonic age of Scholasticism. Aristotle, as we have seen, was at this date known chiefly through the medium of the Arabian scholars, while Plato was known directly by a fragment only, but indirectly through

Neo-Platonic media and Augustin's works. But a Realism as strong as Plato's was supported by Anselm (1033–1109) and others, and this view was tolerated or approved and accepted by the Church. Reason and faith were in process of coming together, but it was an innovation. Scholasticism was struggling to gain its footing. Roscellin (fl. 1092), on the other hand, dared to avow an extreme Nominalism and drove it to an extravagant conclusion.

The second period is the Aristotelian age of Scholasticism, when Aristotle, better known at length in Latin, though not in Greek, came to have more influence over the human mind than at any previous period in history. Way had been made for this evolution by Abelard (1079–1142), that restless, critical, but not constructive spirit, antagonistic to Anselm. Independent and unchecked by rules, he is the first and best representative of freedom of thought in the Middle Ages. A multitude of other circumstances concurred to induce the change of attitude. The beginnings of Scholasticism coincide with the beginnings of the Papal supremacy in Europe—the period from Hildebrand to Innocent III—and the maturity of Scholasticism was attained when the Papacy was putting forth its strongest claims against the civil power—in the days, i.e. of Innocent III (1198–1216)—and when the Church was endeavouring as far as possible to widen the organised ecclesiastical teaching. Now the encyclopædic genius of Aristotle was exactly fitted to satisfy the largest requirements on these lines, and hence Scholasticism, with its ground-principle of reason in the service of faith, flourished at length under Aristotelian influence.

In Thomas Aquinas (1225–1274) the junction was completed. He retained all of Plato that he needed for dogma where Aristotle fell short. But now reason, unlike the first period when she was struggling to enter, not only had entered into the *penetralia* of faith, but was fully recognised, on the condition of yielding aid and reverence to the Church, as the legitimate occupant of the realm of nature. The interest in the natural world felt by Roger Bacon was undoubtedly due to Aristotle's observation of natural phenomena. The watchword of the thought of the day was the Reasonableness of the Faith, and this, Aquinas maintained, was perfectly intelligible even to the smallest particular. But hardly had the generation of Aquinas passed away than this union was seen to be hollow.

The third period is one of rupture and divorce between reason and faith. It is very curious to note how from the two sides equally the fatal change of attitude was effected. John Duns Scotus (1274-1308), who had refined and distinguished beyond all human belief to the extent of twelve folio volumes before he died at the age of 34, was an ardent devoted son of the Church, but he aimed the first blow at Scholasticism by disturbing the concordat of the thirteenth century. He denied that Aquinas had demonstrated the reasonableness of the faith. Christian doctrine transcended reason and had to be believed. Another Briton, William of Ockham, took two strides backward (or forward) for one of Scotus, in reviving the Nominalism of Roscellin, and declaring, like him, that the rational expression of the leading Christian dogmas was impossible. That Roscellin should have beforehand by implication proclaimed the nullity of the Scholastic attempt was as little grateful to the Church as to Anselm, and accordingly Roscellin, who had even exceeded the intellectual licence of Abelard, was condemned and his doctrine banned for two centuries. But the times had changed, and Ockham, milder than Roscellin, could better gain access to men's minds. Professing implicit belief in all the articles of the faith, he proceeded to show, as Kant did later, how impotent was Reason to establish any one of them. Highly gifted, possessing great force of character, and a Franciscan, Ockham gave the Church little cause to love him, and his doctrines did not at once find favour. Nevertheless the times were ready for it, and the Church had gradually to bring herself to support those who declared that the faith could not be explained because it was too high.

But this theory was adopted by independent thinkers as giving, in the mere shadow of restraint it imposed, a chance to get virtually free; and the Church and the world, having agreed to differ, went farther and farther asunder till they turned their backs on each other. The Church might go on believing and exacting what belief it could; but while far from indisposed to believe, men insisted that they would also freely inquire. The influence of the Church was extinguished in different degrees at different places. Events had happened which would have broken Scholasticism even had it been less shaken from within. Human vision and human power were being extended on all sides, in every sphere of human interest. The East had become known through the crusades, and now explorers had unveiled a world and an ancient civilisation in the far West. The reign of darkness, dimly lit hitherto by a circumscribed stock of ideas, once broken, many of those ideas had to be changed or surrendered. Most revolutionising of all were the results of Copernicus's flash of thought. The earth was not fixed and flat, nor the centre of things, but only a revolving satellite, one of many specks in the starry sky, and away on every side, down as well as up, space ran out into the illimitable. Europe was dwarfed in the world; the world was dwarfed in the universe. The heavens existed for other beings than the human race. The right of private judgment was claimed for every separate individuality till, at the beginning of the sixteenth century, Europe was rent in twain. The revival of letters dates from the fall of Constantinople in 1453, when Greek scholars were driven West. The next 150 years witnessed a great revulsion. When through those refugees the true Plato became known, there was a wild wave of Platonic revival. Then attempts were made to understand the true Aristotle, but generally he was decried as the instrument of the Scholastics and, in the heat of reaction, reviled for the artificial supremacy to which they had exalted him. Every Greek school had its adherents who fancied they had lit upon ideas that were all the emancipated world could want. Most remarkable of all were the premature attempts at constructive philosophy by the Italian Nature-philosophers, of whom Telesius was perhaps the most earnest and Giordano Bruno the best known and most imposing. These were endeavours, on a purely secular basis of *objective* consideration, to bring into order and explain the universe in its new vastness. Bruno was burnt at Rome in 1600. Four years previous had seen the birth of Descartes.

Period of Transition.

The Church philosophy, while it ceased to advance in the fifteenth century, lingered on until the modern movement in philosophy took definite shape. After the fourteenth century the best minds were no longer content to be church-philosophers, even if they were friendly to the established religion. A time of intellectual transition supervened, coinciding with the Renaissance, Renascence, or Revival of Letters. But the movement was very gradual. Many among the Schoolmen had been preparing the way for the Renaissance. This transition may be considered as having lasted from 1450 till 1600. It was a time of great intellectual activity, chiefly of a destructive and disintegrating nature, although there were many bold constructive attempts. These, however, were only in revival of past points of view. The destroyers, in this epoch of fermentation, left little of permanent value.

The Modern Period.

With 1600 begins the modern period, properly speaking. Since that time there has been a continuous intellectual flow till now, and there is reason to expect it may continue. The movement has not only been rich in event, it has been European to an extent to which the Church philosophy was not, much less the Greek. The great Scholastic thinkers, it is true, were of different nationalities, chiefly Italian, French, and British, and of these more especially British. The greatest of all, Aquinas, was an Italian, but nearly all the great steps were taken by men of these islands. But whatever nationality they belonged to, they abjured it and became Churchmen. It is only below the surface that we discern the national characteristics. In the modern period, on the other hand, not only do all the cultured races of Europe take part, but the national differences, especially in the British contributors, are far more marked. There is consequently far greater complexity. And whatever else the period has included, there has been a continuous British philosophy.

The Modern Scientific Movement.

Side by side with modern philosophy there has been, to a degree unparalleled before, a properly scientific movement. There is but one name to represent positive science in the preceding period—the name of the Franciscan monk, Roger Bacon (1214–1294). He alone, while the Scholastic mind was turned away from nature and wholly occupied with general philosophy, was profoundly interested in the investigation of natural phenomena. For his pains he was imprisoned twenty or thirty years. Like Archimedes, he stands without known forerunners or successors. It was not till Galileo arose that physical science entered on its modern course.

It is in the modern period that the work of *special* scientific inquiry begins, with ever-increasing subdivision. Some of the leading modern philosophers rank among the scientific discoverers, e.g., Descartes and Leibniz; but modern science commenced its career before modern philosophy. Galileo figures in the first decades of the seventeenth century (1564–1642). Following him there was a continual scientific advance. He was mainly occupied with physics; Harvey, (1578–1657) with physiology. Pascal (1623–1662) devoted himself to physics and mathematics as well as to philosophy. Boyle (1627–1691) is the type of the modern scientific man, of no speculative power, content with eliciting positive results without troubling himself about their relations to other results. Newton (1642–1727) is the supreme representative of special scientific inquiry, though of so wide a range that he is quite above the common rank of inquirers. He laid out what has been accepted as the true physical system of the universe, but becomes confused (in comparison, e.g.

with Locke) when dealing with its speculative aspect. After Newton science branched out and developed gradually into its present high specialisation. At the present time a man must specialise or do nothing. But it was Copernicus (1473–1543) who, in setting the minds of men at the proper point of view for contemplating the universe, prepared the way for Galileo and for Newton, and enabled those that came after to engage in their special inquiries.

By the philosophic movement, as distinct from the scientific, we mean the thinking of men who put themselves essentially at the subjective point of view. They do not exclude the practice of, or the having regard to, a scientific investigation of nature, but they aim at bringing together the results obtained in science, and hold that the study of things must be supplemented by a study of thoughts, the study of nature by a study of things in relation to man.

LECTURE VII.

MODERN PHILOSOPHY.

Divisions.

THE whole movement of Modern Philosophy has been described as an attempt to come at a knowledge of things from a consideration of the conditions and powers of human reason. It starts from the subjective point of view, from that of the knowing mind. Herein it is distinguished from ancient philosophy, which took an objective point of view, as well as from Scholasticism, which was fettered by a system of belief held to be revealed.

Within this movement we meet early with an opposition in thought that admits of greatly varied expression. The German classifications, e. g. Schwegler's and others, are somewhat unsatisfactory. Schwegler, Kuno Fischer, and most of the German historians, divide all schools into Realists and Idealists—those who explain thoughts from things, and those who explain things from thoughts. But this is a bad use of ambiguous, much abused terms. Realist, e. g. has been used both in the question of the perception of an external world and also in that of the reality of 'universals.' It was proposed by Kant to use the term Metaphysical Dogmatists or Dogmatic Metaphysicians, and the usage has become common in Germany; but this does not apply farther than Wolff. Kant, coming after Wolff, it is often said, inaugurated a period of *Critical* Philosophy, appearing as a critical thinker in relation to two movements preceding him—Metaphysical Dogmatism and Empiricism, the latter, he found, having been carried by Hume into Scepticism. Were we at the Kantian point of view this division of modern thought might do; as it is, we must find a place for such as Kant.

Descartes and Bacon.

Modern philosophy, as distinct from the pursuit of modern science, begins as late as the second generation of the seventeenth century with Descartes, and not before. It is in relation to him that we have to understand all who follow. Bacon, who flourished a generation earlier than Descartes, has more relation to the scientific than to the philosophic movement, and had no intellectual succession till long after Descartes. Hobbes caught none of Bacon's enthusiasm for laborious inductive research (though he came into personal contact with him), and showed only a very general agreement with him as to the ultimate springs of human knowledge in sense. Bacon's system fructified later on, mainly in physical science. Whatever philosophy there was in England in the mi 'd'e of the seventeenth century was not truly Baconian. Modern Empirical Philosophy, or Empiricism, took its proper beginning in Locke's *Essay concerning Human Understanding* (1690)—a work which was partly Baconian and regarded experience as the key of knowledge. All the other leaders in the modern movement grow out from Descartes in a continuous philosophic line. Nevertheless, though in Bacon the strictly philosophical ideas and results are a small part of his writings compared with

Descartes', he is without question to be numbered among (mental) philosophers. To proclaim that the human mind must begin, in everything, with simple particular experiences, and that all other knowledge is pretence or error, is a philosophical idea. The study of nature on Baconian principles may be only positive physical science, but in him it was philosophy to call men back from a vain manipulation of words and abstractions to the methodic observation and interpretation of the real phenomena of nature. Moreover, Bacon's idea has its application to mind as well as nature, and therein leads and has led to philosophical results of a sufficiently far-reaching cast.

Rationalism and Experientialism.

There are thus two main lines to be distinguished—those who say that knowledge is explicable from reason[1], and those who hold it is explicable from experience—and these hold good up to Kant, when we begin to get approximations from one line to another: Kant, e. g. approximates to the Experientialists from the Rationalist side; nor is Reid a pure Experientialist. We cannot label the varieties of human thought as exclusively of one kind or the other. Descartes undoubtedly heads the former, and Bacon may be allowed to head the latter, but nowhere must we strain the connexions. We must look only for general similarity in habits of thought. All schools allow the distinction between reason and experience as being, either or both, the ultimate constituents of human knowledge, but in modern times thinkers

[1] The student must distinguish between the narrower peculiarly German connotation of Rationalism used here, and its wider meaning, common in this country, of the revolt of individual reason or judgment against authority in all ultimate questions. ED.

differ in the prominence they assign to one or the other. English philosophers have always put forward experience as that in which to seek an explanation of knowledge. Thinkers of other countries, have, on the whole, been disposed to give pre-eminence to reason; but Rationalists differ much in the relative weight they allow to experience as an additional factor to reason, just as Experientialists differ with respect to reason as an additional factor to experience. Let us survey both lines of thought.

Rationalists.

Descartes began, both in matter and method, a distinct movement during two generations. This was carried on by his (the Cartesian) school—Geulincx, Arnauld, Malebranche, and especially Spinoza. Geulincx, Arnauld and Malebranche sought to be thorough-going Cartesians. Spinoza, while following Descartes, had, besides, distinctly independent views; the most characteristic aspect of him came from the Jewish philosophy of the Middle Ages. Before and after Spinoza's death Leibniz, though bitterly opposed to the former and appealing from Descartes back to the Schoolmen, kept up modern metaphysical Rationalism or *a priori* speculation for yet another generation. Like Spinoza, he was a markedly original thinker, although he thought with reference to the results of Descartes and Spinoza. He was followed by Wolff, who, of less importance, joins Kant to Leibniz, of whom he is a disciple. Wolff had hardly completed his encyclopædic labour of putting form and system into Leibniz's disjointed labours when Kant began his academical career in a state of 'dogmatic slumber,' from which it needed the scepticism of Hume to wake him. Kant called these, his predecessors,

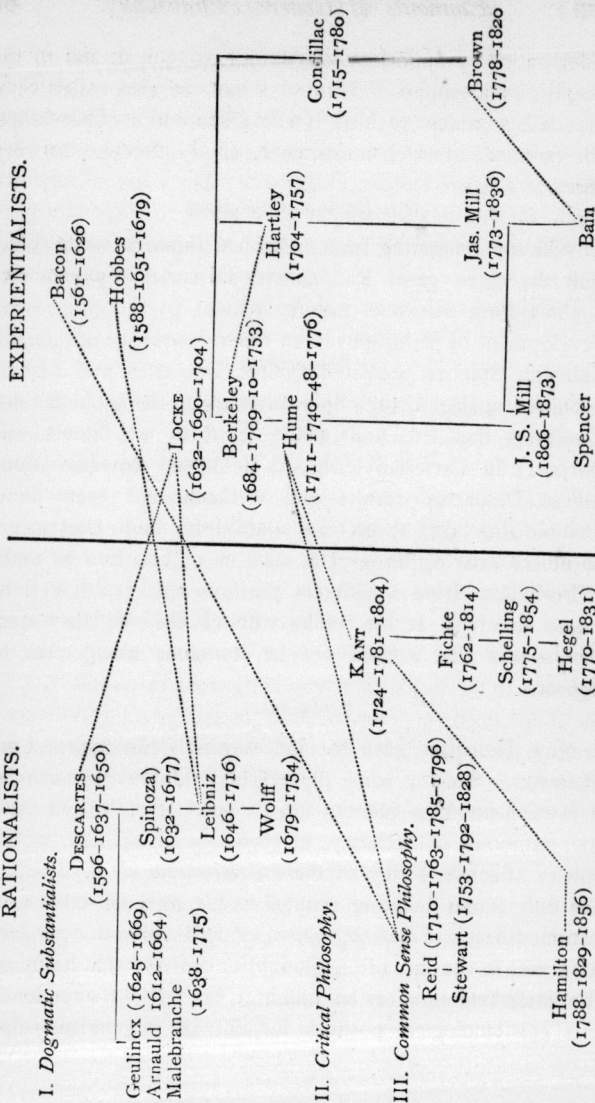

'dogmatic' in opposition to himself as critical, and to the sceptical philosophy of Hume. They are also called Substantialists because each starts with a conception of substance, the variations in which constitute the chief differences between them.

The Rationalist Succession.

Without derogating from individual thinkers, we may say that the three great Rationalists, Descartes, Spinoza and Leibniz, form stages of one movement in the progressive development of philosophy in an orderly sequence of thought, although Spinoza protested against Descartes, and Leibniz protested against both. Spinoza takes up the problems that Descartes had left, and solves them to all intents and purposes in Cartesian terms, as he would not have done unless Descartes' results and methods had been there. Leibniz also takes those results, and from them tries to get to others, arriving however at such as require him to make a fresh start from a different position. And although he began to arrive at his results without Spinoza, they were emphasised and worked out in conscious antagonism to Spinoza.

Cartesianism.

Now Descartes gave to modern philosophy its *subjective* character. Seeking some immediate, irrefutable certainty as a starting-point or fulcrum for all knowledge, he put aside the testimony of authority, of tradition, of opinion, of the sphere of sense, saying of these *dubitandum est de omnibus*. He only found standing ground in his own reflective self-consciousness. *Cogito ergo sum*, or rather *dubito ergo sum*, for it was in the fact of his thought *as doubting* that he found the immediate certainty he sought. But he soon abandoned this epistemological position for one of dogmatism—*Ego sum res cogitans*—and then for the dogmatic Dualism of 'I am a thinking substance, *thinking of a substance that does not think.*' Thus he assumed both mind and matter, the keynote of dogmatic metaphysic being that whatever we clearly and distinctly conceive *is*, or represents, Reality—that thought is the measure of Reality. And the truth of this dual assumption was guaranteed for him, he held, by the existence of a perfect and veracious Deity.

The Development of Cartesianism.

Now this dualism of Descartes is really double, being a dualism as between God and the world, and also as between mind and body. And the problem of the co-existence of substances in either case was carried on by Spinoza and the Occasionalists, Malebranche, Geulincx and Arnauld. The latter concluded that the apparent interaction between mind and body was illusory, the actions of the mind being only so many *occasions* for the intervention of divine power resulting in the corresponding bodily action. But the creature was not only robbed of the power of initiating action, he was also deprived of the ability to know. Knowledge, according to Malebranche, takes place by 'the vision of all things in God,' i.e. it is not we but God that knows through us.

Here we have the consistent development of what was implicit in Descartes. It is the 'death of philosophy.'

Spinoza's central conception was that of substance. He started with it, whereas Descartes worked up to it. But he could not allow more than one substance, all process and all change in the universe being necessarily determined by the nature of that one. 'Besides God,' he wrote, 'no substance can be given or conceived.'

Critical Philosophy.

Kant, on the other hand, raised the question as to whether we can know substance at all, substance being a notion which, while it underlies experience, is not given in experience. He critically examined reason and not experience, yet he approaches nearer to Experientialism than the other Rationalists.

Kant's movement of thought has had a profound influence over all Europe. So much has grown from his philosophy that we cannot here deal with it. Many thinkers have been his disciples, but the great movement in German philosophy of Schelling, Fichte and Hegel was as relatively independent as the departures of Spinoza and Leibniz with reference to Descartes. They philosophise with reference to Kant's critical inquiry, but are not themselves Kantians.

Common Sense Philosophy.

The Scottish school of 'Common Sense' philosophy of Reid and his followers was first of all a protest against the offensive, negative conclusions of Hume, but consisted in a partial departure only from Locke, for it sheltered itself under Bacon as the defender of Experience. Reid sought to make out that, in addition to the senses, there are principles of a common 'sense' inherent in the human mind from the beginning and transcending experience. Dugald Stewart followed Reid, not contributing much original matter, and was followed by Hamilton, who, although he glories in being a disciple of Reid, was influenced in his thought by Kant. Without being a thorough Kantian or well trained in Kantian philosophy, he became through his Kantian studies heir to a larger insight than Reid possessed.

The Experientialists.

There is nothing on the Experientialist side like the definite succession there is upon the side of the Rationalists, although the books are apt to declare the reverse. Bacon was not carried on by Hobbes, nor Hobbes by Locke. Each went on his own way after his own manner. They all start from a consideration of Sense, but do not constitute definite milestones upon a certain track. All are more or less Nominalist. Bacon preached with unsurpassed fervour the necessity of turning to external nature, and it is mainly scientific men who have felt his influence. His general position (v. p. 58) is that knowledge begins with particular experience—that *general* knowledge must be got from *particulars* and tested by experience. But he can scarcely rank as the father of Experiential philosophy. Hobbes's philosophy, again, was markedly provocative to succeeding thinkers, but exercised no regular, systematic influence such as we find on the other side. But when we come to Locke, we encounter a philosophic initiator who may be called so in the same sense as Descartes. He began a new movement which amounted to a definite system of Experientialism. He set himself to prove the problem of human knowledge, and his watchword is Experience as much as Descartes' was Reason. It was the latter who set him thinking, although it was the latter he opposed. Leibniz's *Nouveaux Essais* were written against the *Essay concerning Human Understanding*. Locke stirred up Leibniz to investigate the origin of knowledge from a different standpoint from that taken in the essay.

Locke's essay was present to the mind of Berkeley, who took up human knowledge in the spirit of an Experientialist. Later on he came to be occupied with the question of our knowledge of matter, and solved it in general correspondence with the principles of Locke's philosophy, yet without being more of a Lockian than Spinoza and Leibniz were Cartesians. He took up the question of knowledge as he did because Locke left it where *he* did. Twenty-eight years after the appearance of Berkeley's *Principles of Human Knowledge* Hume wrote his *Treatise of Human Nature*, carrying forward Experientialism as far in some respects as it could be carried, so that in those particular lines there was nothing left for followers to do. He excited more opposition than adherence not only in his own country, but notably in Kant. Hereby English philosophy, as in the case of Locke and Leibniz, came into contact with European thought.

Psychological Philosophy. Associationism.

While his general philosophy was thus carried out by Berkeley and Hume so as to provoke a reaction, Locke set on foot another movement. Although he was a general philosopher and not a psychologist, he nevertheless worked out his philosophy in a psychological spirit. He started from the psychologist's point of view, with the notion of investigating mind in the same scientific way as Newton was investigating nature. This departure had an effect in the very next generation through Berkeley, who carried out special psychological investigation with surprising acuteness in his *New Theory of Vision*. Hume also, without putting forward any system of psychology, worked in a psychological spirit, and discussed particular psychological questions in a notable way, especially the laws of association as containing an explanation of knowledge. Again, Hartley's work on *Man* is of the utmost importance for the so-called

Associationist school, which in psychology tries to get a scientific doctrine of mind as such, and in philosophy tries to solve the general problem of knowledge in connexion with that scientific doctrine.

Now it is usually said that Hume gave a great impulse to the English Associationist movement. My belief, on the contrary, is that James Mill had no special impulse from Hume. If he at all resembled the latter, it was because he started from a similar basis tending to similar conclusions. The origin of the later Associationists is in Hartley and not in Hume. Or, to put it more adequately, the origin of the present English school of the Mills is to be found in the trio, Locke, Berkeley, and Hartley, rather than in Hume[1]. Hartley expressly connected himself with Locke, as Berkeley did. Hume expressly connected himself with Berkeley. We may tabulate them thus:—

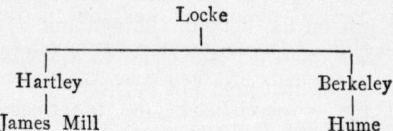

Hartley needs to be connected with Berkeley, though he did not expressly borrow from him.

James Mill's direct descendant is Professor Bain, not John Stuart Mill, who follows somewhat more in the philosophical wake of Hume. Hartley had a philosophy, but not an effective one; he shone as a psychologist. J. S. Mill is, nevertheless, connected with Hartley through his father.

Locke's central idea, viz. that the limits of our knowing

[1] Vide J. S. Mill's introduction to J. Mill's *Analysis of the Human Mind*.

faculty, in regard to the nature and the validity of our knowledge, are only to be understood in reference to a psychological analysis, was introduced into France, together with the Newtonian philosophy of nature, by Voltaire about 1730, supplanting the Cartesian philosophy in both metaphysic and science. Condillac (1715-1780) and Destutt de Tracy (1754-1836), chief among French Sensationalists, greatly affected the Scottish thinker, Thomas Brown. Brown contributed the most important discussion prior to Professor Bain of the part played by muscular sense in objective perception, and still holds the second place.

Of present-day Associationists, Mr. Herbert Spencer is chiefly concerned with a philosophy of evolution on a basis of biological principles. An Experientialist, he approximates as closely to the Rationalist border—by allowing non-experiential elements in knowledge—as Kant did from the Rationalist side in the other direction. Mr. Spencer himself claims to be just on the border. Many think he unites the two sides. Kant, however, laid claim to a similar position, and yet was very distinct from Mr. Spencer.

For LECTURE VIII read Bain, *Mental Science*, App. A. to p. 26.

LECTURE VIII.

UNIVERSALS.

Why Scholasticism was mainly occupied with 'Universalia.'

WE are now in a position to inquire more closely into those great special questions raised by philosophic thought which I enumerated at the close of Lecture III.

From Descartes onward the great question of philosophy has been as to the relation of reason and experience in knowledge. Now, Plato and Aristotle (who practically represent ancient epistemology in the West) were interested both in this problem and in that of the universality of knowledge, while during the whole of the middle period the central question of philosophy was not so much the former as that of the relation between the universal and the particular in knowledge. The more modern question is, after all, the same as the latter, but in another form and with a difference of emphasis; experience is experience of particulars, while reason is concerned with universals.

Why, then, does only one of the two questions occupy the thought of the Middle Period? The fact is that both the middle and modern periods *were* occupied with both questions, or with these two aspects of the more general question, viz. as to the import of human knowledge; but the thought of men in the Middle Ages had been directed to the aspect of the universality of knowledge by an accidental circumstance. This circumstance (v. Bain, App. pp. 23, 24; and *supra*, Lect. V) was that one portion of Porphyry's *Isagoge*, containing an introduction to the Categories of Aristotle, was preserved in translation during the early Middle Ages, whereas it was not till the twelfth and thirteenth centuries that the Schoolmen had a complete translation of Aristotle's works. Now this fragment suggested the question of the relation of different general notions to one another, and hence it came about that this aspect of knowledge occupied philosophers predominantly down to the end of the Scholastic period, till every side of the question had been touched upon and they had come to practical agreement. Modern philosophy also agrees in the main upon the subject, although it was bound in its turn to reconsider it. The difference in modern times is regarding the psychological question.

Concept Psychologically and Philosophically regarded.

We have distinguished knowledge psychologically regarded from knowledge philosophically regarded. Let us now mark off the psychological bearing of knowledge as universal or general from the philosophical aspect. *General* intellection, knowing, or cognition we dealt with under thought or conception (in the wider sense), and for the product of conception we used the term concept. And the psychological question of the concept became for us, How do we come to know generally? How do we arrive, i.e. under what laws of mental action do we arrive, at that kind of knowledge which we call conceptual? Conceiving (*Elements of Psychology*, Lect. XXV, XXVI) arises under certain psychological laws out of historically prior intellectual products. Now of these the percept has corresponding to it an objective thing—at least, we assume that it has—and some images also have a corresponding reality in the realm of being, in so far as they are literal re-percepts, while some again have not. But our question now is, Has the *concept* a corresponding reality? Is there, for instance, a real being to correspond to the concept 'man'? Mill calls 'man' concrete; is it as concrete as 'this man'? No, we cannot generalise save by abstracting, and 'man' is abstract as involving generalisation. What then does this abstract generalisation or 'Universal' portend in the sphere of being? Is it a mere subjective construction, or does the concept represent reality? What is the relation of 'man' the 'universal' to 'this man' or 'that man,' of the General to the Particular, of the One to the Many, of individual changing things to the whole universe? Which has reality? If only

'The One remains, the many change and pass';

as Shelley sang[1], the question arises, Do the Many exist at all?

Platonic Realism.

Now this question, applied by Schoolmen to religious tenets, had been rationally discussed by Plato, who probed the matter deeper than any before him. By Platonic Realism is meant Plato's doctrine of the relation of the One to the Many, of the Universal to the Particular. His standpoint was a development of the question as faced by Socrates. Socrates saw that human knowledge is mainly knowing by way of concepts, and his philosophy was summed up in efforts at getting clear general notions. We arrive at knowledge on a large scale only through the conceptual form; only thus

[1] *Elegy to Keats.*

can we bring together experience as knowledge. If we know for the most part by way of concepts, if all that we can call scientific knowledge is conceptual, i.e. is knowledge of classes or kinds, then the question arises whether that which we know in the form of concepts or ideas does not represent reality, or that which truly is. Thus Plato, following his master's line and holding that knowledge properly so called is of ideas only, declared that therefore ideas and nought else are what really exist, and that, by comparison with the ideas, known and really existing, anything that we commonly speak of as particular things—things of sense—have, in the full sense of the word, no reality, and are only pale shadows of real existence. So far from asking, as might in these times of a developed psychology be asked, whether anything corresponded to the concept objectively in the same sense as is assumed in the case of the percept, Plato maintained that it was the concepts, general notions or ideas, that are the only real beings, and not so-called individuals. Table,' for example, exists; individual tables are mere passing shows, while the idea 'table' exists really and eternally. If any one gets a true knowledge of 'table' it is not by way of sense, but by a reminiscence of a former mental life. Tables—this table, that table—did not exist yesterday, will not exist to-morrow. But 'table' was before all tables, and will be after all tables. In other words, the particulars of sense, whether considered separately or brought together in an aggregate or class, do not really, fully exist. That only can be said really and fully to exist which is THOUGHT.

Platonic Idealism.

This theory—viz. to repeat, that if it is the idea (universal or general notion) which we are dealing with *when we really know*, then it is the idea only that *really exists*—is logically possible on the ground it assumes, and marks a special type of mind. In the Middle Ages it came to be called by the Schoolmen, who were great masters of nomenclature, the doctrine of Realism. Plato's expression of this view has never been surpassed, and never will be. But if he is the greatest of Realists in this the original sense of the term, he none the less remains the typical Idealist in any sense and for all time. For Platonic Realism and Platonic Idealism are one and the same doctrine, Plato being a Realist because of the reality he ascribed to ideas, and an Idealist because it is ideas to which he ascribed reality. He is not the one to the exclusion of the other, unless indeed we attach to Realism and Idealism the meaning they have come to bear in modern times as opposite theories of our perception of an external world[1]. In that case Plato ceases to be a Realist, and is a pure Idealist. In the question of universals, Realism is only another aspect of the more general Idealism.

Aristotelian Realism.

What, then, is the antithesis to Realism in its original sense? The theory which in Aristotle took shape as a doctrine of *essence*, and which became divided against itself as the contrasted theories of Conceptualism and Nominalism (names which are also derived from the nomenclature of Scholasticism), scarcely constitutes an antithesis. Aristotle broke away from the Realism of his master by declaring that particular things have a real existence, but neither they nor universals exist independently of each other; the universal exists *in* the

---

[1] The student must not confound the philosophical connotations of these terms with their modern usage in artistic and literary criticism.—Ed.

particular as its essence. He may thus be considered as a modified Realist. He began by saying that all things which can be thought of or predicated can be brought to ten classes or categories of concepts. But only the first, Substance (οὐσία), can be the subject of predication. Quantity, Quality, and the other seven attributes do not exist in the same sense as Substance. Now we can only predicate existence of a concrete thing, not of an idea. Here he seems to deny reality to the concept. But he further distinguishes between a first and a second substance, the first applicable to a concrete thing of sense which, informed by its universal essence, really and fully exists, and is the subject of a proposition; the second, indicating the general concrete, may be subject or predicate. E. g.

Socrates	is	a man.
(1st Substance)		(2nd Substance)
		Man is mortal.

In this way existence can be predicated of concept. Individual things are substance in the full sense; in essence they *are* universals. But abstractions have no real existence.

Universalia post rem.

Plato's position of extreme Realism being summed up in the scholastic formula, *Universalia ante rem* (*res* = thing of sense), and Aristotle's modified Realism being described as *Universalia in re*, the antithesis to Realism for which there is no inclusive name is best brought out in the corresponding formula, *Universalia post rem*; i.e. it is only from a knowledge of things in particular that we come to know universals, in other words, to form the merely subjective constructions termed concepts, abstract ideas or general notions. Only particular things exist; the universal is a mere instrument of thought for getting at a knowledge of particulars. This was the theory of Epicureans and Stoics.

But, as I have indicated, the formula was interpreted in two ways. When, in the first age of the Schoolmen, Platonic Realism was rampant, an extreme form of Nominalism, viz. that the general thought or universal is a name and nothing else (*vox et praeterea nihil*), was contended for by Roscellin. We cannot think generally without the help of names; what, then, is the universal but a name (*nomen*)? This in fact was the anti-Realism of the Stoics and Epicureans. Later, in the thirteenth century, when Scholasticism was at its height, the predominant Aristotelian Realism shaded off into Conceptualism, viz. that the universal was not a mere word (*flatus vocis*) but a mode of human cognition, though formed from and after the perception of particulars. This was coupled with the doctrine of essences, of 'universalia *in* re.' Some indeed tried to reconcile Platonic Realism with it also by the theory of the real existence of universals in the *divine* mind. When, however, Scholasticism was dying, William of Ockham (a village in Surrey) gave a very decided expression to Nominalism as opposed to Conceptualism, maintaining that the mind arrives at universals through the use of words. And at the end of the Scholastic period the chief thinkers were declared Nominalists.

Harmony between Science and Philosophy.

After two centuries of transition the foremost minds of the seventeenth century, Descartes, for example, turned their attention to physical nature and helped to create modern science. Now the modern science of nature is based on a philosophical view that is antithetic to the Platonic theory. Realism has never regained its importance in the modern period; it was practically overthrown by the growth of positive science. Or we may say that modern science has sprung up *because* the philosophical problem of Realism was fought out. The Realist despises the things of sense as vain shows with no reality. The man of science says they do exist and are worth investigating. With Conceptualism and Nominalism, on the other hand, modern science can get on; they in fact attuned men's minds for scientific research, which goes on the assumption that it is the particular things which really exist, works up from particulars to universals, and refuses to recognise the truth of universals without verifying by particulars. Any one may now be a Platonic Realist, but he must then give up the modern science of nature. In fact there always have been Realists and always will be. It was a mistake for Mill to speak of Realism as exploded (in his *Examination of Hamilton's Philosophy*). Carlyle was a Realist; so also is Ruskin—great men, though not philosophers. And the standpoint, consistently developed, leads to an ascetic doctrine of morals. Carlyle and Ruskin recognise the hostility between modern science and Platonism, and this is why they decry the former. Carlyle hated science, but he excepted mathematics, as did Plato, who said that if a man could not geometrise he could not philosophise. From their point of view science cannot but be absurd. No Realist thinks it worth while to treat of physics and chemistry. If a man prefers to live in the contemplation of Eternal Ideas, this in its way is very good. Theologically such a one will be a Pantheist. But if he would rise to something worth calling knowledge of nature, the right way is that of positive science, with its Inductive Method of working up to general expressions from particulars. Positive science is not all-sufficient for the inquiring mind, and should be supplemented by a philosophy not inconsistent with it. But Realism *is* inconsistent with science. No person who is at heart a Realist can have that kind of interest in particular things upon which thoroughgoing science rests. In external nature we must start from the concrete particular; hence we have in the modern period an anti-Realistic philosophy, instead of an antagonism between our philosophy and our science.

For LECTURE IX read Bain, loc. cit. pp. 26-33.

LECTURE IX.

UNIVERSALS. NOMINALISM AND CONCEPTUALISM.

'Res' *as real*.

MODERN philosophy then, as being in the main concordant with modern science, is anti-Realistic, or, in the wider sense of the word, Nominalistic. Philosophy for the most part, and especially English philosophy, has assumed that the Platonic doctrine is untenable, and that some form of the antithesis, that it is particular things which really exist, must be accepted. Thus in modern times the conflict has been narrowed to the opposition between Nominalism and Conceptualism. The great question now became—Under what conditions does the human mind conceive? What constitutes thinking as opposed to other modes of intellection?

The Ground of the Problem shifted.

Note that the problem has been shifted from metaphysical to psychological ground. It is no longer a question of what may be said really to exist. Conceptualists and Nominalists agree in declaring that the universal has only a subjective existence, that the concept has no objective existence like the percept, but is only arrived at in the mind with a view to the understanding of the particulars. This is the anti-Realistic metaphysic of their position. But if we would give any more positive assertion about them, we must do so in psychological terms. The difference between them is psychological only, and it has played an important part in modern psychology. In England, where, from the time of Locke, the psychological interest began to prevail and where psychology first assumed a scientific form, that difference has been much discussed. Not so abroad. Hamilton, it is true, made light of the difference, but then his psychology is decidedly weak.

Nominalism in England.

The general train of English thought has been in the direction of Nominalism. Now the thorough-going Nominalist says two things:—(1) that it is impossible to think generally without language; (2) that the mind can only represent the concrete particular as such. Hobbes makes both these statements; Berkeley, only the second; nevertheless he as well as Hume and the Mills are distinctly Nominalists, though in different senses. Hobbes seems to say that thought is expression in words and nothing else. Still he is not far wrong. It is since his time that the importance of language in the function of conceiving has been emphasised. Locke, in the immortal third Book of his *Essay*, is strongly Nominalistic and impressed with the necessity of language. In Book IV, however, he shows a strong Conceptualistic vein, maintaining that we can think of 'triangle' which is not isosceles, nor equilateral, nor scalene. (This Berkeley denies.) But this Conceptualism of Locke's is probably only a bad way of distinguishing the intension from the extension of the concept. Because 'triangle' *ex*tends to all three, no one of the three particulars therefore enters into the *in*tension of 'triangle.' He confuses the abstract with the general.

The Scottish school, on the other hand, is more Conceptualistic than the English, Dugald Stewart less so than others. Reid is Conceptualistic. Hamilton's logic is distinctly Conceptualistic, yet in the lectures on metaphysic he adopts Berkeley's view. Hamilton, however, does not so much give his own thinking as get it from certain German authorities.

The Mills, I have said, are Nominalists; so is Professor Bain. Taine's chapter on the Concept is the best statement of good Nominalistic doctrine (see his *Intelligence*).

The Ground of Difference.

The Conceptualists say that the concept is as truly a definite fact of mental construction, an actual subjective somewhat that can be called a representation, as is the percept. Whereas, according to all Nominalists, conceiving is either bringing up a number of particulars one after another, i.e. having a series of percepts, or else we are, when conceiving, only imaging a particular percept, while leaving out of sight the individual particulars.

There are Concepts and Concepts.

But Conceptualists and Nominalists both err in trying to find one uniform expression for a very graduated aggregate. Concepts vary so much in the scale of abstractness (cf. 'tiger,' 'iron,' 'father,' 'nation') that it is hopeless to attempt any uniform representation to suit all. The concept is not a collection, nor a series, of particular images. The concept 'sheep' is not a flock of sheep. Just as we distinguish between the collective and the general, so we must distinguish between the concept and a series of percepts. The former is a means of bringing together a multitude otherwise than as a series, and will vary in definiteness according to the degree of abstractness. In the case of exactly similar objects the concept abstracts from the differences in time and space only. Generic images represent the truth about those concepts where the similarity is very overpowering. Sometimes, finally, conceiving proceeds by way of symbols; i.e. there are concepts of which we have no image unless it be of particulars in succession, and between which the likeness is fixed by a word. We use names of course for individuals as well as for concepts; indeed, we do not know a thing fully till we know its name. But it is remarkable that when a name is a mere adjunct it is apt to be forgotten; but where a conception, e.g. of justice, depends, for any coherence and definiteness it may possess, upon having a name, we do not forget it.

A case of pathology throws light here. Some forms of organic decay are connected with a disturbance of the faculty of speech, or aphasia. And instances of this occur where the intellectual powers are very little affected. The patient, e.g. is able to speak in general language, but forgets the names of particular kinds of things. Emerson in his last years was subject to this. Words like 'table' and 'hat' he could not recollect, but he was quite able to substitute more general expressions, e.g. 'Put the kind of thing that covers head on to the surface that has legs.' Names of definite concretes were forgotten where abstract terms were still within his power. Why? Because for his knowledge of the former he was not dependent upon language. To express the relation he did need language; he had not lost speech where it was indispensable.

The two Types of Nominalism.

Now there are Nominalists and Nominalists. Berkeley, for example, is merely anti-Conceptualistic, and owes his reputation for Nominalism solely to the opinion of Hume. He only takes up the negative attitude, that there is no definite representation of anything but either as perceived or as definitely imaged. He says nothing about the necessity for names. On the contrary, he declares that we can think without language, and that we should think better than we do, could we keep the names of our ideas out of our thoughts —so strangely has knowledge 'been perplexed and darkened by the ... general ways of speech[1].' Whereas extreme Nominalists like Roscellin declare that concepts are nothing more than names.

With regard to the former type of Nominalists, there is this to be said:—So far from it being true that the idea is always of a particular concrete, it might be maintained that our imagining and perceiving are always a kind of abstraction. Do I, in looking at that pillar, perceive all the attributes? No; I fill it in by repeated perceptions. My percept of it at any moment is a perception of it under some one aspect only. Perception of a particular involves abstraction. The generic image, to which I have already alluded, was Mr. Galton's term for that resultant to which, he affirmed, a number of like images give rise—a resultant which is not like any one of them, nor is the whole together, but is yet representative of all (*El. of Psy.* p. 168). This position was supported by the now widely practised composite photography, by which Mr. Galton obtained not a blur of many faces, but an actual portrait, yet not of any one individual. This does not *prove* anything in relation to our conscious experience, but it may well be that the process of conceiving is *analogous*. But in so far as the Conceptualists maintain that we have always a clear

[1] Berkeley, *Principles*, Introduction.

consciousness of a body of concepts as such, they go too far. No Conceptualist has ever given a sufficient and satisfactory analysis of general knowledge.

The Truth in Nominalism.

With regard, on the other hand, to the latter type of Nominalists, whereas their identifying the concept with a name and nothing more is nonsensical and goes too far in the opposite direction, they are right to the extent of maintaining that all the more purely abstract ideas are had through and by, and not without, the help of signs, viz. language. Here—'no speech, no thought.' In proportion as thought becomes more general and more abstract, it needs some kind of instrument to work with. All thinking that is more than rudimentary necessitates language. Savages with poor language have poor thoughts. We must be careful to distinguish. Can we know without speech? Unquestionably. Can we think (know generally, generalise) without speech? Only to an elementary extent. The proper position then to take is that our power of bringing percepts together into concepts depends upon our power of using signs. Science, which is general knowledge, is found to progress according as it becomes embodied in a definite system of symbols. Condillac the Sensationalist had so strong an opinion of the importance of language that he defined a science as *une langue bien faite*. Indeed, Nominalism is often supposed to be connected with Sensationalism, because the two theories are associated in Condillac's philosophy. But it is just sensation that is independent of names and symbols. The error of the Sensationalist school consisted, as Mansel pointed out, in confounding the indispensable instrument of thought with thought itself. Philosophy is so backward because it has not a set of symbols for itself, but has to work with popular names. Nothing can be called an element of knowledge till it is taken up by others and thrown back on the speaker. People who are cut off from the use of language are found to have imperfect powers of generalisation. Even with their manual system the dumb cannot develop any great ability for generalising. The signs no doubt are less pliable, but the chief reason is that they are still cut off from communication with the majority of their fellows. Speech is, as we saw in our psychology, a social, not an individual, product. It is with the need of communicating that speech arises. 'Sheep' may be imaged in general without language, but a variety which we cannot image 'squeezes out,' i.e. expresses, some general sign from us. But this squeezing out would not have taken place but for the requirements of the *common* life. A man does not conceive for himself but in relation to others. Thus the true psychology of conception throws us back on the origin of speech. And hence what a man shall think will depend less on what he is in himself than on his social circumstances. If left to himself, his mental powers would be comparatively undeveloped. If knowledge were a mere aggregate of sensations, the savage might be better off than other people. The superiority of civilised people consists in the fact that there are expressions in force for the new-born individual to avail himself of. It is impossible to over-estimate the importance of this factor, and of late years this idea of the great part played by language in helping us to arrive at knowledge, to which by ourselves we could not have attained, has been gaining ground[1].

[1] Cf. e. g. Professor Sayce's *Introduction to the Science of Language*. See also *Mind*, i. 253, and iv. 149, on the education of Laura Bridgman.

Conclusion.

I do not, then, profess to solve the philosophic question at issue. Any man's philosophy is the expression of his whole being; in every man's thinking there must be a personal subjective element. For me the true doctrine lies partly with Conceptualism and partly with Nominalism. It is a case of the shield with two sides: each theory says it has only one, and therein lies the error as well as the truth of each. Each side makes statements that are too absolute: they are true in what they affirm and false in what they deny. Conception varies too much for any universal statement as to concepts to hold good. But the statement that there may be a representation that is definite without being particular is true.

For LECTURE X read:—
Bain, op. cit. Book IV, ch. viii.
The student may also refer to Professor James's article: 'The Psychology of Belief,' *Mind*, xiv. p. 321.

LECTURE X.

THE NATURE OF KNOWLEDGE. KNOWLEDGE AND BELIEF.

Transition to the Second Question.

Some concepts, then, at least are explicable from sense-perception, i.e. are formed by way of abstraction from particular experiences. Are *all* concepts formed thus, or are some obtained otherwhence? What, in other words, does sense contribute to knowledge? Granted that sense is of account for knowledge, it does not follow that knowledge is mere sense or sense transformed. Thus we connect the question of universals with the controversy on the Nature, or, as it is also called, the Origin of Knowledge, which is the great central problem in dispute among the philosophers of the modern period.

The Origin of Knowledge is not a good name for this question; it is too psychological, and the philosophical question is not answered together with the psychological question. What we have to consider is the Nature of Knowledge—how knowledge is constituted. Whereas in psychology we do not exhaust the consideration of knowledge properly so called.

Knowledge and Belief.

Now the term 'knowledge' is necessary for philosophy, especially modern philosophy, the central thought of which, from its beginning with Descartes, is that we cannot determine the nature of being before we have determined the nature of knowing, and that in any ultimate question we are strictly considering not so much what we are as what we *know* that we are. Hence we see the advantage of getting a word that is purely psychological, like intellection.

We have also asserted that the term 'belief' is of import for philosophy. Belief has both a psychological explanation and a philosophical import very much implicated in the question of the nature or origin of knowledge, and therefore it is that a short consideration of belief under both aspects will serve to show the bond and the distinction between psychology and philosophy, and also to introduce our special subject.

The Psychology of Belief.

Belief is a kind of conscious experience. Our psychological question is to determine *which* kind. Professor Bain appears to treat it as a kind of volition by putting it under the head of Will. This is not so bad as it looks, for by Will he means, as we know, Conation; wherefore he does not mean that when a man is believing he is necessarily willing, or making a voluntary determination. What then does he mean? He places the consideration of belief where he does because he finds it has a certain reference to action. In believing we are ready to act; unless we can show some kind of reference to action we are not believing. Under Will he deals with all activities as set on by feeling, and generally with all motives to action, Belief being taken as one such motive. I excuse the arrangement but do not justify it. Whatever else Belief is, this is not the most fundamental aspect. In willing we are doing something else than believing; in believing we are doing something else than willing. We all believe that life must come to an end, but this is different from willing to die.

Yet, while there is an obvious difference between willing and believing, there is a subtle underlying connexion between the two. How often do we not say, a man believes a thing because he wants it so? How much is not our belief an expression of our wishes? It is quite possible to go on willing so intently that we end by believing. And I think that is at the bottom of Professor Bain's mind in his choice of treatment here. There is something in believing which has a special kind of relation to willing.

But is the fact that what we believe we are prepared to act on a real differential attribute of Belief, marking it off from other conscious experience? Is there any other state of mind where we are prepared to act? Yes; if I am prepared to act on belief, I am still more prepared to act on knowledge; e.g. if I believed there were a tiger in the next room, I might venture to peep in; but if I were 'sure,' if I *knew* there was, I should at once proceed either to lock myself in here or to run downstairs. This reference to action therefore, which unquestionably belongs to belief, is not its distinctive attribute since it is at least equally characteristic of another state.

What else has Professor Bain said? That our beliefs always contain an element of feeling. When we are believing we are always at the same time emotionally affected. Is this the differentia of belief as compared with knowledge? Yes, belief distinctly varies with feeling. Is our tiger heard scratching, the bold one says, Nonsense! the timorous one says, Yes, it *is* there! But knowledge is intellectual expression apart from feeling. $2+2=4$, however you may feel. It is a valuable point in Professor Bain's exposition to have thus connected belief with original spontaneity of feeling, with difference of temperament.

We see then the difference between I imagine, I believe, I know, a tiger is in class-room No. 3. Belief is something like knowledge, but falling short of it. We may know that $9 \times 7 = 63$, but a child who does not yet understand the multiplication table may say, *I feel sure* that $9 \times 7 = 63$. 'Sure' shows the connexion with intellection, 'feel' the emotional aspect. Again, the phrase *morally certain*, another equivalent for 'believe,' brings out the conational aspect: 'certain' is intellective, 'morally' means 'certain so as to act upon it,' but not absolutely certain. Not full knowledge, but probability, and that is after all the guide of life.

This distinctly emotional character of belief may help us to understand the relation of belief to conation. Conation is action under an impulse of feeling, action that is feeling-guided or determined by feeling; it is action for an 'end,' and 'end' always involves feeling. Belief is not action for an end, in order to feeling, but is something that goes on under feeling. Thus we see how easily the one could pass into the other, how action for feeling may result in action under feeling, so that what we will in starting, we end by believing.

Well then, whatever emotional elements there may be in belief, there is something in it non-emotional. Here again we shall find the relation of belief to conation brought out markedly. In the instance of volition employed in our course of Psychology, namely, 'I will to open the door,' can I will to open it without either knowing it can be opened, or believing it can be opened? No, and hence whatever we call volition involves intellection. Believing the door can be opened and willing to open it are not the same, but the difference in my confidence lies between my believing that the door opens in a certain way and my knowing that it does. What then is there common to the belief and the knowledge as such? A fact of intellectual representation. Belief is essentially a representative state of mind, and representation, as we know, enters into all intellection. But willing, or the disposition to act, is as such not representation, is not intellection with its discriminating and assimilating. In believing we are intellective, as in knowing. I believe the moon is round, i.e. I represent the back of it. Were the moon to turn round, I should *know*—at least more than I do now. Belief, then, is fundamentally a mode of intellection. But whereas knowledge is, from the psychological point of view, adequately and exhaustively expressed as intellectual representation, belief, from the same point of view, is not adequately and exhaustively expressed as intellectual representation, because of the feeling involved in it.

The Essential Complexity of Belief.

Since belief is fundamentally a mode of intellection, and to a certain extent a mode of feeling also, it cannot be treated as merely a mode of conation. Professor Bain indeed only seems to do this; his exposition really comes to this, that belief is a kind of intellectual representation, accompanied with, and liable to be modified by, feeling and involving essentially readiness to act. The result for us is, that we cannot refer belief to any one phase of mind. It is an essentially complex mental state, describable in every one of the three phases—a mode of representative intellection, tinged with feeling, having relation to the native tendency to act. I wish not to divorce belief from action. I would assert their connexion more decisively and explicitly even than Professor Bain. We allow in life that a man's belief is justified by his actions. Popular consent and psychological inquiry converge on this point. Where we are not prepared to act we don't believe. Many beliefs, it is true, like many cognitions, seem to have no relation to action, e. g. my belief that the moon is round. But this belief implies that if I were projected thither, I should in exploring be able to make the tour of it. There is no belief and no cognition that cannot, may not, have a reference to action, but cognitions rather than beliefs. Judgment, memory, expectation, all imply a relation to action, while other modes of intellection —reflexion, reverie, imagining (in the narrower sense)—are as such accompanied by a more receptive attitude of mind. It is true that all developed volition also involves feeling and intellection, but that does not prove that the bare fact of volition or conation is anything beyond impulse to act. Therefore we hold by our three phases, and say that volition (will) is complex and belief is complex.

Disbelief and Doubt.

Two other topics connected with belief should be considered, viz. disbelief and doubt. Disbelief is itself belief, namely, in the truth of the opposite; there is nothing to be said of it which has not already been said of belief. Doubt, on the other hand, is the opposite, the contradictory of belief. It is not present when we are believing, or at least in as far as we are believing, but it is only really excluded by knowledge. In proportion as belief is remote from knowledge, doubt tends to be the more present. Doubt is also complex, having its three aspects—it paralyses action, involves wavering representation, is of marked emotional character. We want to know (i.e. to represent clearly, if we cannot attain to presentative consciousness), and we cannot. Consequently representation follows representation, one chasing another and being itself chased away—a wavering intellectual condition which in its emotional aspect is essentially distressing.

The Philosophy of Belief.

Belief and knowledge, then, have each a practical aspect. They are not simply subjective states or mental facts, but are related to a something believed or known, which cannot be adequately expressed in terms of bare subjective experience, i.e. of psychology. Conceiving and thinking may be said to have an object in the concept or thought, but there is nothing in either, nor in the image, that is not fully accounted for by psychology alone. But the object of belief or of knowledge is expressed in terms of *fact, objective fact, real existence, reality*, which cannot be exhausted by psychological inquiry. Now a *real* belief is one we are prepared to act on. Mere imagining is representing what is out of relation to our actions. We may also conceive what is out of such relation, whereas my readiness to act on what I believe determines the reality of that belief. Every cognition and every belief has or may have relation to action—and I can find *no other meaning of Reality*.

We distinguish in ourselves a mental constitution concerned with the functioning of a bodily organism. Let us put ourselves on physiological ground:—the organism is liable to be affected and to send forth impulse; when stimulated, we act; this is the most fundamental fact. Of course we can act apart from external stimuli, and we can be stimulated without ensuing overt action. But, broadly speaking, action follows from stimulus. Now therefore reflex action is the type of action; any act may be expressed in terms of reflex action. The efficacy of the act depends, in the last resort, on the stimulus received. And it is the stimulus received that suggests what we call Real in giving us occasion for acting. There is no mark of unreality more fundamental than the absence of any tendency to produce activity. Here then are philosophical implications: it is the deepest meaning of Reality that it gives occasion for action, that it is that to which action has relation.

So far belief and knowledge are parallel; so far we can only distinguish them both from imagination, &c. We must go further than this. There are two philosophical aspects of the relation of belief to knowledge: (1) of belief as something less than knowledge; (2) of knowledge as based on belief, i.e. as explained by certain principles underlying knowledge which themselves we cannot know, but can only hold as beliefs. We must face both.

Belief as Inadequate Knowledge.

The first is the common usage. Of two intellective acts (to keep to psychological terms) to which we ascribe reality, it is to knowledge that we ascribe it more confidently, inasmuch as knowledge involves less representation and more presentation than belief. As the presentative element preponderates, so does belief merge into knowledge; the attention we give is then called knowledge. Taking my treatment of Seeing and Touch we can generalise therefrom. Sight gives knowledge in regard to some cognitions, but belief relatively to Touch. The difference between belief and knowledge depends on the possibility of verification. In Logic a hypothesis is the best representation we can make under given circumstances. Theory, as opposed to hypothesis, is knowledge as distinct from belief. What is now belief may, at another point of view or time, amount to knowledge. 'Seeing is believing, but touch is the real thing.' Till I touch that pillar, I, strictly speaking, *believe* it is one; much more if I am out of the room. I am then thrown on to representative consciousness. I believe in default of knowing. Not that there is such a thing as pure presentation, or that there is no presentation in belief. Belief is *relative* predominance of representative consciousness. Touch is relatively presentative to Sight. Perception involves belief, yet it is more knowledge than other intellective functions are.

Knowledge as based on Belief.

But if intellection, in so far as it has presentative elements, is knowledge and, in so far as it has representative elements, is belief, how is it that we can speak of knowing anything by re-representative intellection, e.g. when we are reasoning about facts in general terms? Take the argument, 'Kings are mortal because they are men.' This is an act of intellection that would be admitted as a clear case of knowledge, not belief—of reasoned, though not presentative, knowledge. Hence we may have knowledge away from a presentative base when dealing with concepts. This is deductive reasoning, or knowledge of the *why*. If I say 'I know kings are mortal,' and am asked how I know, my answer is, 'Because they are men'; and this is accepted because I know not only the fact but the *why*.

Does this give rise to any further question about the

relation between knowledge and belief? We may say 'Kings are mortal, for kings are men'; but then arises the question, 'Do you *know* men are mortal, or do you only believe it?' One assertion given as the basis of another may be regarded as a ground for knowledge, but it only throws back the difficulty. As to the ground of that fundamental assertion, How do we know men are mortal?—We say, 'Because men are animals.' Now if anybody is prepared to say he accepts the mortality of animals on inductive experience, the question is whether this is to be called belief or knowledge. Certainly whatever we inductively infer (if it be material induction) is belief rather than knowledge. If a material induction goes beyond the experience on which it is based—and to be a real induction it must—then it is a case of belief rather than knowledge. Whatever we have direct experience of we may be said to know; hence an inductive inference is always more or less hypothetical or probable only.

We see, then, that what is confessedly mere belief, viewed with reference to the experience from which it was inferred, becomes the ground of knowledge both in induction and deduction. Our statement is belief or knowledge according to the point of view from which we make our major premise. Thus:—'All men are mortal' is knowledge, if got by deduction from 'All animals are mortal,' but belief, if got as inductive inference from experience. Our knowledge that is got by reasoning may always be looked at in relation to two sources:—first, as experience or generalisation beyond experience, i.e. as belief. But, in the second place, are there not other sources of knowledge? Beside the particular facts of experience we need to assume certain general principles to account for knowledge, allowed even by those who emphasise the sufficiency of experience. It is impossible for me to perform a careful induction from experience without such an assumption as the 'Uniformity of Nature.' Mill, striving here to preserve consistency, maintains that this is itself an induction from particulars; and we must grant that much that is taken by us as generality for controlling individual experience may be seen gradually developing in force as induction based on experience, according as it is in conformity with that experience. But I hold that we should not in the least hesitate to allow, in addition to experience as a source of knowledge, the assumption of some general principles, before or apart from experience, though never to be held independent of verification. In whatever way I have hold of them, e.g. of the uniformity of Nature, whether I believe or know, I believe rather than I know. If the uniformity of Nature *is* an induction from experience, we can but say we believe it; if it be an assumption made by way of pure postulate or hypothesis, we believe still more. To know Nature in detail is found to be impossible except on the ground of the uniformity of Nature; and is not this belief—which is what we assume by way of a postulate for action—postulated because we cannot get on without it? Hence belief much better expresses the uniformity of Nature because of its highly representative character. And so, from our point of view, we come round to the conclusions of Hamilton and Augustin. Knowledge is more than belief, yet involves certain principles held as belief.

It seems strange that belief should thus be something less than knowledge and yet the basis of knowledge, but if we remember the relation to action which is common to both, and which is the ultimate meaning of their reality, then we see how it is that the foundations of knowledge are held rather as belief than as knowledge. Particular facts got by an approximately presentative experience are knowledge, but not *general* knowledge. For that is of the nature of a coherent system with a foundation expressed as general principles; and these are believed in rather than known.

For Lecture XI read:—

Bain, op. cit. App. B, for an able and useful historical exposition of Experience and Intuition.

Locke, *Essay concerning Human Understanding*, Book I.

LECTURE XI.

THE NATURE OF KNOWLEDGE. BEFORE LOCKE.

The Objectivity of Knowledge.

BELIEF and knowledge then are conceptions that are closely intertwined, and the difference between them is one of degree, or lies in the way of looking at the same fact. Let us now see how the whole question has been faced by philosophers; what it is that the problem of knowledge involves. It is a subject that appeals most generally to our interest, and it is suggested by our previous psychology.

Knowledge, as involving more than mere intellection, is a coherent system which we call real, fact, objectively valid. I want to bring prominently forward this Objectivity of Knowledge. The word 'objective' in philosophy is taken in a wider sense than in psychology, where it is the adjective of the perceived object; here it applies to all real, valid knowledge, whether of sense-objects or no. All objects indeed can be shown to be ultimately objects perceived by sense, but we are now concerned with 'objective' as applied to that knowledge which is valid for the consciousness of *all*, not only for mine but also for that of every one. I know that $2 \times 2 = 4$, that the earth attracts stones, that every effect has a cause: these are cognitions and objectively valid, yet not sense-objects; I do not say, without relation to sense at all, but not involving sense as such. Something may be a fact about a particular object or not a fact, but as fact it must hold for all. Do I know objectively? Then I must so think that you can think it too. I know nothing really unless I can show that you are capable of knowing it as well as I. We must not imagine there is any objectivity without a subject; knowledge always involves a knower; still it is possible for me to put together in my mind a synthesis which will not hold good for any but myself; but then I cannot give grounds for it to other people, so that it has no objective validity. Suppose I said, 'The effect always goes before its cause'—this would be an example of a cognition lacking objective validity[1]. No account which fails to bring forward this aspect of knowledge grapples with the question of the nature of knowledge; it may contain good psychology, but it must fall short in philosophy.

How the Problem has been met.

We see, however, that if we have to find subjective representations which can be set forth in such a way as to appeal to all consciousnesses, it is not an easy task. All earnest philosophers have faced it, and I want now to give a notion of how, from different points of view, this definition of the conditions of knowledge has been met. This fact constitutes the central problem—that knowledge is so held that other minds are viewed as participating in it, and that it is communicable to others. Distinctively intellectual philosophy has always been concerned with the problem, meeting it for

[1] Cf. Bain, p. 201, sec. 7. That which he here gives as the distinctive feature of perception of a sense-object applies equally well to all objective knowledge.

the most part from the side of the chief factor or factors in knowledge.

Here we are at once confronted by our antithesis of Rationalism and Experientialism, or Sensationalism as, in its first form, the latter doctrine may be called. According to the former, knowledge is wholly explicable from Intellect or Reason (νοῦς); according to the latter, knowledge is wholly explicable from Sense or Sense-experience. And according to a third position knowledge is explicable from both.

The antithesis to the word Rationalism in the fullest sense is given by the word Sensationalism. If Rationalism is the doctrine of reason, which is one kind of mental function, Sensationalism is the doctrine of sensation, another kind of mental function. Again, experience may mean bare sense-experience, or sense ordered by reason or intellect to form knowledge. Nevertheless Experientialism is on the whole the more accurate term, since no theory of knowledge was ever pure Sensationalism.

Plato's Rationalism.

Plato naturally took the extreme doctrine of Intellectualism, or Rationalism. Sense, he said, is only a hindrance to knowledge; knowledge involves an ignoring of sense. Knowledge is the grasping of ideas with the intellect which never were in sense, were never got from sense, and which therefore the mind must have brought with it; it consists in the mind's possession of innate ideas originally. (He does not use the word 'innate,' but he teaches the doctrine.) Plato was a poet as well as a philosopher, and clothed his philosophical ideas in poetical form. Mythically sometimes and mystically always he expresses the doctrine of knowledge as reminiscence of ideas not formed from sense, but brought from a state of prior existence. In a previous existence men had converse with Ideas. Now they see through a glass darkly, but there was a time, and again will be, when, freed from matter or sense, man will see face to face. Plato's theory of knowledge, then, is a general negation of the import of sense—is a denial that sense can be sublimated into knowledge.

This tendency has been reproduced throughout the history of thought, especially at the beginning of the modern period. Descartes, though he takes sense as a factor of human being, seeks to explain knowledge out of relation to sense, and considers it apart from sense. With Rationalists first and last the burden of the story has been that in knowledge there is obviously something that sense can give no account of—that there are in it notions out of all relation to sense, as for instance 'Cause.' Here is a notion necessary to our knowledge, yet do any of our senses give us an idea of cause as cause? Obviously not, yet we *know* what cause is. 'Substance' is another such notion. We come to know by sense this, that, or the other affection which objects are said to cause in us; but how do we come to know substance as something seemingly apart from us?

Hence it was that Plato looked for some other source to explain knowledge, and found one so fruitful that he denied the value of sense. This source was Reason. Reason knows by way of ideas, and as there was no possible account he could give of how these ideas arose in us, he did not hesitate to imagine that we are carrying on in this life a life that has been begun before, and in a previous stage of which we got our ideas. How much of this was philosophy, how much only poetry, it is hard to say; but we get out of the Dialogues a positive doctrine of Innate Ideas, viz. that the mind comes into the world with a certain means of knowing *in its original constitution*. *I*, according to this view, supply for myself the idea of cause by the constitution of my mind.

Aristotle as Conciliator.

In Plato's time the opposite doctrine had already sprung up, viz. that knowledge is only sense transformed. Later on this found pronounced upholders in the Epicureans, the Stoics and some of the Sceptics. To a certain extent this antithesis was represented and headed by Aristotle, yet not in extreme opposition. He occupied a middle ground, acting as a kind of conciliator between the Platonic doctrine and Experientialism. Never one-sided, he saw the truth in both aspects; hence his great influence on succeeding ages. Those have judged him superficially who, with Coleridge, have said that every man is a Platonist or an Aristotelian. The expression that mind is a smooth tablet or *tabula rasa* occurs in Aristotle[1], but he is no Sensationalist. He does not say that knowledge can be explained from sense, but he does say that it cannot be explained without reference to sense. Neither is it possible to make him out to be an Experientialist of the modern type, as Grote does. There are passages in Aristotle which must be interpreted as implying independence in the intellect as a factor of knowledge. By likening the mind to a tablet written on by experience he meant only that the Noûs was not a fixed body of innate principles, but something *potential* which can be developed by way of experiential realisation. We are provided with such conditions of thought as will enable us to frame ideas in

---

[1] *De Anima*, Bk. III, ch. iv: 'We must suppose, in short, that the process of thought is like that of writing on a writing-tablet on which nothing is yet actually written.' E. Wallace's transl.) *Infra*, p. 230.

connexion with the gradual growth of our experience[1]. It is surprising how Aristotle had begun to conceive how sense becomes worked up by certain definite laws into those cognitions which seem furthest removed from sense.

Scholastic Rationalism.

Most of the Schoolmen, as we have seen, followed Aristotle, but assigned perhaps greater predominance than he did to the intellectual factor, and were apt to bring in 'innate ideas.' Some were pure Intellectualists, declaring sense to be of no account for knowledge. The greatest of them, Aquinas, contended for the importance of sense, but he too admitted innate ideas as co-factors in knowledge.

Bacon outside the Controversy.

Bacon is of no importance for this question. He is a methodologist. He sought for a 'method of discovery,' but prefaced it by no psychological or critical investigation (I use 'critical' here in the Kantian sense), nor did he view the question from the subjective point of view as Descartes did. Had he gone into the question, he must have been a Sensationalist. He speaks of sense as a source of knowledge, but he was no metaphysician.

Cartesian Rationalism.

Descartes was more of a metaphysician than a theorist of knowledge. He made no attempt to give a detailed theory of knowledge, nevertheless the philosophical position he took up has influenced thought till the present day. To him as to Plato sense is the antithesis of knowledge, and is to be discounted and banned as an illusion and a show. He fell back upon the doctrine that we have innate ideas of God,

[1] *De An.* Bk. III, ch. iii.

substance, cause, &c., and interpreted it in a definite way. As a discoverer in mathematics and physics, Descartes came to terms with sense. As a metaphysician he revived and maintained the pre-existing doctrine of Innate Ideas, though in later life he modified it. He distinguished in all mental states three classes of ideas:—(1) Innate, (2) Adventitious, and (3) Factitious or Imaginary Ideas. The last involve a definite mental construction that can be traced. Adventitious ideas come by way of sense. But he insists that there are certain definite concepts or notions which are in no respect adventitious, but are imprinted on the mind from the first as part of its original constitution. Chief among these is the idea of God. On this idea he lays great stress; it plays an important part in his whole philosophy. We know what we mean when we use such a term, yet the idea involves no element of sense.

Intuition and Idea in Descartes.

Another word which Descartes is more especially inclined to use is 'Intuition.' Whenever the knowledge which he cannot conceive to come by way of sense assumes the form of propositions, of the truth of which we are absolutely sure, he uses this term. Through his initiative it has come to be more and more opposed to sense-experience, and thus diverted from its original meaning of inspection, vision, direct apprehension, such as we have in sense. Some philosophers distinguish between 'pure' and 'empirical' intuition, the latter expressing the original meaning. We shall revert to this in dealing with Kant. The student, by the way, should avoid confounding intuition with instinct—the primitive power of conceiving and judging with the primitive tendency or ability to perform certain acts, unlearned action, or action prompted by knowledge that is not got by experience. There is a relation between the two; intuitions may involve activities; instincts may be used with reference to the unlearned knowledge rather than the actions; but there is an approach to a philosophic Malapropism in an indiscriminate use of the terms.

Descartes' use of the term 'idea' is wider than that of Plato; he applies it to *any* kind of conscious experience. (His use of 'thought' (*pensée*) is similar.) He even uses 'idea' for the nervous process accompanying sense-experience. It is only since Hume, who contrasts 'impressions' and 'ideas,' that the latter much-abused term has been restricted to a synonym for representative consciousness.

Cartesianism modified already in Descartes.

Descartes then admitted that sense was a mode of mental experience which the philosopher must account for as entering into some cognitions, viz. Adventitious Ideas; but he had to assume other elements, viz. Innate Ideas, or Intuitions, according as he referred to their primitive character, or to the immediate certitude characterising them. Extension, Number, are for him innate ideas. 'I am a thinking being' is a fundamental intuition; so is 'Out of nothing nothing can come', and 'A cause must contain at least as much reality as its effect.' We have no *sensation* of extension, but we interpret our sense-affections as coming from an extended thing by means of our idea of extension. To the question, 'What guarantee have we that the idea has objective validity?' he answered, 'The existence of a veracious God, incapable of deceiving us.' And to that of 'How is the mind cognisant of these ideas?' he said, 'Mind is a being constantly consciously thinking.' When pushed into a corner by the objection that, if such ideas are innate, children ought to be more conscious of them than adults, he modified his position by saying that the mind has *predispositions* to innate ideas. His 'Innate' theory is really a protest against the Sensationalist position—a protest with which as such I agree—and will not bear direct setting out here.

Locke's Experientialism.

Locke, who really began the English philosophic movement, thinks in relation to Descartes, though he generally opposes him. The first book of his *Essay* is devoted to a hostile criticism of the doctrine of Innate Ideas, all knowledge being traced from experience. Here then is a distinct counter-assertion. Instead of the assertion that the nature and community of knowledge are inexplicable save by way of ideas implanted in the mind, and in all minds alike, together with a theory as to the import of this innate knowing with respect to all minds, a theory in short of the objectivity of knowledge, we have the opposite view, that the mind comes into the world devoid of ideas or of any original means of interpreting experience, analogous in fact to a wax tablet ready for the stylus—that is to say, with a capacity for receiving impressions and with nothing more. Knowledge is that which arises in the mind as the result of the impressions imparted by experience.

It was Locke who objected that if there were innate ideas and principles (intuitions in the form of propositions), then, according to Descartes' axiom, that mind does not exist to the extent that it does not think, every one, but especially children, would be always conscious of them; whereas such is not the case; indeed it would seem that none but Cartesian philosophers were conscious of some of Descartes' innate ideas! Locke probably did not know, when he wrote, how Descartes had (in a letter) modified his theory by admitting predispositions. But Locke used the figure of the *tabula rasa*[1] in a much more dogmatic sense than Aristotle. The notion, on Locke's own line, has long been abandoned.

It must not, however, be supposed that Locke by the metaphor meant to exclude 'natural faculties'[2] or 'natural tendencies imprinted in the minds of men'[3]. It is merely his strong way of saying that without actual experience (either that which comes by way of the senses or that which he calls 'Reflection') there comes to pass nothing of what we call knowledge. In this point of view he need not be supposed to exclude anything that later inquirers contend for under the head of Inherited Predisposition. He does not assert that all tablets alike may be indifferently written upon, or, on the other hand, deny that all human minds are fitted to receive impressions in certain like ways. He may however be charged, by his way of putting the case, with throwing out of view this important element of a complete theory of knowledge, viz. that there is a certain common limit of knowing for the race and a certain personal range for the individual, both predetermined in a manner that admits of investigation (whether by Kant's way of analysis or by the evolutionist historic procedure).

Locke's whole case against innate knowledge has reference to the supposed 'universal consent' respecting it in all men and its express manifestation in the consciousness of each. He seeks to show that no principle, speculative or practical, that has ever been held innate, is as a matter of fact expressly recognised and allowed for by all mankind, as

---

[1] *Essay*, Bk. II, ch. i. 2.
[2] *Ibid.* I, ii. 1. [3] *Ibid.* I, iii. 3.

it must be if innate. The uniformity of knowledge in different men, so far as it exists, he explains by their being exposed to the same experience, by their having the same 'natural faculties,' and by their communication with one another [1]. Thus he does not wholly overlook the influence of the social relation.

Whatever may be said of Locke's polemic against innate knowledge—however he fails to see what really was contended for under that shibboleth (viz. that the fabric of knowledge, for any mind, is never explicable from incidental experience simply)—it must be pronounced good and possible against the doctrine as it had till then been maintained; and this is shown by the necessity laid upon Leibniz to shift ground and maintain the position in quite a new way. Thus a real advance in philosophy was rendered necessary.

Subsequent Mutual Convergence.

While Descartes maintained the extreme position of Rationalism, and while we appear to find an extreme counter-assertion of Sensationalism by Locke, what we discover on tracing the course of subsequent philosophy is mainly in the way of reconciliation and mutual approximation. The Rationalists recognise sense as an indispensable factor of what we call knowledge, the Sensationalists meanwhile progressively deepen and broaden their conception of what enters into or is experience. The dogmatic assertion of innate ideas died slain by Locke's *Essay*, or at least it only lingered on here and there down to our own times. Leibniz, who was most distinctly a Rationalist, finding knowledge inexplicable from anything we can call external experience, never asserted that the mind comes into the world with innate

---

[1] See especially *Essay* I, iii. § 22 ff.

ideas, but declared it has only predispositions, aptitudes, as means of interpreting what comes to it by way of sense—a notion which shows a distinct advance towards an appreciation of the other side. Ideas were only implicit in the infant mind as a statue of Hercules might be said to be implicit in a block of marble. Leibniz's theory of what really enters into knowledge was based on his theory of substance. Descartes had expressed the distinction between mind and matter as between substances the whole character of which can be expressed in *thinking*, and substances the whole character of which can be expressed in *extension*. Leibniz gave up this dualism, and allowed the existence of one substance only, the reality of which lay neither in thinking nor in extension. Trying to get a word deeper than either, he called the ground of its reality *active force*, and the one substance a system of monads, or mental unitary beings. Not all have a self-conscious existence, and those which have do not have it at every moment of their existence. Mind appears at different grades throughout the universe, from the Deity down to inanimate objects—appears, that is to say, as capable of all degrees of subjective apprehension, from full self-conscious apperception to semi- or sub- consciousness and down to unconsciousness. Hence arose the theory of latent mental modifications, springing originally from Locke's objection to Descartes' definition of mind as something constantly self-conscious.

Leibniz and Locke.

In defining his own theory of knowledge, Leibniz took up the formula of the Sensationalists:—*Nihil est in intellectu quod non prius fuerit in sensu*, and gave it a turn noteworthy and original by adding *nisi ipse intellectus*. 'Except the intellect itself.' By this alone, he claimed, do we possess *necessary* knowledge, *necessary* truth. Some truths are merely truths of fact; others are necessary truths. We know sometimes that 'S is P,' but sometimes we know that 'S *must be* P.' And he said, as against Locke, that, while we can account for any mere assertion of fact from experience, to say that anything 'must be' is not explicable from any kind of experience. Locke, on the other hand, with never so blank a tablet, found it necessary to assume beyond sense much else, which he called faculties of analysing, compounding, and the like. Experience for him was either external or internal, i.e. either Sense or Reflexion, meaning by Sense only the five passive senses, or modes of passive affection. What then is Reflexion? Consciousness of the fact of perceiving, imagining, &c. To use modern phraseology— there is an order of objective experience and an order of subjective experience: this expresses Locke's meaning. Knowledge, he found, was altogether made up by experience of Sense and Reflexion. But he has no definite idea how these come together and combine. Compared with Leibniz's profound psychological insight, Locke must be charged with superficiality, with inability to apprehend the complexity of the subject he sets himself to deal with.

Leibniz, however, by reason of his metaphysical start, is in constant danger of diverting real psychological facts into supports for questionable metaphysical positions. The psychological fact that conscious life is composed of elements multitudinous in number and of every degree of intensity may be, should be, recognised quite apart from the metaphysical hypothesis of monads.

Leibniz, while he does not deny that, not only truths of fact, but even necessary truths come into conscious view only upon the occasions supplied by sense, is disposed to lay greater stress, for the explanation of knowledge, upon that which the mind must be in itself in order to be affected so. And as even the most occasional cognition may be viewed in relation to the mind's inherent capacity, he contends for innate knowledge in a sense which, if it departs from the older view against which Locke contends, is not in the least excluded by anything that Locke advances.

The Question advanced by a Step.

Locke thus appears after all as a masked Rationalist. He merely opened up the Experientialist side of the question, and it might well be said that Leibniz was only giving a definite expression to Locke's implicit admission, when he insisted on 'intellectus ipse' as that which had not its origin in sense. It was impossible that the question could remain as Locke left it. Advance was necessary, or else a falling back on Descartes.

When we come to Berkeley we shall see (*infra*, Lect. XVI) that his *Principles* are directed against Locke's dogmatising on matter. Still Locke it was who first began to transform Philosophy into Theory of Knowledge. Philosophy with Descartes was Theory of Being; with Locke it was so only secondarily. And more: his philosophy, if not psychologically based, is at least penetrated through and through with the psychological spirit. In Descartes' science we get some good physics, but of any psychological understanding we get next to no trace. Between his work on vision and that of Berkeley there is all the difference between fancy and science. What then enabled Berkeley in 1709 to do that which Descartes of far greater scientific and philosophical ability had been unable to do in 1637? I can assign no other reason than the appearance in 1690 of Locke's *Essay*. For whatever Spinoza's influence on the time may have been, *he* had no influence upon Berkeley.

Locke's ideas of Sense are crude, but he compelled all subsequent philosophy to admit that into the fabric of knowledge Sense enters as a distinct constituent, and that there is no explanation of knowledge possible which does not take account of Sense as a factor. What else there is in knowledge beside Sense philosophers have since sought to make out. The three chief verdicts are those of the Common Sense or Scottish School, the Critical School, and the Associationist School. These we will proceed to consider.

For LECTURE XII read:—

Hamilton, *Lectures on Metaphysics*, XX and XXXVIII.

Hamilton, *Works of Reid*, with Dissertations by Hamilton—Note A, 'On the Philosophy of Common Sense.'

LECTURE XII.

THE NATURE OF KNOWLEDGE. AFTER LOCKE.

Associationism.

The Associationist doctrine has developed along two lines of thought, both of which may be said to have arisen in Locke—one through Berkeley to Hume, the other through Hartley to the Mills. Its theory of knowledge is that knowledge is explicable from the elements of sense-experience united through the bonds (laws) of association, such connexions being made within the life-experience of the individual. Knowledge is thus an individual construction, and is a compound resulting from the fusion, under certain laws, of sense-elements. It is the product of sense and association. An Associationist must maintain that there is nothing in the mind that could not be developed by the individual for himself. He may be helped to his special associations by others, but he *could* do it all for himself. This is the purest form of Experientialism. Locke himself was an Associationist, not explicitly but by implication. Associationists have not worked out a consistent Theory of Knowledge, but they do make a real attempt to begin at the beginning.

Locke and Berkeley.

Locke's ideas of sense and of the construction of knowledge are, as we have seen, very crude; nevertheless he first opened the question of the *psychological* origin of knowledge. Berkeley, Locke's immediate successor, marks a distinct advance along this line. He began a definite psychological inquiry, while he also took a philosophical position in regard to the knowledge of matter, which is at least more circumspect than that of Locke. He based his philosophy on his psychology; yet he was not set philosophising because he was a psychologist, but because, as a theologian, he wished to get rid of the, to him, pernicious effects of Materialism. Thenceforward philosophy and psychology really began to have a separate history. Berkeley got away from Locke's notion of the five senses as barely passive; and further, he began that definite reference to a principle or principles of intellectual synthesis without which it is hopeless to explain knowledge. Associationism is traced to him though he does not use the word. His theory of knowledge bears more especially on our third problem—the perception of an external world.

Hume.

Hume not only carried out further Locke's theory of knowledge, but put the question into such a shape as to rouse the strongest opposition and so bring about a great advance in thought. In regard to the cognition of extension, Hume is behind Berkeley and not superior to Locke. But he was beyond both in his statement of the formal principles of knowledge. He proceeds wholly upon Locke's individualistic view that there is nothing in the developed knowledge of any mind which is not explicable from the (incidental) experience of that mind; and expresses this (by a modification of Locke's language) in the oft-repeated formula, that whenever we 'really' have any *idea* there is some assignable *impression* from which it is derived—of which it is the copy. By thus distinguishing idea from impression, he gives greater precision to the psychological data which he assumes in common with Locke. But further, when Locke, in order to account for the developed complex of knowledge, is content to assume faculties of 'abstracting,' 'compounding' and the like, Hume formulates definite principles of association under which the synthesis takes place:—(1) Contiguity, (2) Similarity, (3) Association of Cause and Effect. He does not work out the last principle at all, nor the two others at all fully. But not in regard to these can we gauge the importance of Hume. There are two facts in cognition that he set himself to account for—knowledge of substance and knowledge of causation. He was led to the question of cause from the prominence in modern science of the inquiry, 'What is the cause of what?' Berkeley already and the Cartesians before him (e. g. Malebranche) had seen that what science was concerned with was the establishment of uniformity in phenomena. But Hume went so far as to say, that if any phenomenon is by us connected with any other phenomenon in Nature, it is because of the *customary sequence of experience*. A subjective bond is thereby established—and *that is all*, although through 'custom' one phenomenon *comes* to be considered as the objective 'cause' of the other. Thus he decries knowledge, at least from the Rationalist point of view. While his *Treatise of Human Nature* contains an almost complete theory of knowledge, while he vaguely but distinctly recognises intellectual elaboration of sense-data arranged by 'Abstraction,' he stunned the philosophic mind of the century by showing that all previous investigation had, so to speak, led up to a dead wall—that Locke's Experientialism, logically carried out, landed philosophy in scepticism. Besides his Individualism, his Particularism (i.e. that everything complex or general has to be made out of particular elements) is very pronounced as put in the formula which he is constantly referring to :—'All ideas which are different are separable' (i.e. have somehow to be brought together if they appear in one mature consciousness as conjoined).

Hartley.

Hume's contemporary, Hartley, was independent of him, but a follower of Locke. He was the first to formulate the law of Contiguous Association as accounting sufficiently, without other laws of association, for intellectual synthesis. Berkeley did not formulate any such laws; Hume did, as we have seen, but he did not apply them. When later Associationists (the Mills and Professor Bain) faced the problem of knowledge, they worked with reference to Hartley and not to Hume's laws of association. Hartley was the first who distinctly asked how a multitude of sensations, which for us are discretes, come to be fused, or to coalesce into that coherent appearance of an object with a variety of qualities which expresses what our experience really is. It is, he said, by this one associative principle. Thinkers before him, from Aristotle onwards, had used association only in accounting for the imaginative life or representative experience. Hartley was the first to employ it in explaining the synthesis of sensations. He did not give a complete exposition of this theory, or analyse sufficiently the elements of sense, but he first started the Associationist method.

Brown.

Thomas Brown was a strong Associationist, thinking with ultimate relation to Locke, but with modifications due to the influence of the French Sensationalists, Destutt de Tracy and others. They first laid hold decisively on 'muscular sense,' a discovery of great importance in philosophic theories of extension. To this subject Brown's lectures were largely devoted, and to it we shall return. Brown used Hartley's theory of association most earnestly, but was repelled by the latter's introduction of the physiological theory of vibrations.

J. S. Mill.

It is John Stuart Mill and Professor Bain who, as inheritors of the Sensationalist tradition of the eighteenth century, have set up the formulated theory of knowledge, both psychological and philosophical, known as Associationism. The latter gives better data for a true theory, especially in regard to external perception; the former is the better systematiser. In my judgment their Associationism, while it is an approximation to a theory of knowledge, comes evidently short. However important are the factors brought out by Mill, he just fails to solve the problem. He declares that a number of the subjective experiences, had by an individual human being, become for him aggregated according to certain laws (of association), and that these aggregated appearances can come to assume the form of knowledge for the individual *and*—since it is knowledge—to be objective or valid for all. But it is just this last point that he does not account for. Our knowledge, as I have said, is a coherent system of fact and relation held in common by me and equally by others. This objectivity is the distinctive constituent of knowledge, yet Mill never satisfactorily accounts for it—never gets out of the charmed circle, the sphere of the subjective. No doubt this is the right way to begin, but it is the wrong way to end if we want to give an account of knowledge as the common property of all men. Mill never gets off psychological ground. Now I am in sympathy with Associationism as psychology *only*. Mill's psychology is rather defective. He borrows from Professor Bain without comprehending him properly. However, Mill's shortcomings in framing a philosophical theory of knowledge do not detract from his great philosophical merit in his theory of *general* knowledge, viz. his logic. It is as a logician that he is effective, rather than as an epistemologist—not that I always go with him in his logic. In this he gives an account of knowledge in a constructive spirit that is very different from the destructive spirit of Hume. Living in a scientific age, Mill attempted to set up a fundamental theory of positive science involved in all the special sciences. But he does not explain how we come to know the world as consisting of a number of things, of bodies and minds. He works from the phenomenal point of view and from that of *individual* experience. He tries to show how the individual experiences of the mind can become associated so as to enable one man to ask another to accept them as valid.

Even as an inquiry of positive science Mill's work is defective. From one point of view his positive theory may be called no less sceptical than that of Hume. Jevons's *Principles of Science* is more complete though still less philosophical.

Bain.

Professor Bain has been the most important contributor to psychology in England in this century. His pre-eminence extends over the whole field of psychology as distinct from philosophy. Towards the general theory of knowledge he does not contribute any advance on Mill and the Associationists generally. He works from the individual point of view. He makes but little attempt to apply the laws of association to cognition as such. He does not ask, e.g. how we can explain the concreteness of an object on the principles of association, although he gives a careful statement of those laws. Yet he posits an element of personal initiative for the explanation of developed consciousness; he tacitly denies the *tabula rasa* hypothesis. In the mature consciousness he finds an element not derived from the sense-experience of the individual because he considers mental life in connexion with the nervous system. It is recognised that the individual comes into the world organised up to a certain point; and this fact, taken into account on the bodily side, has corresponding to it a certain *pre-determination* of conscious life.

The 'Common Sense' School.

Reid, Stewart and Hamilton put forth their epistemological view in antithesis to Hume's theory of knowledge. The first declared that, while sense was of account for knowledge, knowledge could not be explained out of the elements assumed by the Associationist doctrines. So he fell back on other assumptions. What struck him in the general theory of knowledge, as distinct from the special problem of the cognition of an external world, was the *community* of knowledge—was the fact that while there is more than sense in knowledge, this 'more' is had by all, cultivated or uncultivated, young or old. This he attributed to the subjective factor of *common sense*. Now common sense in psychology is a name for organic or general sensation[1].

---

[1] V. *Elements of Psychology*, p. 62.—ED.

In popular parlance it is the faculty of ready judgment, mother wit. Reid employed it thus:—We are so constituted that we interpret our experience alike. When we are affected through our senses, we refer those sensible impressions to a thing or substance of which they are qualities, by a fundamental principle of judgment or common sense. If we interrogate consciousness we reach this ultimate and objectively valid principle, beyond which we cannot reason.

This was a valuable idea, but Reid's method was haphazard, his assertions too readily made, his elementary principles too easily found. His 'common sense' expresses rather the result, than the means, of the determination of our impressions. It was a kind of revival of the old doctrine of innate ideas, although accompanied by a much more elaborate analysis of knowledge than any preceding Rationalists had given. We may not agree with him, nevertheless his system was an advance on Locke and Hume, if only because it made other thinkers more circumspect.

Dugald Stewart carried on the doctrine on the same lines. Knowledge could not be explained without the assumption of certain fundamental principles of *belief* which determine the objective validity of knowledge.

Hamilton.

Reid, Stewart and Hamilton are the three typical exponents of faculty-psychology. The term 'faculty' is very crudely used by the first two, but definitely by the last. Hamilton, while he justifies his own use of the word by saying that it is merely a way of massing together a number of mental phenomena, points out, as against his predecessors, that the discrepancies in their use of it show a want of principle and are essentially indeterminate. Reid, e.g. is redundant in making two distinct powers of Conception and Abstraction. He and Stewart pretend to fulfil the whole function of psychology, viz. explanation, whereas they only describe. For the only scientific mode of explanation is the bringing phenomena under laws. Explaining facts by faculties is essentially unscientific, for we must ascribe a quasi-independence to these faculties. Even Hamilton, in spite of his having guarded himself, falls into using the word as if for so many mutually independent powers, as though—as some one has said—he were dealing with European Powers. Psychology, as a rule, begins where Reid and Stewart leave off. Still for Hamilton I claim a certain amount of exemption from blame. He is guided, moreover, as to much of his scheme by a scientific principle: he goes from simple to complex. The most salient feature in his classification is that each faculty is explicable from the preceding. His scheme is better than a mere string of beads. But in it psychology and philosophy become hopelessly confused.

His scheme divides intellect into six faculties, in which we find a close correspondence with our own arrangement:—

(1) Presentative (a) External . . . Perception.
    „   (b) Internal . .
(2) Conservative . . . . . ⎫
(3) Reproductive . . . . . ⎬ Representative Imagination.
(4) Representative . . . . ⎭
(5) Elaborative or Discursive . . . Conception, Thought.
(6) Regulative[1].

[1] I am not disposed to reject the prominence given to (2) apart from (3) and (4). Decidedly some retain well, but cannot at will reproduce equally well. I could rather object to separating (3) and (4). The fifth is the most instructive to study. I commend his emphatic use of the word 'thought' as meaning re-representative

Hamilton confuses Psychology and Philosophy.

Now here in faculties (2) to (5) Hamilton is on psychological ground; in (1) and (6) he trespasses on philosophy. For instance, his first faculty he defines as that by which we have (a) consciousness of objects, (b) consciousness of self. This is more than we undertook to find in intellection; it is cognition in the fullest sense. Under the guise of psychology he is already dealing with the problem of knowledge. Now it is hardly fair to speak as though Hamilton professed to give us a work on psychology, when for his title he has Metaphysics. But we must charge him with not making the necessary distinction, any more than Professor Bain does in another direction, between psychology and philosophy. Here he certainly does not pass gradually from simple to complex. And the matter is made worse by the use of the apparently very simple term Presentative. He over-simplifies in one way, over-complicates in another. He himself, when in a psychological mood, sees that Presentation is but a starting-point. I deny (1) that we can start from perception of object and self, (2) that there is purely presentative intellection. The profit to the reader in those lectures on the first faculty lies in the historical information; otherwise there is much that is confusing and inconsistent. It was not a fortunate start.

Then as to the sixth. Till this is exercised, till the results of the other five have been operated upon, regulated, by it,

intellection only, and have sought to establish in the traditions of English psychology this usage, brought in first by Hamilton from Kant. 'Discursive' too is a valuable old term, first showing the function of thought as a 'ranging over' in order to bring together. He calls this faculty also 'understanding,' as opposed to reason or *ratio*, his sixth faculty.

you have not, according to Hamilton, got *knowledge*. Not professedly does he here pass again over to philosophy; he thinks it is all psychology. Yet he himself denies that this is a faculty in the same sense as the others. He calls it by a Latin name, as though English were not good enough for it—the *locus principiorum*—nest or aggregate of principles which have to be made manifest as involved in knowledge.

Hamilton's 'Reason.'

What does he mean by this Regulative Faculty, or the Reason? 'Regulative' is a term he borrowed from Kant, though not exactly the Kantian usage along with it. He did not use it as I do to describe the function of such philosophical doctrines as Logic or Ethics, his generic term for such functioning being *Nomology* (as distinct from Phenomenology). By 'Regulative' he meant ordering or interpreting or conditioning. Certain principles constitute so many forms or conditions under which what we perceive, remember, think, &c. comes to be held as knowledge. For instance, by the action of the principle of Substance we interpret what is presented in consciousness as qualities cohering in a substance. And again, the flow of our representations does not give us cognition till they are ordered by the principle of Causality as effects of certain causes. Not content herewith, he endeavours to reduce all principles to one—the principle of the Conditioned.

Note how he had already begged the sixth faculty to expound the first.

We have now seen what the Common Sense school found wanting in the Associationist doctrine, and how they sought to supply it. In connexion herewith they tend to use belief as being the foundation of knowledge, those fundamental principles of Common Sense or Reason being held in the mind in the form of belief.

No student will lose his time if he study Hamilton. Whatever his faults, his work is unsurpassed for instructive, stimulative value. He really and consciously exhausted intellect no less than is done in Mr. Spencer's scheme and my own. Whereas with the classifications of Reid and Stewart we might ask why they stop where they do.

For LECTURE XIII read :—
Mill, *Logic*, Bk. II, ch. v. vi—'Of Demonstration and Necessary Truths.'

LECTURE XIII.

THE NATURE OF KNOWLEDGE. CRITICAL PHILOSOPHY.

Kant.

KANT was struck and even oppressed by the negative result of Hume's analyses. It seemed to him that, if Hume was right, no explanation of even the plain facts of science was possible. He was prepared to accept Hume against the older doctrines of metaphysics—Platonic realism, innate ideas, and so forth—but he felt that there was that in knowledge which Hume had not touched—that his negation of knowledge was wrong, in that he had not faced the whole problem. So he sought in the *Kritik of Pure Reason* to work out a positive theory of knowledge and to destroy scepticism, not by mere dogmatism like Descartes and Leibniz, but by putting the whole of knowledge on a new footing, and so to find a *via media* between the Experientialism of Locke run out into the scepticism of Hume, and the Rationalism of Descartes and Leibniz.

Kant's Inquiry into the Constituents of Knowledge.

He said that we must first settle what enters into knowledge. That sense is of account for knowledge he takes for granted. Our knowledge is of sensible things. Not that we have not moral convictions of something beyond, but knowledge proper always contains sense-elements. Sense itself does not explain knowledge. Knowledge is not simply sense transformed, but a resultant of certain elements *a posteriori* (empirically given) wrought up with certain other *a priori* elements.

A priori *and* a posteriori.

To these terms, which are to be found in Logic since the time of Aristotle, Kant gave an epistemological significance. The logical *a priori* is cognition of anything on the side of its conditions, of what it can be shown by the laws of thought to depend upon; it is knowledge in deductive form. And it is so called because it can be shown to be dependent, through the laws of thought or consistency, on what has been already known or assumed, i. e. on premises. This is the only kind of conclusion that is absolutely certain. But we can make other inferences, for which we can never claim absolute certainty, and yet which are the most important, viz. inductions, or general assertions about facts. Here, except in Jevons's trivial case of Perfect Induction, the certainty of our inference is technically open to dispute; it is only probable. Such an inference is termed knowledge *a posteriori*.

Kant uses the terms for the two kinds of factors present in knowledge. That which comes from sense, without which no exercise of 'pure' reason has any validity, is knowledge *a posteriori*. But without the *a priori* factor of 'pure reason' (reason not derived from experience) working on experience we cannot get knowledge. For Kant, *a priori* is a general name for 'rational' as opposed to 'empirical;' it is what Leibniz, in correcting Locke, meant by *intellectus*, or that which is furnished by the mind's original constitution.

Kant, be it noted, was very vague in his use of 'experience.' Sometimes it means with him the contribution of sense to knowledge; at other times it stands, not for bare sense-material, but for sense as ordered and interpreted by *a priori* principles—in fact for knowledge.

A priori *Forms*.

Again, just as in Logic a distinction is drawn between matter and form of thought, so Kant distinguished epistemologically between matter and form of cognition generally. The matter of knowledge is the data of sense; these are taken up into, or perceived under, 'pure forms.' The 'forms' of sense are *space* and *time*. When I get external sensations I am so constituted that I order them in space. And I order all my sensations in time. Space and time are pure forms of intuition—a term which Kant was careful to connect with sense-perception only, and not with Reason, seeing how related the words are.

Next, sense-perception, so explained from the conjunction of matter and pure forms, becomes ready for conceptual knowing, i. e. for an orderly scheme or fabric of knowing common to man and man—in other words, objective knowledge. Objective knowledge does not necessarily refer to objects in space. Is it a fact that every event has a cause? If it be agreed that this is so, here is objective knowledge, although it does not refer to objects in space. Such knowledge consists of sense-phenomena subsumed or brought under pure concepts of the understanding or fundamental principles of judgment, by which Kant did not understand so many 'innate ideas,' but postulated certain *necessary* forms of thought.

Universality and Necessity in Knowledge.

For there is a part of our knowledge, there are some of our cognitions, which are not only universal or objective, but also necessary. Some judgments assume the form 'S *is* P,' but some that of 'S *must be* P.' Now no experience can explain—so philosophers said—why a 'must be' is used any more than it can warrant universal validity. Experience deals with particulars only. It cannot tell us that *all* are so, or that all must be so; we only know by it that this, that, and the other are so. We do not hesitate to say 'All men are mortal,' but we only *know* that certain men of whom we have had experience have died. Knowledge may, on the warrant of experience, assume a general form from particulars, but then it is only probable; it is of the nature of belief; it is practical, not theoretical necessity. So for universality. Kant paid most attention to necessity, defining more exactly than had ever been done before the nature of the problem and distinguishing between kinds of necessity. Necessity in knowledge first found explicit statement (as we have seen) in Leibniz. Locke gave an account of necessary truth, and Hume tried to account for the aspect of necessity by the merely subjective explanation that it is habit or custom that determines us to think thus. Mill argued for inseparable association.

Now Kant distinguished between Analytic and Synthetic propositions: these do but correspond to the Essential and Non-essential judgments of the Schoolmen and to Mill's Verbal and Real predication. An analytic proposition is one where P (predicate) is involved in the thought of S (subject). Locke miscalled such propositions 'trivial.' 'Man is rational' is an analytic proposition, because by 'man' we *mean* rational animal. Man *must be* rational or he is not man. Kant saw that all such judgments have the character of *logical* necessity— necessity under the laws of thought (of Identity, Contradiction, Excluded Middle, or generally, of Consistency). Every step in thought that proceeds under the laws of thought may be expressed in terms of necessity. Deny—and, as Aristotle would say, you are a vegetable. This is a kind of necessity experience may give distinct occasion for, e.g. 'Body is extended;' 'Crows are black.' We can put this kind aside.

But, said Kant, we often have judgments which are not analytic and yet are necessary, e.g. 'Two straight lines cannot enclose a space.' This is a synthetic proposition; Professor Bain (in his *Logic*) tried to show it, on no ground whatever, to be analytic. It is also necessary. We may say merely 'do not enclose,' but the necessity, even if excluded from the form of the proposition, lies in its matter. Now Kant found necessities of thought of this kind, not only in mathematics but throughout the whole fabric of knowledge, e.g. 'Every event must have a cause.' And he called such judgments *synthetic propositions a priori*, i.e. necessary because of an *a priori* synthesis formed in the very nature of human reason, and not *a posteriori* or constructed by the light of experience. It was thus that he answered the question, 'How are synthetic propositions *a priori* possible?' 'How is real predication also necessary?' The human mind brings to the results of bare sense-experience certain subjective factors, viz. (1) pure intuitions, in order to perception; (2) pure categories of concepts, in order to understanding; (3) pure ideas, in order to reason.

Of these (1), i.e. space and time, are not general notions, but pure forms for the reception of the bare matter of sensation that arises in us. They are the conditions under which sense-impressions are consciously experienced by us as having the character of definite phenomena mutually related in the way of succession or co-existence. There is nothing in sense to explain sensations *as apart* from each other in space and time. This represents the first stage of cognition as we have it.

The phenomena thus found to be the transformed data of sense now become matter for further elaboration, and get into definite relations with each other, as causes and effects, &c.; and by these new kinds of 'form' applicable to phenomena as their 'matter,' just as space and time are applicable to sense-impressions as *their* matter, the order of nature becomes explicable. If I simply say 'The earth draws a stone,' there is involved this double elaboration of the bare facts of sense as originally given. They are first ordered as phenomena, then ordered into relations. And the forms into which phenomena are thus taken up are twelve 'categories of the understanding[1].' All are involved in physical experience, for these 'forms' of the mind are not cognitions in and for themselves, but apply to phenomena only, and have no meaning out of relation to them. Even what we call experience is saturated with 'reason,' with those highest elaborations or syntheses—the ideas of the self or soul, the cosmos, God—which completed the Kantian account of the subjective factor in knowledge.

Kant's Theory of Space.

So much for general exposition. I will now confine myself to space and those propositions about it which are both necessary and synthetic. Kant maintained that we cannot account

---

[1] 'Discoverable from the common analysis of judgments in logic. (*a*) Three categories of QUANTITY: *Unity, Plurality, Universality* (as involved in Singular, Particular, Universal judgments respectively). (*b*) Three of QUALITY. *Reality, Negation, Limitation* (in Positive, Negative, Infinite judgments). (*c*) Three of RELATION: *Substantiality, Causality, Community* or *Reciprocal action* (in Categorical, Hypothetical, Disjunctive judgments). (*d*) Three of MODALITY: *Possibility, Existence, Necessity* (in Problematic, Assertory, Apodeictic judgments).' Bain, op. cit. App. B, p. 60.—ED

for our knowledge of space by reference to experience, for if we could, we could never form necessary synthetic propositions about it. We have a pure intuition of space; it is a pure form, and we put our experiences into it. In support of this position he adduced psychological evidence both negative and positive—negative, in that he asks us to produce those sources of experience, whence we have notions of space; positive, in that space in relation to sensation stands in a quite peculiar position, thus :—we experience our sensations *as in space*, and while we can think of any of those sensations as eliminated, *we cannot think away space*. We can think of a pillar as having colour, as emitting sound when struck, but we cannot think away its extension. We may colour our space as we like, but it must always remain extended. Space, then, is one of the two 'forms' of sensibility, a form to which sense supplies the matter; it is there before experience, and therefore we can utter synthetic propositions not built up by experience.

Associationist Explanation of Necessity in Knowledge.

Kant's insight into this question surpassed that of his predecessors both Rationalist and Experientialist. I think that we may yield him this pre-eminence and yet, in the light of our more advanced psychology, be able to explain those aspects of our cognition of space which led him to deny its experiential origin. Let us face him with the developed position of his Associationist opponents as best seen in Mill and Professor Bain. The latter in his Psychology gives the very data which we shall use to show where Kant was wrong, yet he does not make use of them as he might have done. Had he seen the full import of what he makes out, he would have had a better argument against the Kantian position. Take

Mill:—For him there is nothing in our knowledge of space which may not be accounted for by the amount and constancy of our experience going to form the cognition. If we find that we cannot think of colour except as in space, it is because we find that they always do go together. Associations, though formed within experience, may become inseparable. 'Space a form in which we receive colour as matter?' No, said Mill; we have always apprehended colour as extended, extension as coloured. Necessity depends upon the amount of experience, which is here of a peculiarly simple kind. Experience that is frequent and constant enough can give rise to a 'must be,' a 'cannot be.'

Criticism of both Positions.

Now I have thrown doubt on how Associationism can ever account for the necessity of synthetic propositions. I take a middle position, neither Kantian nor Associationist, finding neither view perfectly valid. *Is* Space a form for all external sensations? (I omit Time—for lack of it.) Yes, said Kant, sensations are by us ordered in space. Well, I have shown, in dealing with perception[1], that every sensation does come to have some kind of spatial reference—*more or less*. But there is all the difference in the world, of DEGREE. For that difference of degree we must account in detail, and this puts a check on our agreeing with Kant's superficial assertion, that space is form for all sensations alike. Do the notes in the scale of an octave or in a chord appear to us spread out in space like the colour-spectrum? It is true that we should hear them as 'in space,' yet the spatial order is very different.

On the other hand, I protest against ranking our experience of space on a level with that of colour or sound, as the Associationists do. How can we have experience of colour?

[1] V. *Elements of Psychology*, p. 96.—ED.

By way of sensations passively received. How of space? There is no such simple source of space-experience. Inseparable association exists, it is true, as a psychological fact, and explains much that looks like necessity. Mill uses it to account for mathematical necessity. The ideas, e.g., of 'two straight lines' and 'what cannot enclose a space' have come, through personal experience, to be so closely associated as to be practically inseparable. But however that may be, colour and extension do not constitute a case of inseparable association. We must find one where the associates were first known in separation, e.g. the name 'hat' and the thing 'hat.' Inseparable association refers to what is practically inseparable, not to what is *theoretically* inseparable. And if we look at how the human organism is constituted, we see that the relation of colour and extension *cannot* be a case of two more or less indifferent elements being brought together by chance-experience and fused. It lies in the constitution of our perceptive faculty that we cannot but have the experience of extended colour if we have eyes. I am so constituted that when I am affected by *colour* I *move* my eyes. This is a necessity of the constitution, and not of acquired experience. Inseparable association can never explain necessity in knowledge.

But have we not seen, it may be asked, how extension is explicable by 'muscular sense'? This is really important, though more is required. It is by reference to 'active sense,' the resultant of muscular sense in conjunction with passive sense, that we do get an actual experiential origin of our perception of space. Space, as we have seen, is no simple experience, but a complex product of data given by colours and touch. Thus space is a 'form'—I have no objection to the term as expressing the relation of space to simple sensations—but it is not therefore a 'pure intuition,' since we can psychologically explain it. Nor is it the universal form of external sensation.

Organic Necessity.

Now if, constituted as we are, some sense-organs only are muscular, and if it is the fact of muscularity whereby we have apprehension of extension, it becomes a necessity for us to have *those* sensations 'in' space. We are so ordered, through the mobility of our hands, eyes, &c., as to have those sensations so. Here is the explanation of this necessity—*because of our organic constitution.* And this is not to explain mind from matter; I use 'eyes,' 'muscles,' &c., to designate the factors, not to explain them. The material differences in the brains of different men suggest differences of mental ability. Kant, then, was right in maintaining that our reference of colours to space was of our original constitution, though what he called pure intuition I term bodily organs. Whether the tendency be innate I know not, not knowing the consciousness of myself as an infant or that of other infants. Even were it not so, the psychological facts we have mentioned can account for the development of the cognition within the lifetime of the individual. And if it were so, the tendency would still be not a pure intuition, but the result of the principle of *heredity.* Pure intuition cannot satisfy; we must inquire further. I am far from dogmatically asserting that the idea of space is got in the life of the individual; it may, or may not, be so. It were possible to go deeper than Mill or Bain, and yet give a psychologically based explanation. Enough here to say that the line is fruitful, and that more may be done therein by English psychologists than Kant ever achieved. I am not hostile to Mill's exposition on demonstrative science in the second book of the *Logic.* It is good as far as it goes, and is the best explanation yet made from the point of view of individual experience. Professor Bain gives his adhesion to Mill's mathematical theory, but extraordinary is the way in which in his *Logic*[1] he throws away the advantages got from his position in psychology as to our unique apprehension of extension, and never refers to it. For if extension is not had merely by experience from without, but by activity of ours put forth, springing from within, it is absurd to say that we are reduced to the same conditions for our knowledge of space as for that of the qualities of things. It is always possible for us to perform movement of some sort, and this movement is involved in our apprehension of extension. My knowledge of space depends upon my acting when I like; other perception depends upon whenever, in a broken, limited way, I happen to be sensibly affected. We make, we determine space; we come to know it by way of construction—not of *a priori* construction, not of spontaneity of thought, as Kant said, but by conscious bodily exertion, not limited by occasions of passive sense-impressions. And this is because we are what we are. We are thrown back on our original constitution. Hence it is that the science of space is different from the inductive sciences of nature; hence it is that mathematics is a demonstrative science. The explanation applies to all sciences in so far as they are demonstrative—to Arithmetic and Physics, e.g. as well as to Geometry—for all are to that extent concerned with matter as apprehended by activity, by construction; and herein lies their 'necessity.' Other sciences we form piecemeal from experience[2].

[1] 'Deduction,' Bk. II. ch. v.
[2] The lecturer referred students, for a fuller explanation, to his article 'Axiom' in the *Encyclopædia Britannica*. (Reprinted in *Philosophical Remains*, pp. 119–132.)—ED.

LECTURE XIV.

THE NATURE OF KNOWLEDGE. CAUSATION.

The Category of Causality.

WE will now proceed to Kant's Categories of the Understanding, and single out for examination and comparison that one which the growth of modern science has brought most prominently under discussion. When things are sensibly perceived they are ordered in space or in time; but when thought or *generally* known, i.e. when in the form of concept, we say they must have a *cause*. Now according to Kant this is a synthetic assertion *a priori*. Cause, or cause and effect, is a pure concept not got by experience. We are naturally determined to look for something before and after an action. With cause, as with space, a necessity is laid upon us in the act of knowing. This was an immense step beyond earlier views; it is perfectly intelligible and satisfactory also—as far as it goes. Before Kant's time no one took the trouble fully to analyse knowing as we find it.

The Growth of the Notion of Cause.

The question of causation is as old as Plato, but the epistemological aspect of it—'How do we, in our knowledge, come to relate phenomena to one another as cause and effect?'—has (in addition to the consideration of space) only come to the front since the time of Hume and Kant in connexion with the establishment and progress of modern science. Through that, Nature has come to be regarded as a realm within which law reigns universally. Nature has always, it is true, been considered as a realm in which there are things having a fixed occurrence, and a law of universal causation is no new thing in philosophy. Without the acceptance of the law there could be no science as science is now constituted. Yet it is only lately that Nature has been scientifically investigated in a thorough-going manner, and the law applied to every kind of phenomena. People have not always referred every thing and every happening to cause and effect. Even Aristotle expressly distinguished a region of cause from a region of chance. And there are some who still deny that mental phenomena are regulated by it. For example, it is a question still raised whether human action, the action of beings having a conscious volition, is a fixed and orderly action which can be investigated and forecast like other facts in nature. This is the famous free-will controversy (v. *infra*, Lecture XIX). The difference of opinion which we see yet prevailing with regard to this sphere of occurrence formerly prevailed with regard to all nature. It was held that things would happen otherwise than under the condition of strict uniformity.

Causation as Universal.

Generally speaking, however, the causal connexion may now be considered as established. In regard practically to anything that happens, we are prepared to make one presupposition if none other, namely, that it is caused, or *determined to happen*, and that it does not happen except as it is caused. When anything happens, I say, we also assume that it follows on something else, not as on a bare antecedent in time, but as on a cause or determinant. We assume that Nature is an aggregate of events all determined to happen as they do happen, i.e. that Nature is uniform in respect to cause and effect. When an event happens we seek to conjoin it with some other event as cause. On this assumption is based all scientific generalisation, all inductive inference, every real and complete induction. For a complete induction is one where the nature of the instances is such that any *other* result than the universal assertion we commit ourselves to would run contrary to the universality of the law of causation[1]. The causal connexion then being at this time of day established, we have to account for it.

Rationalist and Experientialist Explanations of Cause.

Now Hume was the first to account for the causal connexion on the ground of *experience*, there being nothing beyond experience that he can find to explain it from. Locke was too far back in time to touch the subject. Science was then too little established as a system of knowledge to draw the attention of philosophers. But Kant, who professed to account for science as we find it, had specially to occupy himself with this question. And since his time Rationalists have held cause to be a 'pure concept.' Hamilton indeed thought to advance beyond Kant in saying that the judgment of causality is a work not of the Elaborative, but of the Regulative Faculty—an act of reason as opposed to the understanding. We are, according to him, to account for universal causation, not by a pure concept brought by the mind, i.e. by the mind's *ability*, but as due

[1] Cf. J. S. Mill, *Examination of Hamilton's Philosophy*, p. 402, *note*.

rather to its *impotence*. It is owing to the limitation of the mind that we bring everything in relation to something else. Every event must have a cause; we cannot help it. This is in connexion with his fundamental 'Law of the Conditioned.' Hamilton's turn to the argument should be studied, but his doctrine of causation is not good. Kant's position is preferable. He best represents the Rationalist position, Hume and Mill that of Experientialism.

I throw up a stone, and it falls to the ground. I say, 'The earth attracts the stone.' Now the Experientialist explains this judgment, as made on the strength of the individual's countless experiences of this sequence of phenomena. He asserts causation as a generalisation from experience. Whereas Kant maintained that, unless he could first pass an *a priori* judgment of causality, he could never have the experience at all—that we bring our category of causality to bear on, and elaborate the judgment out of, the bare experience of the stone falling to earth. (Notice that Kant—and he is not alone in this usage—employs experience ambiguously as meaning either raw sense-material, or phenomena ordered in certain ways, i.e. according to the categories.) According to Kant, I repeat, unless we knew *a priori* that every event must have a cause, we should never have got so far as to say 'The earth attracts the stone.' According to Mill the phenomenon is a simple particular by which we rise to the universal assertion.

Criticism of both Positions.

Now I am wholly dissatisfied with this common-place Experientialism of Mill and others. Not thus can we account for knowledge. On the other hand, we are not driven to Kant's alternative, to assert cause as a pure concept of the understanding. For as we found that his pure form of intuition was not pure—since space has a development—so we find that cause is not a pure concept. It comes by way of sense, although not given by experience already developed. Nevertheless, as against crude Experientialism, I side with Kant, who gives a much profounder analysis of knowledge.

Cause in Science and in Popular Usage.

Before suggesting a solution of the question, it is necessary to make a distinction. There is a real difference between cause as understood in science and cause as used in everyday speech. The cause of anything that science seeks to account for is the set of conditions of a phenomenon; it tries, in assigning cause and effect, to establish a certain fixed relation among phenomena—a certain kind of uniformity. Science has nothing to say of the reason *why* one phenomenon should be followed by another, and in no way professes to account for the relation except as a mere uniformity of occurrence. Thus when oxygen and hydrogen in combination are exploded by a spark there results water. For the purposes of science the cause of this is explained by proving the presence of oxygen and hydrogen, and the application of the spark. But no one can say what ultimately brings about the result. Science has only words to denote a certain fixed succession.

Popular speech is, however, much more definite in assigning a cause. Where a stone falls to the earth it says at once, 'The earth *draws, attracts* the stone,' i.e. has *power* to produce this effect. Science only points to the fixed relation or succession of phenomena. *Any* succession is not causal, but causation is only succession of a certain kind. Now what else is there besides succession when the principle of causality is assumed? There seems an implication in the philosophical principle resembling that in common speech, namely, of power in one thing to bring about another thing. Our language certainly commits us to more than the bare scientific notion.

The scientific conception of cause has grown up lately, because it is only of late that nature has been regarded phenomenally. Before positive science grew up nature was regarded as an aggregate, not of inter-related phenomena, but of active beings. No science came to pass until men looked away from this view and established definite relations among facts as they found them.

As this aspect of phenomenal relation, of co-existences and successions, developed, the popular notion of cause and effect, with its implied assumption of power, became attenuated to indicate merely a special kind of phenomenal succession, and theorists began to dispute the propriety of using the word 'cause' in this connexion as misleading. Hume's philosophy centres entirely round this part of the subject, namely, the great question: Can this relation among phenomena that science takes account of be properly called *causal*? Mill answered this affirmatively, and tried to show that the notion of *power* (in cause to produce effect) ought to be excluded from the notion of causation. This is equivalent to asserting that a causal relation, as it is made out in science, is purely phenomenal. Both Hume and Kant agree with him here. Berkeley regarded cause not as a phenomenal antecedent, but as a spiritual reality, as the connexion between the real being (mind) and what appears. He spoke of the scientific cause as a 'phenomenal sign' of the true cause, science dealing with ideas (phenomena) that are significant of other ideas. Comte was the most thorough phenomenalist of them all; he would not even raise the question as to any reality beyond phenomena. And just because he was a phenomenalist, he wanted to get rid of the notion of cause altogether, and asserted that the utmost object of science was to determine uniformities of phenomena or laws. According to Mill, scientific relations, though all phenomenal, may yet be called causal. According to Comte, because they are phenomenal they must not be called causal. Comte agrees in expression, though not in thought, with Berkeley and also with Dr. Martineau. These two concur in saying that science is concerned only with the signification of phenomena by phenomena, in order to show that, beyond all considerations of phenomenal relation, there is a deeper consideration of cause, viz. as to how any phenomenon is related as effect to a cause in the sphere of metaphysical reality or ultimate being. They hold that when we have got science we are only at the beginning of our investigation and not, as Comte believed, at the end of all possible inquiry.

Cause in Cartesianism.

The attenuated notion of cause that we find in science had already been anticipated in philosophic thought by Occasionalism, although based on different premises from those of Hume and Mill. Occasionalism explained *all* change in Nature as mere sequence, the full working of cause being only between God and every creature. The creature was robbed of causal efficiency [1], this being placed to the credit of the account of the Deity. Geulincx especially came near to scientific Pheno-

---

[1] In Aristotle 'efficient cause' includes the notion of power, but, as opposed to 'final,' 'formal,' and 'material' causes, is equivalent to the modern idea of causation.

menalism in seeking to account for the apparent interaction of two such opposed substances as mind and body. Malebranche also explained every event as due to direct divine intervention, finding in the world only phenomenal conjunction. Descartes himself went nearly as far as this in controversy. They tended to the Pantheism, with its notion of immanent causation, which was fully developed by Spinoza.

The Logical Weakness of Mill's Theory.

What account do we give of this problem? Can we say with Mill that every human mind, from seeing things happen, develops the conviction that every event must have a cause? If we study what Mill says in his *Logic* for this position, we find it gives strength to Kant's view. Data that he assumes to account for causation are *already* co-ordinated by the application of the pre-existent principle, for we are naturally determined to interpret our experiences by way of causation. The difficulties in the way of accepting Mill's view are insuperable.

Universal Causation a Postulate in Science.

For purposes of science, I think that at present it is a sufficient explanation of the universality of causation when it is set out as a *postulate*, without which it is impossible to have science at all. If things happened now in one way and now in another we could make no general assertion about them. We must postulate a fixity in the occurrence of phenomena. This will be sufficient to account for the universality of causation in science. If with some we doubt whether it be universal there is so much of science blotted out for us. We may use the word 'cause' for the mere phenomenal relation, but it must be without misunderstanding it. The question whether cause has *power* to produce an effect has no meaning in science. But this is not accounting philosophically for the notion.

The Truth in Mill's Theory.

Having excluded the notion of 'efficient cause' from science, Mill seeks the origin of our notion of cause and effect in generalisation from the phenomenal relation. He argues that the principle of causation on which induction is based is itself an induction. This is to beg the question. And he reckons this generalisation from experience of cause and effect as, according to Bacon's term, an induction 'by simple enumeration of instances,' i.e by the weakest, the least scientific method of induction, Mill himself allowing, as we have seen, that he cannot make a good induction until he has got the principle of causation. Hence he gets the principle by a bad induction. This is not worked out as well as it might have been. Nevertheless there is reason in his position. He arrives at his primary assertion tentatively, and it is strengthened by every fresh induction. We may trust simple enumeration in regard to the general *fact* of causation in Nature, but not in regard to cause in a special case; in the latter we need to base our inquiry on the law of causation itself.

In point of fact it *must* have been from experience that people arrived at the idea of universal causation, because it is only lately that universal causation has become recognised. Whereas if it were a pure concept, why was it not recognised before? Kant does not face this evolution in thought. An experiential origin of the notion of cause may be defended as against his view.

Yet I do not put the case like Mill. The notion of cause is *not* derived from a consideration of the phenomenal relation, because this is not a natural but an artificial view of the question, whereas the notion of cause has grown up with men from the beginning. It is from the popular idea, whence the scientific sense of causation has been derived by attenuation, that the philosophical notion of cause was first got, and it is in reference to *that*, that the question of ground should be raised. For we do ultimately think of cause as something with power to produce an effect. Whence then does this arise? Through external experience or apart from it?

The Psychological Basis of the Notion of Cause.

Exactly that which Mill protests against Reid's adducing to account for the notion of cause may be maintained in explanation of the popular idea. The notion of power in the conception of cause is got from our consciousness of *being able to put forth activity*, from our consciousness of *volition*. Both Hume and Mill argue that actual experience of cause and effect shows only a relation between phenomena either from the objective or the subjective point of view. I demur. However necessary it may be for scientific purposes to regard our subjective states as phenomena, no man regards himself simply as a phenomenon or series of phenomena. We know ourselves as beings that may or may not exert a definite energy, and this quite takes our actions out of the category of phenomenal successions. Now just as, in regard to movements of my body, I come to consider them as depending on my will, so I come to conceive there is a similar 'causal' power determining other movements in nature.

Mansel thought this not enough, and that to find the root of the notion it was necessary to go down to the power of man to determine the successive states of his mind. This is of course one case of the exercise of our volition, but it is better to take the more general and the older view. So when we say that the earth draws a stone we ascribe a personality to the earth just as we are conscious of our own personality, in the same way as I ascribe to another personality the power of moving the arm. If I credit *you* and *the earth* with being reservoirs of power, it is because I have read my own consciousness into everything that I say acts. I have read into my experience what is not directly in it. Not that we really *think* that the earth is endowed with a personality like ourselves, but we have a tendency to read it into the earth, despite our real convictions.

The Larger Experientialism.

Thus there is a good ground for urging that we do not get the notion of cause from strictly phenomenal experience. The Rationalist position is so far good. Yet if we consider the circumstances fully, we shall come to see that this mode of interpretation is not fixed and fast, but has gradually grown up, and, like the constitution of the human mind, has been developed with the human race, or anterior to it in the succession of animal life. This mode of interpreting our experience as a world of active causes, however natural for all of us now, even for the uninstructed—more perhaps for them—has only, as there is every reason to believe, come to be developed gradually, as men have awaked to full consciousness. Man came to interpret the world in this way after the experience of ages, and not within the experience of the individual. In this way only may the Experientialist position be justified. It does seem to me that, despite the position taken up by the English Associationists, we can find no sufficient explanation of our view of the world, as an aggregate of active agents in relation to one another, in terms of their principles only. My view of the world as known is not explained by my simple sense-experiences becoming aggregated under principles of association. There is more in my knowledge than my experience can account for.

For LECTURE XV read:—

G. C. Robertson, *Philosophical Remains*, pp. 63-74:—'How we come by our Knowledge' (or *Nineteenth Century*, March, 1877).—ED.

LECTURE XV.

THE NATURE OF KNOWLEDGE. EVOLUTION.

The Principle of Heredity applied to the Problem of Knowledge.

THE problem of knowledge, then, cannot be solved without reference not only to our consciousness but to our organic structure and functions, either according to Kant's view of the constitution of the mind, or according to the scientific point of view which takes into account our nervous system. Now here we see how entirely the philosophical question of knowledge has changed in consequence of our wider scientific view. Evolution has given the problem quite a new expression. I do not say that the evolution of our physical organisation explains consciousness, but it yields us a statement of external conditions. Our experience is determined from the first, and definitely combined in certain ways. Anything more inappropriate, more ludicrous than the *tabula rasa* theory, with its implication that all minds are at starting alike and, if exposed to the same conditions, would all develop alike, is not to be found. Allowance must be made for the predetermining of primitive endowment: aptitudes must be recognised, as Leibniz saw better than Locke. No child's knowledge is explicable from its own experience. This no doubt involves a starting-point somewhere, but scientific explanation does not pretend to give absolute beginnings. We need not assume the primitive endowment of a child as something inexplicable. Heredity is a real factor, and accounts for facts in knowledge which Associationists cannot explain. Breed was always allowed to count for something, but prior to Darwin and Mr. Spencer there was no formulated theory of it. The organism, more especially the nervous system, becomes modified by a change of environment. What one generation acquires in the way of adaptation to environment another gets the benefit of. An accommodation takes place in the individual and modifies the character of the progeny. The individual inherits the experience, or the effects of the experience, of the race. Mr. Spencer, it is true, is not so effective in applying it as he makes out : he should have gone to school under Kant, whose is the insight if not the power of explaining : his theory of knowledge halts, because he fails to see the problem of knowledge in its fullness. The principle of heredity, if applied intelligently, would account for more than he has made it do. By it we can not only explain the difference between your constitution and mine, but we can partly account for the community of knowledge by the fact of common ancestry, a common inheritance of mental and nervous constitution. This fact, properly understood, is of the greatest importance in explaining. It is a dim fore-feeling of this that we get in Plato's ideas had in a prior existence, and in the theory of innate ideas generally. Experience has gone before us. It is quite evident that our own experience does not determine us to perform acts we do perform before experience can teach us. The mere study of the individual organism will give no explanation of knowledge as we find it. There are factors to be sought outside of the experience of the individual.

This does not cut us off from Experientialism, but it does cut us off from Individualism. Heredity explains both the individual element in the conscious living organism and also its element of relation to the conscious life of others.

The Social Factor.

When we have made every allowance for heredity in the Evolutionist sense, and for experience in the Associationist sense, we have accounted for but a very small part of our knowledge. What the knowledge of an individual comes to be is not to be accounted for by accidental experience alone, nor by heredity, nor by the original constitution of the mind. There is something, principally speech, passed on from generation to generation, which has gone on increasing as it has passed. This the individual finds ready for him to take hold of; it takes hold of him, and through *this* we have our knowledge. The child comes into the world in a social relation; when it begins to act for itself, then it is that it comes under the influence of the Social Factor.

No; the question of knowledge is not to be resolved in terms of individualistic experience. The eighteenth century theorists of knowledge—Locke, Hume, Berkeley, Kant— none of them take into account the social conditions of the individual. Hegel, the great Rationalist, recognised that man has his being determined and moulded by social circumstances. But it was Comte who first clearly apprehended the 'solidarity' of the individual in society, and the debt we owe to our fellows and especially to past generations, not by way of organic inheritance, but by way of intercourse, and chiefly by the social engine of thought expressed in language. Lewes's thought too was impregnated with this doctrine. It was he who brought it to the front in this country. Man is no mere unit with independent development, but depends for that development on his environment and the overpowering influence of social tradition. It is when he has passed through the training imposed by society that he first begins to assert himself.

Speech and Knowledge.

Now this social influence, I say, is exerted chiefly by the medium of language. The Nominalists, e.g. Hobbes, Locke and Hume, denying that we have any, or any save very imperfect, powers of general thinking except by means of verbal signs, have always recognised the importance of language. But they were mainly concerned with the special psychological question, 'how we think generally.' They did not discern the far more widely pervading function of language. Whatever the individual develops into can be shown to be a product of his relations with others through the moulding medium of language. For language is a natural social product of the mind, which is not come at or elaborated by any one person, but consists of expressions caught up between man and man and become current. No child coming into being is allowed to follow his own bent, save in a limited degree. For awhile a spontaneous language is allowed free course, but very soon progress in language consists not in his own creations, but in what he shows aptitude in getting from others. Imitation is natural. Through it he is laid hold of by society and moulded after its kind. For the language that is its chief instrument has been developed by accumulated deposits of the countless experiences of the society of the past. The more he works into that language the more he adopts what transforms his whole being, involving as it does an entire theory of the universe.

The simple fact of an active verb implying, involving, a subject and object, cause and effect, and the like, embodies such a theory, and becomes a way of interpreting his experience which that experience itself does not adequately provide. Experience is interpreted *for* him, in spite of him, so as to compel his explanations into the course they take.

Here is, for the individual, a non-empirical factor within sense; not a mere system of sounds, but also an *a priori* factor of knowledge. But not on Kantian lines. There is no need to fall back on pure intuitions and concepts that cannot be accounted for. The child thinks with concepts formed prior to its own experience, concepts which have been developed and which were in past times different from what they are.

We have seen that the notion of the world as a realm of cause and effect has developed with the human race. That language has moulded and dictated its development is no justification of Mill's theory, that invariable sequence teaches us to distinguish causal action. Relatively to the individual the concept *is* pure: it is not developed by him; others have done this and handed it on ready made. Well then, is the concept absolutely pure from the first? Was it intuitive? Or has it been developed in the history of the race? The question is unanswerable: and yet does there not lie a pretty strong suggestion in the development of languages themselves, with systems of metaphysic variously developed in each? Kant said that effect and cause can never have been developed in the individual or in the race; such a necessity of thought as that—never! *I* say, the gradual development of the conviction that nature is a realm of law, that everything is caused, is a historical fact. Even Aristotle's mind, as I pointed out, had no full notion of universal causation; some things, he held, happened by chance, causelessly. Necessities of thought *can* be explained in terms of experience, *if* we let experience include accreted racial experience. This is an extension of Experientialism. Mr. Spencer's Heredity or 'organised experience,' on the one hand, and the fact of growing language on the other, as an impersonal factor, seem to go much further to explain knowledge than unbelievers think. Scientific psychological data, if sound and wide, will answer philosophical questions.

In Conclusion.

One word more. Kant's importance in the history of philosophy can never be overrated, and, in his own line, no one can go beyond him. No serious study of him is ever lost, for through no thinker can the student be so well led into the heart of the philosophical questions of the day. He is the first philosopher who fully understood the complexity of the problem of knowledge, however mystical his ultimate assumptions may appear in the light of the advance of science. Working on independent lines, although a Rationalist, he went as far in the direction of reconciliation between the two opposed standpoints as was possible a century ago.

On the other hand, it is the great merit of the English school that, with its feet firmly planted on psychological ground, it has answered as to the nature of knowledge in conformity with this ground. It is true that biological advance has rendered for ever impossible the older Experientialist position, that knowledge with its objectivity, its universality, its necessity, has to be acquired by every individual for himself, in the course of his own experience, from the beginning. But the Experientialism of to-day is far in advance of that of the last century. We have advanced all round,

e. g. psychologically, by the distinction drawn between active sense and passive sense—a discovery which has completely altered the state of the question. Thus the means are now present for working out a systematic theory of knowledge from the point of view of modern Experientialism. Philosophy is not science, but its problems should be solved as far as possible from a scientific point of view.

For LECTURE XVI read :—

Bain, p. cit. 'The ries of a Material World' (p. 202).

Mill, *Examination of Hamilton's Philosophy*, ch. xi. 'The Psychological Theory of the Belief in an External World.'

Hamilton, *Works of Reid*, Notes C and D.

Berkeley, *Principles of Human Knowledge*.

LECTURE XVI.

THE PERCEPTION OF AN EXTERNAL (OR MATERIAL) WORLD.

Berkeley's Influence.

WITH this our third problem we have been dealing more or less by implication. In considering how we come by our knowledge, what are the psychological factors in our cognition, it only remained to add the special emphasis—knowledge, cognition, *of objects*. Objectivity as applied to percepts is only a case of the objectivity of knowledge. What account can we give of the existence, in our system of knowledge, of an external, extended, material world? Is there a real pillar corresponding to my individual percept of it? The question is specially an English one, and it was Berkeley who first gave this direction to English thought. The same Berkeley who denied the existence of things of sense, as a philosopher and Immaterialist, was the first man to begin a perfectly scientific doctrine of sense-perception as a psychologist. He approached the philosophical question through his psychology. Yet although he was foremost in the psychology of his century and made great positive additions to science, he is almost the only first-rate modern thinker who set to work with a definite religious and even theological purpose; for the note of modern philosophy is that it leaves out religion as such in its explanations. I said 'first-rate,' for some second-rate thinkers, e.g. Butler, did have a religious purpose; whereas Berkeley psychologised for philosophy, and philosophised for theology.

Before Berkeley.

Descartes' position was that mind and matter are utterly differentiated, the former by thought, the latter by extension. Mind exists and thinks and is not extended. Matter exists and is extended and does not think. The resultant problem was, How, in the human constitution, can mind be conjoined with a body? Further: if matter exists in so far as it is extended, is there or is there not much in material things that can be proved not to exist in the same sense, e.g. colour, sound, &c?

Locke was not, like Descartes, a dogmatic metaphysician—at least, not to the same extent. Philosophy with Descartes was theory of being, and his fundamental assumption was substance either extended or thinking. With Locke it tended to become theory of knowledge, constructed if not on a psychological basis, at least in a psychological spirit. Nevertheless Locke's psychological view of external things is largely coloured by Cartesian metaphysical dogmatism. He asserted at times the existence of matter in a manner as absolute as that of the growing materialistic science of his day. Locke's doctrine of matter as known was that, of our ideas of external things, some correspond to qualities really existing in external bodies, while some are of qualities wrongly imputed by us to those bodies, and which have no objective existence. The former are 'extension, figure, motion, rest, solidity or impenetrability, and number;' the latter are 'all other sensible qualities, as colours, sounds, tastes, and so forth[1].' Those he calls primary, these, secondary qualities. The latter are not in things, but are sensations of ours interpreted as absolute qualities of things. Primary qualities exist absolutely, but of them too we have sensible apprehension. These primary and secondary qualities were the equivalents of Aristotle's Common and Special Sensibles. The special sensibles were the impressions conveyed each by a special sense to consciousness, but the common sensibles, e.g. extension, were the result of a number of senses being affected together, or rather of what Aristotle called common sense, a sense over and above the special senses. Now Locke thought of extension only as something apprehensible by different senses at the same time, and so he translated common sensibles into primary qualities, holding that all those aspects thus apprehended are fundamental or primary, as representing qualities of objects as they really are. Locke was bound to assume an absolute matter in which these qualities cohered. But if primary qualities are such as we have sensible apprehension of, they are not so different from secondary qualities.

Berkeley on Locke.

It was here that Berkeley stepped in and broke up this absolute distinction between primary and secondary qualities of matter. He contended that the former are as much explainable in terms of ideas as the latter. All are agreed that colour, sound, heat, &c., are things we impute to matter on the strength of our sensible experience. Berkeley maintained that this was equally and in the same way true of

[1] Locke, *Essay*, Bk. II, ch. viii; Berkeley, *Principles of Human Knowledge*, Pt. I, § 9.

the former. *They* also are ideas, and just as little representative of any reality in matter as colour, sound, &c., are. If colour is something we impute to external things, there is a sense in which we impute extension to them also. *All qualities of things, primary as well as secondary, are for philosophy phenomenal.*

Berkeley's Theory of Matter.

Now this was Berkeley's reason for denying that material things exist at all apart from mind. He regards them as mere aggregates of sensations. All that we mean by matter is uniformity of sense-experience. All that absolutely exists is mind. External things only exist for mind. *Esse est percipi.* Nothing can *be* except as *perceived.* Being, apart from being perceived, is 'a direct repugnancy and altogether inconceivable.' 'The absolute existence of unthinking things are words without a meaning, or which include a contradiction[1].' As we know everything through our senses, and cannot know in any other way, it follows that nothing perceived is absolute, and that matter can only exist if the sense is there. Berkeley does not get rid of the reality to each perceiving mind of the external world, but he does claim to have got rid of its *absolute* reality, i.e. of its existence apart from perceiving minds. Granted the existence of mind, there is nothing that we cannot express as orderly experience of mind.

Such was Berkeley's doctrine of Immaterialism—a less ambiguous term than Idealism—by which he thought,

---

[1] *Principles of Human Knowledge*, Pt. I, §§ 17, 24. 'A "contradiction" if it means that sensible objects are at once ... phenomenal and yet not phenomenal.' Fraser's *Selections from Berkeley*, 3rd ed. pp. 48, 53 note.—ED.

in a community of pure Materialists, to get rid of the matter which was their one fundamental assumption, and at the same time to confute the half-hearted dogmatism of Locke. Berkeley was born in the century which saw the beginning of modern science, and at the end of it, when that science was tending to be very materialistic. Matter was not only assumed, for science as for the practical purposes of life, as an absolute, as something extended and consisting of minute invisible parts having motion in relation to each other—a fact which accounted for colour, sound, heat, &c.—but was posited as the one thing that really did exist. Locke, on the other hand, as we have seen, allowed only a partial accounting for matter as mental construction. Berkeley contended that, if it can be shown that object is a psychological construction in regard to its secondary qualities, it is equally a psychological construction in regard to its primary qualities. We are not to regard our senses as giving absolute copies, as Locke did, of objects; we must explain how objects come to appear extended, figured, and moved just as much as how they appear coloured, heated, and so forth. This it was Berkeley's great merit to be the first to put forward.

Berkeley fails in legitimate Psychological Explanation.

The psychologist has no right to assume object, viz. the object he is going to explain. By this I do not mean that the psychologist, beginning his scientific procedure with an account of the senses, has no right to assume an external world affecting his body and senses. He is bound, for instance, to assume the sun and his own eye before he can give any account of sense-experience in regard to vision. Thinkers of the Hegelian, or, as it is sometimes called, the neo-Kantian, school of Green are constantly insisting that the psychologist assumes what he afterwards professes to explain, and that it is only thus that he contrives to explain. Green made out very cleverly that this was the case with Locke, but though the charge is here well founded, it is not so when made against philosophers who seek to reason on a psychological basis. It is one thing to assume sun and eye in order to get language to explain sensation; it is another to assume that we have explained what the sun ultimately is. We go on afterwards as philosophers to explain in subjective terms the very things which as psychologists we were bound to assume, and I say that Berkeley's great merit was to see that nothing was present in primary qualities of object which we cannot explain. But then he did not go on to give this explanation: he did not see that primary qualities *are* different from secondary, and why they are so. Why are some forms of our experience of more account for making up our knowledge of that pillar than others?

Berkeley's Fundamental Assumption.

So far Berkeley's statements have appeared as negative criticism, but he had constructive aims. He felt it necessary to give a consistent theory of things, a theory which would sufficiently explain the facts of science and also satisfy all the demands of religious conceptions and of every-day experience. Now the fundamental necessary assumption on which he grounds his theory is the existence of one infinite spirit and other finite spirits. What we call Nature is only a mere orderly sequence of 'ideas,' and these are brought to pass by the real causation of the infinite spirit in the minds of finite spirits, these being so far like the infinite spirit that they too can have ideas.

After Berkeley. Hume.

Berkeley's argument against the validity of the distinction between primary and secondary qualities was completely accepted by Hume. He did not dwell on this side of the problem, regarding it as finally made out that, from the point of view of psychology, or, as he would have expressed it, of philosophical consideration, there was no ultimate ground for Locke's division. But he went on to assert that, on the same grounds on which Berkeley had declared that beyond ideas aggregated in certain ways we could get no knowledge of matter, it would be no less incontestably established that it was impossible to get below ideas, or subjective states in general, or subjective phenomenal experience, to the existence of mind. Just as matter was resolved by Berkeley into ideas expressed in certain ways, so by the same kind of resolution was mind reduced by Hume to what we may call a phenomenal expression.

Hume worked this out as a part of his general dialectic, in which he was really concerned not to set up any positive theory of knowledge, but rather to follow the bent of his mind and show that when philosophers attempted from their reasoning to make out the ultimate nature of things and dogmatically to determine all that is, they were going a great deal beyond the legitimate sphere of knowledge. His theory of Substance is the first serious and anything like sufficient attempt to give a psychological explanation. He dwells especially upon the amount of representation (work of imagination) involved in objective perception, but fails in not distinguishing either the psychological factor of muscular activity, as lying at the basis of all objective synthesis, or the 'social factor.' As a positive theory it is to be described as an inadequately filled-in Phenomenalism. I am not concerned here to defend Hume's argument, which to me is imperfect in the last degree. But it is irrefutably true in maintaining that all our knowledge, whether of matter or of mind, is confined to phenomenal aspects. Of either, save in their phenomenal aspects, we know nothing.

Kant's Idealism.

Now Hume argued sceptically, so as to imply that human knowledge was next to nothing. Kant, on the other hand, while he accepted Hume's general position in this matter, was of those who hold that human knowledge is of a very positive nature. Kant distinctly declared that all our knowledge was of phenomena. He declared indeed that for our knowledge of physical phenomena we are not wholly dependent upon experience, inasmuch as we can make *a priori* determinations about nature; nevertheless these determinations are always about nature as phenomenal. But in regard to our knowledge of mind, we are positively confined to experience. However much we ascribe our subjective states to an Ego, we commit a 'paralogism' if we claim to *know* mind otherwise than in its manifestations.

Kant takes up the question in quite a different way from the English thinkers. He is concerned mainly with the general theory of knowledge, within which theory he has of course a view about the material world as such. And that view I bring into relation not only with Hume, but also with Berkeley. Kant agrees with the latter in refusing to allow the distinction between primary and secondary qualities, declaring that the former are—to use his own terms—just as subjective or phenomenal as the latter. And though he has by no means the same explanation of extension as Berkeley, though he does not declare, as Berkeley does, that for our apprehension of extension we are dependent entirely upon experience, and that it is developed by association of touches and sights, yet he, even more expressly than Berkeley, declares that the extension of things is no real objective quality of them. For, as we saw, he declares that space is a mere subjective form of sensibility. According to Kant there is positively nothing in our perception of this table which is not subjective. Kant in this respect is an Idealist—not an empirical Idealist, since he does not suppose that all the (subjective) elements into which we could analyse this table are such as come to us by way of experience. And he even accuses Berkeley's Idealism of making matter out to be illusory because it is phenomenal, showing herein a very imperfect apprehension of the latter's theory.

Kant's Realism.

But Kant does not rest in this Idealism. Beyond phenomena knowledge, for him, cannot go; nevertheless he declared that phenomena imply an underlying reality which he called the *thing in itself*, or noümenon. The former is the less misleading term, since noümenon suggests a knowing subject no less than phenomenon. Thing-in-itself, then, for him underlay the double stream of experience, subjective and objective, constituting probably a single existence or entity, if that might be called existence or entity which he admitted was an *unknown* quantity. Self as a particular entity with a possibly immortal future we could hold only as a *moral* conviction.

The Ding an sich *an inconsistent Theory.*

Now Kant declared that all things in themselves are in relation to, or ideas of, 'pure reason;' it is on the ground of this pure reason that we hold them to exist; in other words, it is a necessity of reason that gives a foundation for noümena. But then he is placed under this difficulty: if it is upon the ground of reason that we assert these things to exist, have we any *rational knowledge* of them? This he was forward to deny, saying that through reason as such no knowledge proper is possible. In the same breath, then, in which he posits, as beyond phenomena, the thing in itself as what cannot be theoretically known, he assumes it as the cause of sensations in us, which we group and interpret in various ways as knowledge. He supposed therefore that when we have a sensation, say, of colour, received according to the law of our being in time and space, and worked up into knowledge according to the categories or laws of the understanding, this phenomenon of colour was really explicable from a thing in itself, the character of which he did not pretend further to define, which he most confidently asserted was not in space or time, nor subject to the categories, and yet to which he applied the category of cause. This seems to me the fundamental inconsistency in his philosophy.

Reid's and Hamilton's Eclecticism.

I now come to the English stream of thought to show what followed upon Hume's scepticism. Reid, while he contested Hume's philosophy altogether and, like Kant, set up a general theory of knowledge, was more especially moved to criticise both Berkeley and Hume in their theories of the external world. His whole philosophy was accommodated to his own theory of this problem. And his theory is that, however philosophers may give a subjective expression to the qualities of matter, yet at the last the philosophical position should be that of common sense, namely, that underneath qualities there is a real entity existing apart from the mind. You do not want, he said, a *theory* of the external world. Open your eyes and see it! In the very fact of perception there is a present apprehension both of subject and of object, opposed entities, real existences. This view is also called Natural Realism and Natural Dualism, because it agrees with the common view. It may be said that this after all is only Kantianism, with its assertion of our conviction that things exist in themselves. But Reid went further and declared; as against Berkeley and Hume, that, however it might be with secondary qualities—and these he gave up—this real entity outside of us had as inherent qualities of its own those called primary. Thus he directly took up the position declared by Berkeley to be untenable.

But the champion of common sense was, as Hamilton pointed out (v. p. 820 of his edition of Reid), by no means always consistent with himself. At times he declared that on the ground of common sense real things exist outside of us, with qualities of extension and so forth; at other times he falls back upon the position which Hamilton called Representationism, namely, that our sensible apprehension of things, our mental experience, is a mere substitute or representative for a reality beyond, for which we cannot find an expression—that both primary and secondary qualities, instead of being at once subjective and objective facts, or in other words mental experience and real qualities, merely represent that ultimate undefinable reality.

And while I bring here no charge against Reid that is not brought against him by his follower Hamilton, I bring this further charge against both, that they depart from the position of common sense to the extent of depriving matter of all secondary qualities. Now it is unquestionable that, in the apprehension of every-day life, we ascribe colour as confidently to external things as we ascribe form. If in philosophising we are to go by common sense at all, we must go by it altogether. This reserve then is objectionable and opens their whole theory to doubt. Hamilton often says that if the testimony of consciousness is false in one thing it is false in everything. But my consciousness gives me the same evidence for the secondary as for the primary qualities. His eclecticism shows that the views of 'the man in the street' are not necessarily correct. And his theory of the immediateness and intuitiveness of our knowledge of an external world involve an absolute element that is at variance with the philosophical doctrine of the Relativity of Knowledge[1]—'Everything known is only known in relation to a knowing mind'—which he assents to and asserts.

We cannot take either common sense or consciousness as our ultimate referendum, and then accept or reject this or that in its testimony as we please. My opinion is that whatever common sense may say, it is *common* sense that says it, and common sense is one thing and philosophic insight another.

Ferrier in this generation has with very great force done over again the work accomplished by Berkeley in the last century. He has done it, if not in the full light of modern psychology, and rather in a metaphysical than a psychological way, yet with a force of thought and expression not to be surpassed. He may be studied either in his *Institutes of Metaphysic* or his *Posthumous Works*.

[1] Distinguish from the *psychological* theory of Relativity, viz. in knowing a thing we know it as distinct from something else.

Spencerian 'Transfigured Realism.'

Mr. Herbert Spencer's Transfigured Realism (as he himself classes it) is really nothing more than what, in Hamilton's classification of theories of External Perception, is called Cosmothetic Idealism. Mr. Spencer himself, it is true, says, Realist I am, only not a crude Realist, i. e. with the Realism of popular opinion which imputes all my special sensations to things outside of me. But he goes further and, like Kant, denies that even primary qualities are inherent in real substances, noümena, or things in themselves. And he ends by saying, not professedly in the language of common sense, which he rather scouts, and yet in language which practically comes to that, that we have a fundamental certainty, the deepest certainty of our being, that object exists as opposed to subject, and subject exists as opposed to object. He does not, like Hamilton, insist on the essence of object being extension, but he declares that in any act of perception there is involved the ultimate certainty that there is an object outside of and apart from the percipient.

Now if a thinker like, e. g. Hamilton or Reid asserts this opposition of object and subject with the view of establishing a duality of substances, I can understand the position and see the force of it. This is what we certainly do assume in daily life, and it is open for any philosopher to say that his object is to give a philosophical expression to that assumption. But in the case of Mr. Spencer, who scouts the notion of a human being consisting of two entities, mind and body, mutually opposed, all the pother that he makes on this point (in ch. xviii of Vol. II of his *Psychology*) seems to me, I must confess, to come to no more than much ado about nothing. Why *he* should be so anxious to make out an opposition of object and subject outside of consciousness to explain what is in consciousness I cannot, from his point of view, for a moment understand. Take the passage: 'Realism, then, would be positively justified even were the genesis of this consciousness of existence beyond consciousness inexplicable' (ch. xix). I say that this is a contradiction in terms, and so much so, that when he comes afterwards to give an explanation of this consciousness of existence out of consciousness, it turns out to be after all altogether in terms of consciousness and he has not got to it at all! He has only got consciousness of existence that is *in* consciousness.

For LECTURE XVII read:—

Bain, op. cit. 'Perception of a Material World,' pp. 197 et seq.

The student may with profit consult also Leibniz's essays *La Monadologie* and *Principes de la Nature et de la Grâce fondés en Raison* (*Œuvres*, ed. Paul Janet, vol. ii. pp. 594-617).—ED.

LECTURE XVII.

THE PERCEPTION OF AN EXTERNAL (OR MATERIAL) WORLD (*continued*).

The Circle of Consciousness.

For my own part I agree in this matter essentially with Professor Bain and also with Mill. I hold with them, with Berkeley, Ferrier and others, that outside of the circle of our consciousness it is perfectly impossible to get. Mr. Spencer aims at doing so, at getting a consciousness of object outside of consciousness, claiming this as a more certain, fundamental testimony of consciousness than anything else. I cannot understand the words. I do not see how we can work with a conception like that. I go further. In daily life we *do* work with such a conception, we do really suppose things to be outside of us with qualities that demonstrably can *not* be outside of us. But however we may 'in the street' get on with this, from the point of view of philosophical consideration I cannot but call it with Berkeley a self-contradiction, and I frankly confess that I do not pretend to give any account of an object not in consciousness, nor of a subject not in consciousness. I cannot help it. I would if I could; but I do not think it can be done. The whole of this discussion can take place only from the point of view of consciousness, and we can never get away from that point of view. What is the good of trying to get away from it and pretending by mere words that we do so?

That we do so in daily life does not alter the philosophical truth of the matter. Any object that I can make out in the universe, I cannot pretend to make out except with regard to my mind. So Professor Bain (p. 197):—'There is no such thing known as a tree wholly detached from perception,' &c. But within that circle I am anxious to make out—and more anxious than either he or Mill, for I think the treatment in both writers is incomplete—that there *is* an opposition of what cannot better be expressed than by 'subject' and 'object.' And I think that this is an opposition which should find expression in such terms as psychological inquiry can justify, and such as, in respect of philosophical import, may be admitted to contain the ultimate rationale of what undoubtedly is the fact in our common every-day experience, the fact that we do posit mind and matter as independent existences apart from consciousness, out of consciousness, or even without the slightest reference thereto. In common life when we see anything we usually leave ourselves entirely out of account. It never for a moment occurs to us that we have anything to do with it.

Berkeley claimed that his Idealism really expressed the thought of people in common: that to the popular mind external object is really whatever can be felt, seen, &c., of it[1], and that the kind of abstract substance supposed by metaphysicians to underlie the qualities of matter is really made no account of in the popular conception. There is some foundation for his view. If we abstract from our table

---

[1] Cf. op. cit. I, § 6: 'Some truths there are so near and obvious to the mind that a man need only open his eyes to see them. Such ... that all the choir of heaven and furniture of the earth ... have not any subsistence without a mind—that their *being* is *to be perceived or known*,' &c.—ED.

all its qualities and yet retain for it a metaphysical entity, this is clearly what the popular mind cannot or does not take account of. Still I do not think what Berkeley said is correct. However true it may be that the popular mind expresses in terms of sensation the character of external things, I think it is unquestionable that, in the popular apprehension of us all, we do ascribe a perfectly independent existence to these aggregates. Berkeley said, to be is to be perceived. This cannot be said to be the popular apprehension. Perception is an accident in the popular mind. Commonly we conceive the qualities as real objective qualities of a real existing thing.

And I think that this popular apprehension must find its explanation. If psychology leads us to take up another position from that of common sense, it is bound to give some kind of explanation of this. If it holds that there is an unwarrantable assumption in these things, it must yet give some explanation of how it came to be made. I am not saying that we are bound to do this for perceptions of daily life. If we did, we should not get on as well as we do. Human action, human life, is one thing, philosophical insight, I repeat, is another. I have no disposition to hide the difficulties of the case, but I think that psychology should be able not only to give a scientific explanation of subject in relation to object circumspectly expressed, but also to explain how it is that this opposition of subject and object within consciousness *becomes aggrandised* into an opposition of mind and matter apart from each other, and which, generally speaking, rather leaves mind out of account and ascribes to matter, erroneously as I think, an absolute existence. For this is the way of the, to me, utterly unphilosophical doctrine of Materialism: it assumes matter to be a real existence apart from mind, and then pretends from this to explain mind. The most monstrous inversion of the rational course that can possibly be conceived! First through mind to get a notion of matter, then to objectify it and give it absolute existence, and then from this to explain mind! The very term 'phenomenon' used in science implies that the assumptions it makes are not ultimate.

Object developed by way of Active Sense.

Now I think that Professor Bain, better than many thinkers, lays hold of that element of difference, that means of differentiation within the circle of consciousness through which the opposition of object and subject is developed. He lays his finger on this when he brings out, first, as the fundamental element in the object-consciousness, the difference in our experience between passive sensations and consciousness of energy put forth, and next that all passive sensations, which in themselves fall to subject as opposed to object, like colour or sound, since they are found to vary definitely with our consciousness of activity put forth, come to be transferred from the subject to the object side of the account. We come to project them, and so absolutely, that we cannot now have them otherwise than as qualities outside of us. So that when we have made this transfer, we have left for subject all those sensations that do *not* vary with our movements as well as the whole of our representative and emotional life (using emotional to correspond with emotion only and not with sense-feeling as well).

Explanation of the Distinction between Primary and Secondary Qualities.

It is this consciousness that we have in connexion with muscular activity, or rather, active sense, which gives the real psychological explanation of the difference between so-called primary and secondary qualities of matter. The latter are the result of our passive sense; all the former, except the dubious case of 'number,' being the result of complex active sense. So Locke was only exaggerating a distinction of real importance, while Berkeley, in trying to break down *all* distinction, was not doing well. He never gave prominence to the fact that we cannot apprehend primary qualities of matter without activity of ours put forth. He approximates towards an analysis of touch in his *Theory of Vision* (§ 45), but does not clearly distinguish between active and passive touch.

Mill's Contribution.

While Professor Bain takes good account of the material elements in explaining the development of this opposition of subject and object, he scarcely brings forward sufficiently the intellectual laws that are involved. Mill, on the other hand, in his *Psychological Theory of the External World*, while he gives a much less careful statement of the material factors, gives a careful and relatively correct statement of the laws under which this development takes place. The two taken together, read with discernment, will afford the kind of explanation that can be given from the psychological point of view of the development of the opposition.

Object and Subject in the Germ.

I say *development*, implying that originally this opposition was not present in consciousness—that, even in the lifetime of the individual, there is a time when in the growing experience of the child this opposition begins to develop. I hold that the vague, discrete consciousness of the infant, while it may be called consciousness, is not to be distinguished as subjective or as objective consciousness in the sense afterwards meant by these words. It is discrete, else there would not be the fundamental condition of consciousness, i.e. discrimination, but it is too vague to admit of that opposition being present. Probably this comes to be at different times in different minds. At some moment in the history of every mind the confused, vague consciousness centres itself, or a beginning of separation is made, and thenceforth to one term or the other all experiences begin to be referred. I do not say that it is not possible for us, and possible with a certain scientific ground, to interpret our experiences, before the separation takes place, as having a subjective meaning. Unless what afterwards comes to be object had arisen within our individual experience and in that sense been subjective, we never could have got to the separation at all. And I accept the relativity of knowledge in the fullest sense—that we can have an experience of object only in relation to subject. But I assert also that there is no subject-experience until there is object-experience. Each implies the other.

Now philosophers who have laid stress upon this and made object and subject, or matter and mind, two separate entities, have in one way aggrandised this opposition developed within our psychological experience, but not so aggrandised it as to have overlooked the mutual implication. In popular apprehension this *is* overlooked. And the scientific excuse for maintaining this exaggerated separation is that it affords an excellent working hypothesis for the purposes of objective science.

Projected Personality fills up the Import of Object.

And there is this important element still:—When we talk about an object outside of us we give but an inadequate account of it if we express it psychologically in terms of movements of ours and so forth. To each such object we ascribe more or less a subjective existence for itself. Everything to me is object primarily, and my subject is as it were to me alone. But I come to see, in the first place, that of all my objective experience there is a certain part more constantly in connexion with my special subjective states than any other; and that is my body. I come to think of myself as a composite entity, and not only as two kinds of experience, but as a prominent subject in relation to a relatively prominent object.

Next, I find amongst other outside objects various objective experiences resembling those I have from my own body, but not quite similar, else I should mistake them for my own body, and for that matter rendered distinct by the absence of the double touches afforded by my own body. To the sources of these, on the ground of the similar experiences they afford me, I ascribe conscious states resembling my own—a subjective and also an objective experience.

Finally, even when there is no such similarity, I ascribe an adumbration of subjective life. I do not ascribe to this table the power of putting forth activity, or the feelings that I ascribe to my hearers or claim for myself. But in as far as I talk about the table as a thing able to enter into relation with other things, and in particular with myself, I do give it a kind of quasi-personality; and I believe that this element can never be absent from object entirely. In primitive minds we have the tendency to ascribe full life to everything, as we see happen in fetish-worship. Children too have this anthropomorphic interpretation of experience, e.g. when they kick the chair they have hurt their shins against. It is a natural tendency that we have--this interpreting what we experience as analogous to our own subject. And I believe that this is only an exaggeration of what each of us does, and needs to do, in order fully to body out any object. Unless I give the table as it were a highly attenuated personality, I do not think I get full objective experience, I do not think I get at that in my consciousness of object which is metaphysically expressed as *substance*.

The Psychological Explanation of Substance.

For we may insist that all qualities have their psychological expression in terms of sensible experience, we may insist, with respect to qualities, on the historically fundamental character of resistance—how that object is first *obstacle*, or impediment in the way of activity, and that object so got is interpreted through experience as extended, so that space is body attenuated rather than body is space filled in—and yet, when we have finished this analysis of the psychological conception of perception, it may be urged that from the point of view of the *metaphysical* conception of perception the question may still be asked, Is the object 'there' *real*? Is it anything *for itself*? This is a question not to be answered apart from psychology, but it should not therefore be evaded. Popularly judged, there is in our pillar something more than resistance, extension, colour, and any number of qualities. It is said, there is a substance there. Psychology then has to explain substance as well as attribute.

Now, as we have seen, my consciousness presents me to myself under a subjective as well as under an objective aspect. I am an extended object and I have a subjective life, a consciousness, a personal identity. And I attribute to you both body and consciousness. But it is your consciousness that is to me the *reality of you*. You are not so much a bundle of qualities which give me impressions as the conscious being who *has* these sensible aspects. Turning to animals, we find ourselves attributing subjective life to them also. And, going lower still, what we ascribe to the pillar as reality or substance is something analogous to that which in us is personality. Its substantiality, as opposed to its qualities, is a pale reflexion of our own subjective experience. Substance is at bottom subjectivity. This is the psychological explanation of the popular notion of difference of substance and quality, which was overlooked by Berkeley, Hume, Mill, and Professor Bain.

The Weakness in Berkeley's Theory.

Berkeley said that supposing it were the case, that the qualities of matter were to occur to us in a certain orderly and definite manner, and yet suppose that there was no substance there, would you miss this '*substratum* or support'? His answer is No, we should not, even as we do not in dreams (op. cit. I, 18). Then, he says, we have no right to assume it; and he claims that all he has to account for in perception is the orderliness of experience, which he does by assuming an Infinite Spirit. And he works round to his original position by the argument:—If the only account which scientific men can give of substance is a confused idea of something supporting sensible qualities, what shadow of right have they to say that matter is the only real thing in the universe, and that where there is no matter there is nothing at all? His demonstration then is that there is nothing whatsoever in the notion of substance which is not accountable for as sensible quality, or if there is, it is nothing at all.

Has Berkeley got rid of substance altogether in overturning either the crude materialism of scientific men or Locke's unsatisfactory account? Have we come to this, that there is in the world only an Infinite Spirit and a certain number of other spirits, and can we not ascribe a real existence to anything but God, Berkeley and other spirits like himself? To me his theory comes as short here as it does in the explanation of primary and secondary qualities. There is no doubt that the notion of substance is reasonable, and that while the common sense, which has found Berkeleianism repugnant, is no final criterion, it is yet a fact that philosophy must take into account, and that too when it says, 'A pillar *is there.*' Berkeley can get a coherent universe only by *supposing* a number of other minds *plus* the Deity. Here is rank assumption! Where are all these minds? He may be conscious of his own mind, but how then can he be sure of other minds? He ought to be able, from the point of view of his psychological experience, to account for this conviction. He would have given another answer had he faced the question, How can a mind allow other minds as existing?

Through Mind to Bodies; through Bodies to other Minds.

My own conviction, as I have already shown, is that I infer consciousness in others *through my sense-perception of them as bodies.* Let me be mind only, and I could never get out of myself. If I assume that minds like mine are, so to say, present, it is because I perceive bodies like mine. If *your* bodies do not exist, why, mine does not. My conviction of the double phase of my existence is strengthened by finding that I have objective experience of other bodies, which suggests the existence of other minds. And this conviction, by way of inference that material bodies like mine exist, is extended to animals, to which mind is ascribed because of external manifestations. It is only an extension of the same notion to posit the existence of all living things.

Then where may we draw the line? There is no material object perceived by me which is not for me something more than an aggregate of (Berkeleian) ideas. By what way I become sure of you, I become sure of all objects, because I interpret my experience upon the distinction I make between body and mind. In a sense my body is real enough, just as animals, trees, pillars, &c., have all in a very real sense a substantial existence, which is not adequately accounted for by merely assuming the Deity and a few human subjects. But bodily processes are explainable as mental facts, and not vice versa: these are for us ultimate; these explain. Though I am body as well as mind, the reality of me lies in the continuity of my conscious being. *I am* because I am subjectively conscious—there is my reality. And where I can infer subjective consciousness I say '*you* too are real.' This, extended further, is for me the explanation of the metaphysical notion of substance. We may express substance in terms of quality, viz. as Resistance, but quality in terms of substance needs Subject. Let no one say that because that pillar is perceived as substance by analogy of my consciousness of myself as subject, it is therefore taken up into my own being. If I fritter away the reality of substance, what remains of my own reality and that of others? There is just the same reason for accepting the reality of external objects apart from the thinker as there is for accepting other consciousnesses. The world of sense is just as real to Berkeley as it is to the man in the street. The truth in his teaching suggests to fresh students a distressful sense of a desolate universe with the ground cut away from under their feet.

Any philosophic satisfaction that they win will, it may be, come slowly through struggle, wrestling and trial. The transition, however won through, is a necessary process, but it leaves us with quite as real a world, nay, a world more real than we had before. If I say, I am and none other is—the motto of Solipsism—this is a position from which I cannot be dislodged, and it is the only logical position for Berkeley. But once I allow other minds, then by the same argument I allow other things, since it is through perception of bodies that I get at minds. Mind, then, is that which is absolutely existing; mind is the ultimate expression.

Ago ergo sum.

Let us pursue the analogy between subject and substance one step further and deeper. If we resolve the material thing into its physical constituents and stop at molecules, we are still at the stage of qualities. But if we go beyond sense to inference and come to the theoretic atom, we no longer apprehend matter by way of qualities, yet we are compelled to consider the atom as endowed with a certain inherent *activity*, with force or energy. Matter is not dead when thus considered; it is only in mass that it deports itself as relatively dead. Now here, in this energy, we get a mean term relating to matter in its ultimate being and our own personality as we subjectively know it. For the reality of our being consists most fully in putting forth activity, in *willing*. I *am*, in another and fuller sense, as I *will* or put forth activity. So too as far as atoms exert energy they really are. Force then in the atom and force in the individual constitutes real existence, and is the fullest expression of mind. Mind exists everywhere, and must be carried down to explain any true reality.

Thus we may take advantage of all material phenomena in order to help in the consideration of mind. This is in no sense a materialistic position. Atoms when in combination appear so extended, yet the atom is not extended. Extension is only the ultimate phenomenal appearance of matter. I assume that the universe consists of elements which are not extended, which appear when in conjunction as extended, and which are ultimately expressible in terms of mind. This is the Leibnizian conception of monads, which in conjunction appear to a conscious mind as extended, but taken alone are not extended, and whose ultimate expression is in terms of activity. Monadology is the ultimate philosophical analysis of the universe, with its fundamental postulate of real beings, immaterial, unextended, having power to act, of which conscious activity is a higher phase. Here is the platform of philosophical agreement.

LECTURE XVIII.

REGULATIVE PHILOSOPHICAL DOCTRINE.

The Regulation of the Three Phases of Mind.

I HAVE made allusion in the first lecture of this course to philosophy as connoting, under the aspect of 'love of wisdom,' a reference to practice; I also claimed in the psychological course that philosophy included logic as well as ethics; and I spoke later on of a 'regulative doctrine' of feeling. Not only feeling, but also intellection and conation admit of being regulated in order to an end or ideal. We may think, for instance, amiss or well. Now logic deals with the conditions of good and bad, i.e. true and false, thinking—with thought so as to make it true. Again, action can be made good and feeling beautiful. Ethics, accordingly, is regulative doctrine with a view to making action good. And æsthetics considers feelings, sees which of them admit of development towards a certain end, namely, beauty or refinement.

The fact that we *can* distinguish these three regulative bodies of doctrine, mutually independent, mutually unresolvable, exhaustive, is to be regarded as one of the strongest arguments for the tripartite division of mind. In psychology it is often hard to isolate them and secure their independence. But we can distinguish well enough that intellection in the end has to be made true, conation in the end has to be made good, feeling has to be raised to the grade of the beautiful. And we cannot add hereto; the summary is exhaustive.

Law as Generalisation and Law as Norm.

Whereas psychology explains mind, these doctrines are occupied with the regulation of mental functions. In the one case we explain what *is* (or rather *appears*), in the other we regulate the phenomenon with a view to an end. Clearly then in the latter case we are beyond psychology. We have passed from Phenomenology—to use Hamilton's terms—to Nomology; we are dealing with norms, which, it is true, are laws, but not laws in the scientific sense. Scientific law explains, i. e. expresses the complex in terms of the simple, the particular in terms more general. Thus the function of psychology is to explain by classing mental phenomena together, or generalising with respect to them. For instance, according to the law of similarity, whenever we form concepts we are assimilating. But in the logical sense thinking is being consistent. If you are not consistent, you are 'a vegetable.' Here then is law as *norm*. Psychology has nothing to do with action as good, any more than it has with thought as true, but simply with any kind of action. It deals with mental action as it naturally comes to pass.

The Connexion between Psychology and Practical Philosophy.

These three doctrines then come under philosophy, not as a certain deeper kind of knowledge, but as involving that certain practical bearing as implied by wisdom, which philosophy had at first and will have again. They are departments of philosophy in its practical reference, ethics being the branch most closely identified with philosophy thus considered. Ethics is philosophy as regulative of conduct, logic and æsthetics being philosophy as regulative of thought and of feeling. Philosophy results, eventuates, is consummated in ethics, inasmuch as philosophical consideration always in the end must be regarded as having an ethical direction, as having its outcome in guidance of conduct, whether the Ethics be blended with religion or not. Wisdom has reference to conduct; good conduct is wise; wise conduct is good; hence ethics is a philosophical discipline.

Logic regarded as a Science.

From a certain point of view these doctrines may be regarded as science and treated advisedly from the scientific point of view. Let us take logic first and classify the sciences as once before (v. Appendix) into objective and subjective sciences. Now though logic is not a science when considered as in any way dependent upon psychology, yet, considered by itself, it *is* a science, and moreover it must be placed at the head of the *objective* sciences. For just as chemistry is more special than physics, and physics more special than mathematics, so is mathematics more special than logic. Every one of the sciences, so far as it is a 'logy,' is a *specialised logic*; and before logic there can be nothing. But when it is thus considered, it must not be said to be conversant with thought, since this is essentially a subjective notion. It becomes the science of *relation*[1], and relation is as wide objectively as thought is subjectively. Things as

[1] Not of *quality*, which, as it includes *quantity*, would include mathematics as well.

thinkable are, objectively considered, things as relateable. Nevertheless logic is not so much a science as a *condition* of science.

Ethics regarded as a Science.

Ethics again may be considered as the science investigating the various ways in which men have been found to act in relation to men, and on this basis of historical investigation rules how to act in the best way may be framed. This scientific view of ethics has followed from the evolution theory and rather holds the field, Messrs. Spencer and Leslie Stephen being the chief exponents. Ethics is concerned with good conduct followed by not all individuals and nations. To get a science we must examine the meanings of good and bad, what good, and what bad, men do. Facts have to be collected from all times and a progressive or regressive development sought. This view is an extension of evolution as first applied only to biological, and then to anthropological conceptions; man as considered in respect of his origin, as evolved, and morality as a product of evolution, appearing in time.

Unquestionably we may proceed thus. Ethics may be regarded as the science dealing with moral conduct as manifesting itself throughout time, and the development of ethical notions as the business of the ethical philosopher. Mr. Spencer too, the great systematiser of evolution, says, with Comte, that ethics is a science dependent upon sociology and not upon psychology, although his work on psychology is put first. Morality is regarded as a historical social fact—an affair between man and man. The theory of man's social relations is sociology, and some only of those relations are moral. Ethics is a more specialised sociology. As logic may be regarded as the science of things as related, so ethics may be considered as the science of action as practicable, of such actions as men can get on with amongst themselves. Indeed much ethical matter *can* and *ought*, much more than it has been, to be treated scientifically, inductively, with verification from history.

Scientific Treatment does not exhaust Ethics.

But no ultimate problems can be thus fairly gone into. Unawares the scientific moralist is ever making philosophical assumptions which he ought to justify there and then. For instance, 'whatever is, is right;' 'if a moral custom is found in use, it is because it is right.' Here is an assumption which may not be justified by scientific consideration alone. Again, 'the conditions of human welfare are those of human being;—why need men be dissatisfied with what they find?'—this is a philosophical consideration. The ideal morality, the morality of the future, is an inevitable point in ethics, but it cannot be prescribed without pronouncing some one goal preferable. Now why any one in particular? This is not a question of matter of fact, but of what were better or worse, and needing a *criterion* of the same. It may not be adequately answered by direct facts of sociological experience, but needs deeper consideration—even philosophical. There is room, I say, for plentiful investigation of manners, for inductive inquiry into human relations down the course of history. Already we see a development of ethical conceptions, an ethical progress, a change of ideals. But *what is* an ideal? What is good? And what, we ask at this time of day, as ask we must—what direction ought human action to take? The problem of ethics is not soluble by purely scientific analysis; we cannot help being philosophical. Very much from evolutionary science we can accept, but it just misses the point in that it does not adequately treat of the 'consciously aimed at,' the ideal.

Finally, let not this view (of ethics as a science) be made light of; let the works of its exponents be read, but critically, and it will be seen how Mr. Leslie Stephen, scouting metaphysic as he does, is as much a metaphysician as any one, and how Mr. Spencer really deals not only with facts, but also with aims, ends, ideals.

Logic and Psychology—the Bond and the Distinction.

Logic derives the materials it works upon from psychology; it has to regulate that function of mind which, psychologically, we distinguish as intellection. It does not however deal with the whole of intellection, but only with that higher or more complex mode which we have termed 'thought.' Now why is thought the only part of intellection that can be logically regulated?

Let us first consider some of the definitions of logic:—

(*a*) The science of reasoning;

(*b*) The art of reasoning;

(*c*) The science of the operations of the understanding which are subservient to the estimation of evidence, i.e. in the pursuit of truth.

Of these (*a*) is not quite acceptable, for surely psychology as the science of *mind* includes the science of *reasoning*; and the statement is now admitted to be insufficient. It confuses logic with psychology. (*b*) avoids the error of (*a*); psychology can under no circumstances be termed an art. An art has a practical outcome, and logic tells us how we ought to reason in order to reason correctly or effectively. An art is a science definitely applied, and this sort of applied science is what logicians most probably wished to assert as the nature of logical procedure. Any confusion between the two is really only verbal. Nobody pretends that logic and psychology deal with reasoning in the same way. But logic has to do with much besides 'reasoning,' namely, with judgment, as expressed in propositions, and with names or terms which correspond to concepts. Hence Hamilton's definition, that logic has to do with *thought, as thought* is a real advance towards justice and accuracy. Logic, he also said, is the science of the necessary laws of thought. Bare thought as explained by psychology is all very well, but it is not as real or effective thought that psychology can take account of it. In order to be effective, valid, true, thought has to conform to certain definite conditions, to 'necessary' rather than to natural laws. But it is in Mill's definition (*c*) that we may best gather how logic differs from psychology. 'Understanding' has of late become more popular than scientific, but it once corresponded to thought (or to Hamilton's fifth faculty—the Discursive, Elaborative or Comparative). The definition more tersely put is that 'logic deals with *true* understanding.' Logic deals with thought as true, while psychology deals with thought as it naturally proceeds within us. With the question whether thought has any validity, psychology has nothing whatever to do.

What is Truth?

Now what is this truth of which logic seeks to give an account? This is about the deepest of philosophical questions and cannot be thoroughly answered. But we do not need to go to the bottom of it in this connexion. The full question is thus to be stated:—What is the relation between thought and being? Is there a reality apart from thought which thinking represents? And how does thinking represent it? These questions, as we have seen, fall within the province of epistemology, which is really another face of ontology. When however we consider truth in logic we do not need to determine what ultimately is, and how that reality can be known; we do not need a theory of knowledge or an ontology to start with. In logic we hold that to be true which is valid not only for my consciousness, but for all consciousnesses like mine. A thing is not true if it only holds good for me. Psychology deals only with the fact of intellection going on in my consciousness for me or in yours for you; it does not touch upon truth as such at all. A thing may be psychologically explicable though not logically grounded. Intellection regulated with a view to truth is logically grounded knowledge. 'All men are mortal' is logically grounded knowledge. When psychology has explained to me how I come to connect 'man' and 'mortal,' these notions are then further connected upon a basis of logical ground which holds for others beside myself. Hence we say 'Man is mortal' is *true*; it holds for all consciousnesses upon ground that can be assigned, i.e. evidence.

Self-consistency; Conformity to Fact.

Truth is, then, what holds intellectually for all minds alike. But we distinguish two kinds of truth, viz. *truth to self* and *truth to fact*. 'All men are mortal'—this holds for all consciousnesses in the sense that our thought in the case is taken to represent fact. Any assertion that flows from this will also be truth of fact, e.g. 'No immortal is a man.' Now let us assume 'All men are cats.' Then if a man were to enter this room, we must expect to see him furry and on all fours. If you cannot accept this, you are untrue to yourself; but if in this case you are true to yourself, you cannot be true to fact. We can have truth to self entirely apart from fact; and again, we can have truth to fact which is not true to self. A really effective mind is both true to self and true to fact.

Departments of Logic.

Now Pure or Formal Logic is the doctrine that determines the conditions that regulate truth to self apart from fact, the doctrine, in other words, of mere *consistency;* whereas Applied, Material or Modified Logic is a doctrine that lays down the conditions that regulate truth of fact. Hamilton's Logic, e.g. is chiefly Formal; Mill's aims always at being Real or Material. Jevons jumbles up the two quite hopelessly. Consistency really covers both kinds of logic. The internal, intrinsic truth of thought is that it shall be consistent with itself. The external, extrinsic truth of thought is that it shall be consistent with fact; that subject shall correspond to object. The business of most of us in life is mainly to be consistent with ourselves. For very few of us are destined to widen the bounds of knowledge; we come into the world 'the heirs of time,' and have enough to do with truly applying the knowledge we find. Herein logic tells us to do explicitly what we have hitherto done implicitly.

Truth is a Question of Judgment.

Now to answer our question why thought is the only part of intellection that can be logically regulated. Intellection includes perception, imagination, and thought. Why can we not logically regulate our perceiving and imagining? Strictly speaking, we cannot speak of *true* perception or *true* imagination, whereas *thought* can be true or false. Neither our perception *as such*, nor our imagination (which is only perceiving over again) is grounded; we do not *find reasons* in the case of either. It is only when knowledge is *general* that we can speak of it as true. Perceiving and thinking both proceed unreflectively and naturally, but thinking may also proceed reflectively; we can watch it as it comes to pass, and regulate it; it can be modified and corrected as perceiving cannot. Perception involves to some extent thinking; to the extent that there is explicit thinking perception may be regulated. Scientific observation is perception involving explicit thinking; thought is brought to bear on the sense-experience we are having, and so far this admits of logical control and may be improved and corrected. The Fröbel system helps children to perceive in a definite way more accurately and effectively. The help thus given to perception may be compared to the logical regulation of thought. But we cannot think logically before we can perceive, any more than we can be taught to dance before we have practically taught ourselves to walk. We come to think, and think, it may be, in a regulated fashion, upon a basis of perception.

For LECTURE XIX consult:—

G. C. Robertson, *Philosophical Remains*, 'On the Action of so-called Motives;' and Bain, Bk. IV, ch. xi.—ED.

LECTURE XIX.

THE BASIS AND THE END OF ETHICS.

Conation, Ethics, and Conduct.

As I have already pointed out, the fact of logic, ethics, and æsthetics being all on the same level with respect to their all having distinct regulative work to do for the mind is really one of the strongest indirect proofs that we have of the existence of a third distinguishable phase of mind, namely, conation. And of these three doctrines ethics, at any rate, has at no time lacked full consideration. It has indeed tended to be identified with practical philosophy. In the end all practice ends and culminates in acting *rightly*. For conduct involves others, whereas thought and feeling directly concern the individual only.

Ethics and Psychology.

Ethics is related to psychology not as a cognate science, but in that it depends for its material upon the psychology of conation. English writers are always confusing ethics and psychology, e.g. Butler and Reid. Professor Sidgwick seemed, in the earlier editions of his *Methods of Ethics*, to be so anxious to separate ethics and psychology that he almost said the former had nothing to do with the latter, e.g. 'The investigation of the historical antecedents of moral cognition and of its relations to other states of mind has no more to do with ethics than the corresponding investigation of the nature of space has to do with geometry[1]'—a view he has since modified. It was a mistaken view, for the psychological solution *has* a bearing on the ethical. Ethics deals with that which has to be brought to pass as an end *consciously conceived*, and thus we see the subjective aspect, the relation to psychology, of ethics. The leading ethical topics, viz. the springs of action and the moral faculty or conscience, can only be understood in their relation to psychology. Again the question of the freedom of the will, which belongs to the metaphysics of ethics, is discussed largely on a psychological basis.

The Question of the Freedom of the Will.

It has been asserted that we must posit a power of action in the human mind wholly antecedent to and independent of all psychological experience whatever. This has naturally been connected with a metaphysical consideration of what mind is in itself. There has been much discussion as to whether the terms 'free will' and 'necessity' are good and appropriate words to be used in regard to will at all, the pertinency of the former term especially being declared against generally by those who deny the 'freedom' of the will in the sense in which others assert it. Let us put aside these words, in which the question has commonly been treated in English controversy, and give attention to other terms more in recent use—'Determinism' and 'Indeterminism.' The latter is a strictly definable term and is synonymous with the doctrine of

---

[1] *Methods of Ethics*, 1st edition, Preface. In the 3rd edition Professor Sidgwick has appended this note: 'This statement now appears to me to require a slight modification.' Cf. also his art. 'Ethics,' *Encyc. Britannica.*—ED.

free will, while what has commonly been called the doctrine of philosophical necessity, or also Necessitarianism, is more scientifically expressed by the theory of Determinism. *Both* views, while opposed in themselves, are opposed to another view, the supporters of which have been confused by being classed with either side. These are theorists who do not consider the question from the point of view of psychology at all, but from that of man's position in the universe. And they assert, as related to and yet different from Determinism, that there is fatalism or perfect fatality in human actions, that everything in the world is as it cannot but be, that all is predetermined by external causes. This fatalistic theory may also assume the theological form of predestination, viz. that the Creator has determined exactly what shall come about in the world in general and in each human mind. By opposition to fatalism or predestination we have the assertion that the foreknowledge of the Deity determines nothing absolutely or necessarily with regard to any particular event or action of men. The necessity of fatalism may be said to be a cosmical necessity. The necessity of predestination is cosmical too, but more determined, not falling back upon a mere abstraction like fate or cosmos, but connected expressly with a personal Being or Providence. On the other hand, there is the view asserting absolute freedom from cosmical necessity of any sort, and of course from providential determination. Theologians like John Calvin, or, to a great extent, Augustin, were much more concerned with the question as between fatalism and predestination and the opposite than with the more scientific problem depending on the nature of Will. Their views we exclude from present discussion, the question for us lying between Determinism, or philosophical necessity, and Indeterminism.

The Ground of each Position.

The Determinist declares that, as in nature generally so among human actions, the same circumstances being present the same effect will follow. Or, as it is often expressed, since motives are productive of actions, the same motives being present, the same action will always follow. The view of the Indeterminist is that motives never wholly, or need not ever wholly, determine human action; that with the same motives present at different times different actions may follow; that in motives we do not get the full expression of the conditions of human action; that beyond all motives there is the activity of the ego itself; that there is a source of internal force, a self-initiating power in the human mind itself, a power of self-determination of the ego apart from the circumstances in which the ego is placed, which may determine action in the teeth of any quantity of motive. Hence it is called Indeterminism, meaning that action is not, or need not ever be, wholly determined by motives.

Now it is easy to see what sort of grounds the different theories rely upon.

The Determinists say that it is a *fact* that human actions proceed uniformly, and they point to statistics in proof of this. All human actions, they declare, are determined wholly by motives; unless we knew that people would act, under particular circumstances, in definite ways we could never get on at all. Unless there is this uniformity in human action as in everything else, between volition and its antecedent, it is impossible to have a science of the human mind at all. I think this is the strongest thing the Determinist can urge.

What the Indeterminists dwell on chiefly is the *consciousness of freedom* that we have in volition; we are conscious of a power of acting against any motives. Not that we do so always or often, but let the motives be never so strong or so weak, by a pure act of will, as it is sometimes called, it is possible for the man or ego to act for himself and of himself. So much do they rely on this that one of them, Hamilton, declared that, however much, on the ground of psychology, he was bound to allow that any action ever put forth can be said to follow from particular motives (of course widely extending the notion of motive to cover cases of action through so-called sheer caprice), we must yet in the last resort rely upon this simple and fundamental deliverance of consciousness, viz. that we are free agents, that our actions proceed, or may proceed, from a source within us wholly undetermined.

Choice as determined by the prevailing 'Motive.'

It is easy to see how a Determinist would answer this. I might have a strong inducement to go out of that door and yet say 'No, I will stay'—and stay. Now here, he would point out, I should only have yielded to a motive of a different kind, which motive may be sheer caprice, or obstinacy, or laziness, or the desire to show you that one need not act from particular motives, and so forth, and which is just in this case the more powerful motive, or motives. All this Hamilton allowed with full force, and was angry with Reid, who did not see what Determinists aim at in declaring that every action can be expressed in terms of motives of some sort or other. Yet he would not therefore give up free will in the strict sense, and indeed points to this case of apparent contradiction between necessity to act under motives and consciousness of perfect freedom as a clear case of contradiction within consciousness, and as illustrating his Law of the Conditioned.

The Argument in terms of Motives is a Logomachy.

Now just one word about the controversy before I pass on and close. I cannot help thinking that here, as elsewhere, the difference between the two views is greatly affected by the language in which the discussion has taken place. I am not arguing in the sense in which Professor Bain argues, not ineffectively, against the language that has been employed in this question. He objects to the use of 'free and 'necessary' as applied to will, and there is much force in his remarks. But I want to make a deeper charge against language than that, and especially against all this talk of 'motives' with regard to the question of choice of action. Such language is not scientific but merely metaphorical, and prejudices the issue. Both sides are to blame herein. And I think that, if the question had to be decided in terms of motives, the Determinists get into a very bad position. 'Motive' implies an ego or subject who is 'moved.' If this terminology is used and regarded as an ultimately satisfactory way of stating the case, then we must fall back with the Indeterminists on the assumption of an undetermined ego, in which case motives no longer amount to a sufficient explanation of actions. On the other hand, and granting still the language of motives, I must with the Determinists, as well as with Hamilton, assert that the determining causes or antecedents of every act can well be expressed in terms of motive. And I certainly think that those cases where we talk about the self-initiation of movements and their proceeding from the ego and so forth are as much acts determined by 'motives' as any of the simplest are.

'Motive' is a mere popular Metaphor.

How then shall we get out of this difficulty? We have proved the Determinist theory and also the Indeterminist theory under this language of 'motives.' We must lay the difficulty on the language. If motives were something external to the mind, as from the language used one might well conclude, then indeed we must take account of a mind or ego. But what sort of thing is a motive affecting the mind and yet external to it? What *is* motive after all? It may be a feeling. It may be an idea. It may be a resolution or vow, or a great many other mental states. 'Motive' is only a popular or loose way of stating certain mental states involving action. Well then, if motives are after all mental states, and not something external to the mind, as is commonly implied, then the question becomes altered at once. We cannot say that a state of mind is anything apart from mind. It is mind *in that state*. When I say, I have a conflict of motives, it means that I have now one tendency to act and now another. And when I say, I hold to a particular motive, the truer expression for this is that, amid a variety of conscious conditions succeeding one another, one becomes prominent or predominant and has a particular action following upon it.

The Determinist view I am constrained to accept; its ground of universal uniformity is sounder. But just as the Sensationalists used to express experience in terms of sense in such a way as to render any explanation of knowledge from sense impossible, so does Determinism by the terms of its statement render itself inadmissible and make a surrender to the opposite side.

Altruistic Considerations.

In ethical problems, then, we are on a basis of psychology, but not psychologising. If, e.g. we consider appetites and desires, it is not to make out anything by way of psychological explanation about them, but to account for what they are with regard for self and for others. Ethical questions are wholly concerned with the consideration of self and others, with relations between man and man—with *liberty* to develop the subject in either direction, viz. of the relations between man and higher minds (religion), and between man and lower minds, of relations, i.e. either humanistic or to the universe. For 'springs of action' it were better, in ethics, to substitute 'springs of conduct,' conduct being the actions of an individual considered in relation to anything which involves himself and others as related to himself.

The Ethical Standard.

The properly ethical question is that of the standard of right and wrong. A man's view of this is enough of itself to determine his whole ethical theory; and there is no other question that is sufficient in itself for this. Men may agree as to the nature of the moral faculty, and yet admit different views as to the standard or criterion of right and wrong. Whereas a view of the standard will carry a man right through. It is to ethics what truth of thought is to logic.

Ethics and Politics.

In modern times ethics has acquired a great independence of politics, and has come more and more to rise supreme above the latter. Plato and Aristotle made out ethics to be a department of politics. This was because the Greeks, in a highly developed political system within a small territory, were politicians first and moralists afterwards. Only a few saw that there was room for a further consideration of man's action as man and not as citizen. When Greek political life became extinct the ethical question in turn came uppermost, e.g. in

Stoicism and Epicureanism, in which ethics began to be differentiated as a theory of individual action. At a time when the traditional religious conceptions had lost their hold on cultivated minds, it became of primary importance that some Theory of Life and Conduct should be developed as a substitute for a religious creed. With the progress of time a more highly analytical study of human nature has arisen, hence we distinguish more sharply between ethical and political principles.

Ethics and Christianity.

Again, the influence of Christianity on ethics is extremely marked. Christianity inculcated the notion of the individual life or soul as having infinite value. The man, in and for himself, once swamped in the citizen, has become the fact of greatest moment. What *a man is* and what *a man ought to do* are questions that have become prominent in the Christian era as they never did in Greek or Roman civilisation.

Ethics and Theology. Cogency of the Social Factor.

In so far as ethics has helped to develop ethical principles, it has done so inevitably in relation to certain theological considerations. Yet this does not make ethics necessarily dependent upon theology. One ought to be able to determine the rule of life merely from a consideration of human nature. Morality proper depends upon the exclusion of theology. To seek a constraining power in order to good conduct impeaches the very notion of morality and trangresses the province of ethics. Morality can only give *intelligible reasons*. Conscience, the impulse to do right from a purely ethical point of view, arises from the fact that man is no mere individual but a member of the social organism. What a man becomes, he becomes not of himself but through others. Therefore, while it is natural that he should act out of regard to self *un*reflectively, when his actions begin to be done reflectively, it is *impossible* for him not to allow that he is bound to sacrifice himself in all cases where there is a conflict between self-interests and the common good. There is a law upon him not to be thrown off. Not to allow this is for a man to claim to have created, by and for himself, life and knowledge and all that makes life worth having.

PART II.

SPECIAL LECTURES

LECTURE XX.

ON THE EPISTEMOLOGY OF PLATO IN THE
PHÆDO, REPUBLIC, THEÆTETUS AND TIMÆUS[1].

READING—Plato's *Dialogues*, Jowett's Translation; Plato's *Timæus*, edited by Archer-Hind.

THE stages in Plato's life are well marked. The date of his birth being B.C. 427, we note (*a*) the Socratic stage (407–399)—his *Lehrjahre* as they have been called—when he was the pupil of Socrates till the latter was put to death. (*b*) Twelve years of travel (399–387)—his *Wanderjahre*—when he visited Magna Græcia (S. Italy), Sicily, Egypt, with occasional returns to Athens, when he began his relations with Dionysius of Syracuse, and which include his first period of productive activity (i. e. of the Socratic dialogues). (*c*) The stage of supreme effective thinking and teaching, as a philosopher, with his school in the grove of Academus (387–367). (*d*) To Syracuse again, visiting the younger

---

[1] From a special course on the *Theætetus*, &c., February, March, 1892.

Dionysius (367–365). In 361 he visited Syracuse yet again.
(*e*) Third period of philosophising and teaching, during which he gave the last development to his theory of ideas, and his cosmology. The chief productions of this period were the *Laws*, probably the *Philebus*, the *Parmenides*, and the *Sophistes*, leading up to the *Timæus*.

We have already seen (*supra*, Lecture IV) what was the heritage of thought to be entered into by Plato: first, the physical philosophy of the Pre-Socratics; then in Protagoras a despair of physical and also of moral science, withal a highly refined argumentation as to practical life; next the teaching of Socrates, also despairing of physical science, but aiming at a science of moral conceptions and identifying virtue with knowledge, or with the outcome of knowledge. Into the mind of his predecessors and contemporaries Plato entered generally, combining the high moral purpose of Socrates, and, at first, the Socratic method with a wider and bolder sweep of constructive thinking. He asked, in its widest generality, as the great question for a philosopher, What is knowlege? Though ethical purpose is always present as his final aim, yet the problem of conduct was to be solved by him through previous consideration of the *universal* problem of knowledge, and not of knowledge in a limited sphere as with Socrates.

The *Theætetus* is a dialogue of research without the positive results characterising the *Republic*. Many points are raised, but not settled. The subject is of the greatest difficulty, and one on which Plato's writings show a continuous development. It is occupied with epistemology—with knowledge as such—here treated more independently than elsewhere of his dogmatic theory of Ideas. It sums up and destructively criticises all previous views on the problem of knowledge, making reference, explicit or implicit, to Plato's predecessors. His own theory it leaves indeterminate. Had he thought out a reasoned solution, his positive philosophy would have been complete. Some suppose the dialogue was written before 367, but revised in the third period, because of the view that philosophers should stand aloof from practical life. This, it is said, will have been in connexion with his unfortunate experiences during his later visits to Syracuse and his own isolation from practical life. On the other hand, the *Laws*, his latest work, shows the philosopher in close relation with practical life.

The *Republic* is Plato's greatest achievement in its combination of range of thinking with literary effect. Close inspection, however, shows signs of aggregation at different times. Books I and II on Justice are quite Socratic, and may well have been written in his first period of production. After Book I, which leads to no positive result, we have two great divisions: (i) a complete political theory (II–IV and most of V; Books VIII and IX are also political); (ii) in relation to (i), a *theory of knowledge* (V–VIII and X). In this second division the *Republic* should be taken in conjunction with the *Theætetus*; it takes a positive dogmatic attitude with regard to those points which the latter treats in form of search. It is probable that this (excepting Book X) is the only part of the *Republic* written in the third period, showing Plato's theory as it does, in the more developed stage.

The German line of thought tends to regard Plato as a connected and consistent thinker. Grote, on the other hand, finds him inconsistent with himself at different stages of his philosophy. It is for us to distinguish him in his negative attitude (*Theætetus*) and his positive attitude (*Republic*).

It is in the philosophical part of the *Republic* that the latter, viz. his dogmatic Idealism, is most fixed and characteristic, though not yet in its final form. It undergoes further development in the *Parmenides*, *Sophistes*, *Philebus*, and *Timæus*, certain parts of the *Republic* theory being dropped, others exclusively developed and emphasised, though nothing is added.

Now the *Theætetus* is obviously preparatory to a possible solution of the question of the problem of knowledge universally put, first in *Phædo* and *Republic*, later in *Parmenides*, *Sophistes*, *Philebus*, and *Timæus*, which four embody the earlier solution in a modified form. It sweeps away previous insufficient solutions as a preparation for one that shall be complete, while itself containing no direct statement of his ideas. Is then the *Theætetus* preparatory to the *Republic* and *Phædo* (*ante* B.C. 367), or to the remaining four (*post* 360)?

We must distinguish, in the dialogue, the essential from the unessential. It has two episodes, very striking but not related to the general argument, viz. an artistic description of the Socratic method, and a comparison of the man of the world with the philosopher. The brilliancy of these episodes makes many call the dialogue an early work, the later dialogues not containing writings of this kind, but this does not prove much. However that may be, apart from these episodes we get a consideration of three answers to the question What is knowledge ($\dot{\epsilon}\pi\iota\sigma\tau\acute{\eta}\mu\eta$)? current in Plato's day:—(1) Knowledge is sense-perception; (2) Knowledge is true opinion; (3) Knowledge is true opinion, $\mu\epsilon\tau\grave{\alpha}$ $\lambda\acute{o}\gamma o\upsilon$, i.e. with a rational explanation or definition. All these views had unquestionably found expression before Plato wrote, though, except the first, not before Socrates lived. Plato found them all insufficient. He first assigns (1) to Protagoras, then connects it with the Heracleitean doctrine of perpetual flux. All the physicists, so far as they touched on the problem of knowledge at all, gave the first answer. It is doubtful whether it really coincided with all that Protagoras meant when he put forward his doctrine of *homo mensura*; it remains the obvious answer of practical every-day men.

Note in passing the remarkable affinity of Protagoras and Hume. Both were Individualists and Relativists; and Protagoras anticipated many of Hume's sceptical results. His treatise on Truth, from which Plato quotes, was probably not a developed consideration of the subject, or we should have more of it in the *Theætetus*. Plato himself developed the view of Protagoras, imputing to him a more thorough-going notion of the relativity of sense than even the latter held, and thus makes way for his own position. By exaggerating the relativity of sense he throws us back on something opposed to sense; whereas modern philosophy has shown that, even though sense as such is not knowledge, there is no real knowledge apart from sense.

The third view of knowledge belongs in a sense to Socrates and Plato themselves, μετὰ λόγου referring either to the Socratic definition by enumeration of elements, or to the earlier Platonic definition by characteristic difference. The second view joins closely to the first and belongs to no particular thinker. In explaining it Plato shows pyschologically that opinion is sense intelligently interpreted, i e. is perception involving representation. (This he illustrates by the metaphors of wax and the pigeons.) Here, while he makes light of the view as answering his epistemological question, he shows great psychological insight, his explanation of perception being worthy of ranking beside Hume's account of imagination.

The argument that knowledge is sensation, is disposed of by Plato through the fact that knowledge is the activity of the soul itself. If we see, it is through the soul's instrument. The cognition of the soul, i.e. its powers of comparison, are not attainable through sense. Sense is not even an element of knowledge.

This last assertion is Plato's characteristic exaggeration, and leads up to his theory that knowledge consists in merely thinking of our ideas. How this position was taken up and modified by modern Rationalist thought, how Locke and his school vindicated sense, how for Condillac knowledge was sense transformed, how Kant developed Leibniz's conception of knowledge as arising from intellectual predispositions into 'forms,' while requiring sense to furnish 'matter,' we have already seen. After all Plato may be said to have adumbrated modern views, for he practically committed himself to the doctrine that knowledge is an affair of mental activity, the furnishing forth of certain ideas (κοινά) on occasion, and by comparison, of sensations.

Into his discussion of 'Knowledge is true opinion,' Plato again insinuates much acute psychology, especially as to the imagination that is present in perception (true opinion), and distinguishes the latter from illusion (false opinion). Opinion, for him, is intellectual representation of sense. Note the grounds on which, namely, in the example of the lawyer, he bases his rejection of this definition of knowledge: the argument is another preparation for his theory of ideas. True opinion rests on intelligent perception of sense (answer 2 being resolved into answer 1), and therefore, being concerned with sense, is not knowledge. On his distinction between opinion (δόξα) and thinking (διάνοια) he bases his whole theory of ideas.

The *third* view breaks down because λόγος, in any of its three senses, viz. description, induction of particulars, division (bringing species under genus), is shown to be involved in the meaning of opinion—is a working with sense, i. e. with particular experience relative to the individual —and is therefore no adequate expression of knowledge. Hence answer (3) is resolved into answers (1) and (2). The dialogue ends abruptly.

Plato's theory of knowledge in the *Republic* is set forth in connexion with the education of the Guardian or philosopher. Thus this epistemology is linked with his doctrine of the state and the notion of virtue. Here (end of Book V) he recognises knowledge and opinion as opposed. But afterwards we find him opposing knowledge (having being for its object) to ignorance (as related to the non-existent), opinion coming midway (having as its object multiplex experience). Later on, however (end of Book VI), ignorance is dropped from consideration. None of the difficulties discussed in the *Theætetus* occur here; they have either vanished or not yet arisen, according to the date of the latter. Plato dwells rather on multiplicity than on becoming, distinguishing the Idea from its manifold manifestations. His great positive doctrine grew up in him in relation to the view of Socrates, that knowledge is of the universal. Socrates cared only for general ethical conceptions; and he sought to get at our concepts or universal notions, for purposes of regulation, by means of analysis or definition. Plato applied the Socratic analysis (explication, definition) of the ethical notion to metaphysic. The object of knowledge, he maintained, is more *real* than the object of opinion or of sense. The idea is what *really is*, though the object of opinion is related to the idea. Nevertheless the ethical conception is uppermost with Plato also. The idea of the Good is the highest with which knowledge is conversant, and is its ultimate end.

In the sixth book Plato works out the philosopher's position in the world and the state. We may in this connexion compare the first two-thirds of the book with the episode of the philosopher and the man of the world in the *Theætetus*. The strain is the same, although in the *Republic* there is the additional and apparently inconsistent conception that the philosopher, even if unpractical, ought to be ruler. After this episode Plato again reverts to epistemology in a passage of great importance. Note how he dwells on the idea of the Good as the highest with which knowledge is conversant, how it is related to other ideas, and finally the illustration of the sun. Good is the ultimate end of knowledge, the true aim of all real philosophy.

In the last pages of this book he advances beyond his position, at the end of Book V, as to knowledge and opinion (illustrated by the section of a line), in distinguishing between the work of reason (νοῦς) and that of understanding (διάνοια), and between opinion as belief (πίστις) and as conjecture (εἰκασία), both belief and conjecture being concerned with particulars, that is, with sense-experience. In both reason and understanding we are occupied with ideas, with the abstract, with knowledge, but in understanding we bring in certain sensible manifestations, namely, in mathematics, the highest of the special sciences, while in purely rational knowledge we are occupied with pure ideas (dialectic). Thus the doctrine given in Book V is here expanded and developed. But distinguish carefully the method of dialectic and the method of dianoetic (special science). Plato is very modern here, and it was he who originated the distinction between reason and understanding. He practically marked out the whole sphere of philosophy. In the seventh book he gives a most remarkable classification of the sciences, which holds against some of the present day [1].

Dialectic is rational conversance with ideas, is in fact philosophy. As method Plato opposes it to that of the sciences, taking mathematics as representing the latter. Mathematics, he said, starts from hypotheses, working deductively by synthetic combination, without going back to question the fundamental data (axioms and definitions) whence it starts, whereas the philosopher is concerned to inquire into these. Philosophy is conversant with ideas as such; science, with ideas as they may be sensibly represented.

Mathematics is often spoken of as the only differentiated science in ancient time; in Plato, however, a multiplicity of sciences is mentioned. And note the order of study in the sciences prescribed, after music and gymnastics, under the system of training for a philosopher. The philosopher is to be trained in the abstract consideration of sensible things, as suggestive of reality beyond sense. Scientific considerations should lead up to philosophy. Under the former the most prominent is the numerical aspect of things. It was not till Post-Platonic thought that arithmetic was subordinated to geometry. Euclid, for example, gives his arithmetical theory of proportions (Books VI–IX) after treating (in Books I–IV) of notions of space. But arithmetic is more general, and Comte followed Plato in giving it priority as an abstract science of wider application than geometry. Plato, again,

[1] The simile of the cave in Book VII is an application of the end of Book VI.

saw that before we pass from the formal to the actual consideration of things we must deal with solid geometry and astronomy. Comte followed him here also, including physics. Plato's statements show that physics was studied in his time, but it was not till Galileo that its position was rightly recognised.

In Book X of the *Republic* we have a statement of Plato's theory of ideas (see *ante*, Lecture VIII). The meaning attached by him to idea is not the more modern one of merely 'something before the mind,' but that of something objectively real—a meaning that comes out in the equivalent term 'form.' Corresponding to any concept, which we form psychologically by bringing together a multitude of particular experiences, there is in the region of existence, of reality, a Form or Idea. We get, for example, a concept of 'bad' by comparison of particular bad things, but there is a real Bad to which our concept is related. Six different kinds of Ideas are put forward in the *Republic* :—(1) The supreme Idea, that of the Good. Plato sought to establish a hierarchy of ideas, headed by this one, but when he tries to fix the relation of the Good to other ideas, he betrays uncertainty and incompleteness. (2) Ideas of qualities akin to the Good, e.g. the just, the honourable, &c. (3) Ideas of natural objects—man, horse, &c. (4) Ideas of artificial things, e. g. bed. (5) Ideas of relations, such as equal, like, &c. (6) Ideas of qualities antagonistic to the Good, e. g. unjust.

Such is the only way in which he could account for knowledge. In the *Phædo*, where the epistemological position is parallel to that in the *Republic*, he entered more closely into the relation of the particular to the universal, of the particular thing of sense to the pure form or idea. Things of sense have a reality, he found, only to the extent that they have participation in (μέθεξις), or presence of (παρουσία), the idea, or communion (κοινωνία) of the idea with the thing. And because there are ultimate realities in which sensible things participate, *therefore* knowledge is possible. From sense we may mount up to the real, using especially mathematics as an aid.

Aristotle, in his theorising concerning knowledge, which occurs especially in the *Metaphysica*, criticises Plato's epistemology and sets up a counter-theory. Reality appeared to him an ambiguous term, but lay rather in the concrete particular thing than in the universal or Platonic Idea, yet for him too, although he allowed that the particular does really exist, knowledge is of the universal only. Again, therefore, there arises the question of the relation between universal and particular, which he settled by his theory of essence.

Now Aristotle's criticisms referred to a later development of Plato's theory than that given in the *Republic*, for according to Aristotle the Ideas were of natural things, but not of artificial things or relations. Already in this dialogue and the *Phædo*, Plato expresses dissatisfaction with his theory, and proceeds in the *Parmenides*, as well as in the *Sophistes*, *Philebus*, and *Timæus*, to criticise it, his criticism in the first-named being more shrewd and trenchant than Aristotle's. We find him, for instance, anticipating the latter's objection of the 'third man.' But his treatment here is negative only; the self-criticism is not final, as Grote suggested; yet he maintains that knowledge is impossible without a theory of ideas as real existences. It is in the *Timæus* that we find the ultimate expression of his doctrine, propounded with more confidence and definiteness, although in mythological form, than in any other dialogue, and in a way intended to evade the objections raised in the *Parmenides*. Here all Ideas are discarded save those of the

Good and of Natural Kinds, and it is a question whether from these he does not exclude all that are not *living* things (including plants). Again in opposing things that are to things that are merely becoming, i.e. things of sense, he no longer looks askance at the latter as in the *Republic*, but attempts to show how, by positing the Ideas of the Good and of Natural Kinds, we can account for things as we find them— for the coming into existence of the natural world. He gives us in fact a cosmogony. He is eager no longer to get from the things of sense to reality, but from the region of reality to come down to an explanation of our actual experience. The crude position taken up in the *Republic* has been transformed into an absolute Idealism. The only thing that really is, is mind—Mind the Universal, and finite minds in relation to, being the outcome of, the Universal Mind. Experience is the mode in which particular minds can take in the ultimate reality that is concentrated in the Universal Mind. Thus the form of doctrine in the *Timæus* is more mystical, more removed from actual experience, and yet it is given to account for this experience, and not as in the *Republic* to shun all explanation. The Idea is no longer a reality apart; ultimate reality is now for him certain types of things in the universal mind, and particular things are related to these types, not as participating in them—that theory has dropped out—but as images or likenesses of a pattern, model or archetype (παράδειγμα). They are the way in which the finite mind of man represents to itself the thought of the universal or divine mind. Only Hegel reached a more extreme form of Idealism than this.

We see then that between the earlier position of the *Republic* and the later one of the *Timæus*, the *Theætetus* is important as indicating transition. The *Parmenides* is destructive; the *Theætetus* points the way to reconstruction. With the final view given in the *Timæus* Plato never shows dissatisfaction. His position is constant to this extent, that knowledge for him from first to last is conversance of mind with ideas as such, is an affair of the soul's activity: we know by something furnished forth by the mind. The theory of knowledge being attained by way of reminiscence derived from previous existence as held in the *Phædo*, makes way for what is the relatively sane doctrine of the *Timæus*.

Now the *Theætetus* is preparatory to a theory of ideas. The question is, which theory? The earlier or the later? Its form connects the dialogue with the *Republic*, but close inspection reveals declarations inconsistent with this, viz. Mind knows common notions (κοινά) by comparison of particulars, and knows them only through this process. Whereas in the *Republic* we find relations (of likeness, &c.) existing already as ideas side by side with ideas of things. In the *Theætetus* Socrates tests his own size by comparing himself with different people. In the *Phædo* Socrates is said to discover his own relative size through *participating in the Ideas* of smallness and largeness. In such ways the *Theætetus* may be shown as inconsistent with the *Republic* and *Phædo*, but not with the *Timæus*.

Hence it is probable that the first draft of the *Theætetus* was a *negative* preparation for the *Republic*, written about the same time, but recast later when Plato had otherwise or more fully developed his theory of ideas. The suggestions in it that are assignable to Plato himself are developed not in the *Republic* but in later dialogues. Plato could not have committed himself to certain positions in the *Republic* after those he assumed in the *Theætetus*. Moreover the *Sophist* carries on the argument of the latter, and is again connected with the *Politicus*, the three forming a trilogy. Thus the stage of thought in the *Theætetus* is later than that in the *Republic*.

LECTURE XXI.

ON THE PSYCHOLOGY OF ARISTOTLE [1].

READING.—*Aristotle's Psychology.* Greek and English, with Introduction and Notes by Edwin Wallace, 1882. *Aristotle*, by George Grote, edited by Alexander Bain and G. C. Robertson, 1883, ch. xii. *Mental Science*, by Alexander Bain, 1884, Appendix B, pp. 33-42, (written by Grote). *Reid's Works*, edited by Hamilton. Note D, pp. 826-30. Also Ueberweg's, Erdmann's or Schwegler's (latest German edition) histories of philosophy on Aristotle.

ARISTOTLE, truly named 'the master of those who know,' the most encyclopaedic of thinkers, was a great pathfinder in both science and philosophy. He is the creator of Logic, and he knew it (v. Grote, pp. 419-20); he also laid the foundations of scientific psychology. The condition of the advancement of a science is that it shall be broken off from its surroundings and worked at separately. The first to be separated, Mathematics, is also the most highly perfected. Psychology till the last generation had not been broken off; to the circumstance that it has now been singled out for separate treatment it owes its advance within recent years. Aristotle had an overpowering sense of the relation of psychology to philosophy, yet to a great extent he separates psychology in a manner that is very modern; unfortunately his successors did not do so. There is hardly a suggestion

[1] From a special course on the *De Anima*, Oct.-Dec., 1890.

made by modern psychologists as to the lines on which psychology might have advanced that was not anticipated by Aristotle. Psychology is a science apart, of a special character, self-contained. It is science in respect of method, philosophy in respect of scope. Philosophy depends on psychological insight, but psychology itself is concerned with mind as it appears, and does not deal with the question of the ultimate nature of the soul. Aristotle however includes this question in his psychology, treating the science both as empirical and as rational (i.e. metaphysically).

He commences his analysis in the *De Anima* with a metaphysical definition of 'soul,' his psychological notions being overridden by his desire to fit soul into that 'First Philosophy,' as he called it, which for him was not the crown but the basis of his system of knowledge. It is possibly a pity that he committed himself at the start, instead of building up his metaphysic inductively, for his metaphysic is the most developed part of his work. Herein successive philosophers have been no wiser than he, with the exception of the school of modern psychology, the impetus of which was given by England and Scotland, but which, no longer as at one time a national study, is now chiefly, though by no means exclusively, carried on by Germans. Scholars of other nations have broken up that national characteristic just because, and in as far as, they have put aside metaphysical presuppositions. On the other hand, all in this country who have come under the Kantian influence have inverted the order of English thought. Even Mr. Spencer, our most scientific philosopher, has broken away from English tradition, and begins his system with an attempted solution of the riddle of the universe. Whereas psychology that is scientific in method, from the outset takes mental facts as they are found, and treats them as far as possible apart from a metaphysical basis. Agreement is so much more likely in psychology—though desirable enough in philosophy—that it is best to carry on psychological research, and be patient in philosophical conclusions. For example, how does Aristotle's definition of soul help us in his psychology, however intelligible that definition by his first philosophy may be? It had been better had he limited his psychological inquiry to the manifestations of mind or soul in all living things.

As to the method of psychology, he asks, (1) Can we get at the truths of psychology as with mathematics by demonstration (ἀπόδειξις) or the synthetic method? Or (2) can we by analysis (διαίρεσις, to be taken in its evident meaning and not, as Wallace says, as the Platonic division), i.e. take consciousness as it is and break it up? Or (3) may the two be combined? His answer to (1) is, No; psychology is not a pure deductive science, and cannot therefore be so treated. But if we cannot start with what a thing is and work down to the properties of it, we can start from the properties and go up from them to the complete conception[1].

Consider now Aristotle's account of the traditions of thought he had inherited. Greek philosophy before Aristotle culminates in Plato and Democritus. By these two philosophers Aristotle thinks; to both he is related: to Democritus, whose chief theory is the 'moving' power of soul, and to

[1] I do not approve in this connexion (Bk. I, ch. i. § 11) of Wallace's translating διαλεκτικός by transcendentalist. A dialectician is a logician chiefly on the side on which the latter deals with *words*. He also deals with probabilities; he is a bare speculator as opposed to one dealing with facts; he is occupied with playing with words as opposed to real science. He works deductively apart from facts. A φυσικός on the other hand is one who buries himself in facts and works inductively. Aristotle's business is with facts.

Plato, whose chief stress is laid on soul as thinking. Plato also supports the theory of the moving power of soul. And though they are mutually antithetical, both together form an antithesis to Aristotle. He puts forward Democritus as the typical upholder of the theory of soul as moving, and Plato as the emphasiser of soul as cognitive (as well as of soul as moving). Thus, from Aristotle's opposition to both these theories, the antithesis between the Idealism or Spiritualism of the one and the Materialism or Atomism of the other does not appear in his works. Aristotle allowed that all movement in the organism has a mental basis, yet this power of motion is not, he considered, the chief characteristic of soul. Nor, again, does he deny that mind (or soul) is cognitive, but he rejected the then prevalent doctrine of *how* mind moves and knows. The prevalent doctrine of cognition, followed by Democritus and Plato, and set forth by Empedocles (of Agrigentum, fl. B.C. 444), lay in the supposed likeness or homogeneity between the elements of mind and those of which external things consist, in virtue of which, on occasion of contact between effluent mental elements and effluent external things, perception could and did come to pass. In his opposition to these three thinkers Aristotle seems to have been working towards the modern distinction between subjective and objective. Subjectivity as the characteristic of mind is not stated by him, yet he implies it. The characteristic of mind lay for him neither in power to move body, nor in cognition, nor in knowing like through being like. Refusing to consider mind as body, or yet apart from body, he opposed to the physical side what was in reality the subjective side, although he termed it form ($\epsilon\tilde{\iota}\delta o s$) or entelechy, as that which, in forming body, gives reality or actuality to it (I, ii–II, i).

There was at first in the history of Greek philosophy no thought of opposing mind to matter; that idea was of very gradual development; in Pythagoras we get more away from object; in the *noûs* of Anaxagoras we get the first suggestion of subject. And note how Socrates, the contemporary of Anaxagoras, gets on to concepts and away from the external, though without any distinct theory. Here then it is that Greek philosophy properly so called—at least as I understand philosophy—may be said to begin. In his pre-philosophic thinking however, proceeding as this does by way of Animism, man does not refuse to consider mind, nor does he wait to make the distinction between mind and body, which again emerges when he has begun to philosophise. And this distinction he makes not only in himself but in everything. Not only has he a soul, but so also have all, even inanimate, things—stones, rivers, &c. What for him *is* soul? Another kind of body, ethereal, attenuated, but still a body within the body. The idea will first have sprung from the thought of dream-life, when the body is stationary, but the spirit goes abroad, hunts, fights, &c., in the man's own shape. The ghost-story is a survival of this.

Now how far are there traces of this in early Greek philosophy? We find all Aristotle's criticism of Democritus (in the *De Anima*) directed against a kind of semi-scientific animism. And we may suppose that Thales and his successors, by occupying themselves with the object-world *alone*, and dropping all reference to the soul, emerged from the prevailing animism, till in this respect and to this extent Democritus, with his atomistic theory, set forth what was an unconsciously transformed animism. Plato, again, Immaterialist as he was, making the soul's immateriality a ground for its immortality, has remnants of primitive animism in him. He speaks, metaphorically if not literally, of the soul being extended in the body, and so he too incurs Aristotle's criticism. Both Aristotle, however, and in modern times Grote, have taken Plato too literally to do justice to his poetical mode of exposition. But wherever Plato stands as to animism, Aristotle at least is absolutely free from it, as is shown by his attacks on Plato and Democritus. Modern science in speaking of mind as subjective is non-animistic, but not more so than Aristotle was.

Not that animism died through Aristotle! It reappears in Epicurus, and in the early Christian Fathers—in Tertullian, e.g., who even ridiculed the non-animistic position—and in Jewish thought both before and in the Christian era. In proportion as mediæval thinkers follow Aristotle they are rid of animism. But it was not till Descartes that for philosophy at least the idea was destroyed, and the notion of mind as non-extended finally accepted. To-day students of physical science are in the position of the earliest Greek thinkers, setting aside mind altogether in order to consider external facts.

Yet Aristotle, Immaterialist as he was, would not take soul apart from body, but held that we can only study mind in relation to body, and as manifested in all sentient beings[1]. See how, in default of the notion of subjective, he brings out *logos*, in calling mental states λόγοι ἔνυλοι—a logical, as opposed to a physical view[2]. It is true that in relating mind to body he makes some reservation in the case of the νοῦς, and almost commits himself to saying that thinking has no relation to body. Yet his meaning is rather that thought is

[1] Cf. e.g. his allusion to anger. *De Anima*, I, ch. i. §§ 10, 11.
[2] '... it is clear that the feelings (πάθη) are materialised notions (λόγοι ἔνυλοι).' Ibid.

distinguishable, not χωριστόν, or separable, from body. Never does he say, like Plato, that mind is incorporeal, immaterial[1].

Plato, for that matter, is inconsistent on this point. In the *Phædo* he says that mind or soul is absolutely incorporeal; in the *Republic* and *Timæus* he lodges it about the body and holds that only thinking goes on in the brain. This was owing to Plato's psychology being so far unscientific as to serve a purpose, either political, ethical or theological. In the *Timæus* he is a speculative theologian, considering the self-manifestation of God; in the *Republic* he is philosophising, ethically and politically. Hence his concepts and language vary with his different standpoints. Whereas Aristotle, as far as he went, was thoroughgoing and consistent.

As to Aristotle's definition of mind as entelechy, or 'first entelechy,' no word perhaps better interprets this in its bearing upon body than that generally adopted of realisation or actualisation. Mind as form gives reality or actuality to body, which without its in-working (ἐνέργεια) remains merely a potentiality (δύναμις) like unhewn stone. Mind is implicated in body, but is distinguishable from, superior, prior to it. Mind is not body, nor yet a harmony resulting from body, but is necessary to give body a real existence (II, ch. i).

The force however in the term entelechy lay for Aristotle in the *telos*—end or purpose. What most struck him in the universe was end or purpose everywhere inherent. A thing, he held, was real in so far as it had an end or purpose—of its own, more or less, if animate; if inanimate, not of its own. And the higher animate beings are conscious of their

---

[1] This is said with reference to the individual human mind, and not to the νοῦς χωριστός or cosmic mind, which as an ontologically prior reality Aristotle calls ἀπαθής καὶ ἀμιγής (*De An.* iii. 5). See *infra*, p. 227, and p. 229.—ED.

end; they are self-realising. Now in proportion as there is the getting an end to the individual existence and the working towards it, there is mind manifested. Mind or soul is a kind of life, and life as mentally endowed is self-realising. Aristotle first introduced the idea of an organ, of something formed to carry out a particular purpose or function. The notion of organism as distinct from a mechanical aggregate was that which subserves a purpose, and, in a mental organism, its own purpose. Object subjectively realised, object realised by a subject who knows—this was what he was really groping after and working towards. This comes out, for instance, in his theory of sensation, and, by rendering it epistemological, spoils it as psychology (II, ch. iv. §§ 1–6).

Aristotle's division or scheme of soul—nutritive, sentient, cognitive (the last I have condensed, since the division is practically threefold)—is not a logical division under a genus, but is in the order of increasing connotation. Its divisions are rather to be described as stages in the development of soul, constituting an evolutionary concept, as Grote might have called it, or concept of the gradual differentiation or progressive development of mind—a wonderful stroke of insight, and a striking advance on Plato's psychology[1]. There is a verbal likeness to Plato's three-fold phase or division of soul—the appetitive, the passionate, the rational—but this distinction was intended to subserve an ethical purpose, and is not fertile scientifically. Aristotle's scheme is good psychology. His kinds of soul are stages of psychic development, just as we call sense not a division in psychic

---

[1] Note him, in I, i. § 6 and elsewhere, 'worrying' over the choice between a faculty-theory and an inquiry into facts and laws determining facts; now keeping clear of the former and now getting entangled.

life but a stage, inasmuch as children feel, will and know in relation to sense alone (*Elements of Psychology*, Lect. VIII).

The chapters on Sense (Book III, i–ii) are very remarkable. The first serious attempt to form a theory of sense in Greece was that made by Democritus—a theory so effectively striking that we still use his terms. Things, he held, are constantly throwing off images (εἴδωλα), which pass into the body through the peripheries of the sense-organs and are stored up in the *brain* to be produced by memory. This he connects with his general atomistic theory. He makes all the organs of sense developments of Touch, a view that is to a great extent borne out by modern biology with regard to taste and smell, and perhaps to hearing and sight, although with regard to sight embryology presents difficulties.

Plato had no proper doctrine of sense; he considered the subject rather from an ascetic point of view. The Sophists however had anticipated some of the modern theories, especially that of primary and secondary qualities, and generally of qualities as subjective experiences of our own which we project into objects. This was pre-eminently the case with Protagoras in his sceptical conclusion as to reality— that 'truth is what each man troweth.' Their doctrine, it is true, was not based on any scientific theory of sense. Plato, as we know, understood this doctrine of sense, but cared not for it. Knowledge, as he conceived it, lay elsewhere.

Now Aristotle, while he is unanticipated in the account he gives of the different kinds of sensation, is reactionary with respect to the Sophistic theory of the relativity of sense. He does not distinguish between primary and secondary qualities of matter; all qualities for him are primary, embedded in things. He upholds the immanence, for example, of colour. The deficiencies in his doctrine of sense arise from his total ignorance of the physiology of the nervous system as involved in sensation. Of this Plato had gathered some notion from Hippocrates and others.

Again he makes no distinction between sensation and perception. But his account of sense is very good and in earnest, complicated though it is by the philosophical question of the relation of subject to object[1]. He insists on the fundamental importance, psychological and philosophical, of Touch, and opposes to it the other senses as not needing a medium. Yet even in Touch there is a kind of medium, namely, the skin.

He saw in sensation a process to be explained in terms of motion, the transmission of a movement from object to organ. Nevertheless he had no clear physical doctrines of medium or movement; his concepts are metaphysical. Do not be beguiled into seeking parallels with modern mechanical concepts: Aristotle had no notion of the part played by nerve-centres, while *we* cannot define sensation out of relation to these. On molecular transmission he has fallen back from the position reached by Democritus, Hippocrates and Plato, who discerned atomic motion continued *inside*. He also has fallen behind them with respect to the subjectivity of sensation, a theory, for that matter, not fully developed till the days of Descartes, Locke and Berkeley. He got instead into bad metaphysic as to the relation of object and subject, finding colour, sound, &c., really *in* things; he expressly rejected Protagoreanism, and saved himself by juggling more or less with δυναμεῖ, and ἐνεργείᾳ. In our day it is said that colour, physically speaking, is the result of

[1] E.g. Book II, ch. v. That Aristotle neglects to distinguish in either case is overlooked by Wallace, whose psychology is not his strongest point.

molecular motion in object, medium and brain, and that, when these movements are propagated up to the brain, then, psychologically speaking, a state of consciousness follows. And we find that we ought not to pretend to get farther towards bringing nerves and consciousness together; indeed that we never shall. Aristotle's theory was that there is a potency in the object and a potency in the organism, and that by contact we get an actuality through both, a ratio established between object and organism by way of a medium. Grote will here be found helpful, but he is not justified in identifying the visual medium with ether, nor with our concept of mode of motion. Aristotle was only able to invent the abstraction 'transparency.' Note too with caution Grote's big words for the medium in hearing and in smell. Aristotle gives good description but no scientific account; he gives no efficient *explanation*, metaphysical, scientific or any other. We do not want a 'logos' between sensation and object.

Some of the questions raised in the third Book (chh. i, ii) are of great psychological import; some are trivial, e.g. the first:—why we can have only five senses, the answer connecting them with the 'four elements.' We actually have more; animals may have more; we may be developing more. But in Aristotle's day there was no fund of positive knowledge as a basis for further inquiry.

Part of his doctrine of sensation Aristotle only indicates here; it is to be sought in the *De Sensu*. Grote's references to it should be attended to, especially the passages concerning our apprehension of the 'common sensibles' (τὰ κοινὰ αἰσθητά) and our associations of two 'sensibles.' Aristotle there treats of the 'first sentient' (πρῶτον αἰσθητικόν), or 'sensorium commune,' the medium between soul and sense-organ. This, physically speaking, is for him the heart. All the streams of movement contributed by the senses go to the heart by way not of the blood but of the hot air in the blood, and when the heart is reached by the disturbance then there is consciousness. Thus he conceived sense as one, fed by many currents, or as one stem with many branches. Hence, he thought, we can have sensations common to different senses, while we can also distinguish between sensations of different senses. Here we have the herald of the expression *sensus communis*, or general sense (Cf. *Elements of Psychology*, Lect. IX). In the *De Sensu* the term κοινὴ αἴσθησις is used with a purely psychological meaning.

Note how, though in a crude way, he raises the question of self-consciousness:—seeing, e. g., and 'perceiving' that we see (Book II, ch. ii).

Grote's very cursory notice of Aristotle's 'common sensibles' is a defect. No doctrine has had a more remarkable development than this. Hamilton (in his 'Note D' on Reid) brings out a complete coincidence between it and the doctrine of Primary and Secondary Qualities. He goes so far as to think that the *Koina aistheta* may be reconciled with Reid's common sense. Perhaps so, yet Aristotle is never metaphysical on this point. Democritus and Protagoras had some such distinction, viz. between qualities that were really *in* things, such as motion, and qualities imputed to things, such as colour, which were derived from the former and are thus really modes of motion. Aristotle called them (III, chapter ii, § 8) partly right, partly wrong. Not wholly rejecting their Relativism he did not like it, and evaded it by rendering all sensations in terms of matter and form. This, though it was a large, coherent doctrine, was scientifically retrograde. All progress since Descartes has been on Democritean lines. Aristotle's matter and form is no real advance, is not his strong point.

But if this is so, if Aristotle denies subjectivity not only in primary but also in secondary qualities, then Hamilton's parallel is upset. For the latter there is a reason, if not an excuse. Aristotle's *Koina* happen to coincide in the main with primary qualities. But the doctrine of the Qualities is metaphysical with a psychological basis, whereas Aristotle's distinction between common and particular 'sensibles' is purely psychological. He has plenty of metaphysic, but this special distinction was not made by him psychologically as a basis for metaphysic as we make it, or rather as Reid and Hamilton made it. But both these thinkers invariably confused psychology with philosophy. Aristotle dimly sees the force there is in the term *Koina*, but does not realise it (as, e. g. in his allusion to touch and sight, Grote, p. 465 *c*.). Since Berkeley we have denied that the distinction between primary and secondary qualities is valid; Protagoras saw this too. Knowing what we do as to the coefficient of muscular sense in sight and touch we say, as against Descartes, Locke, Berkeley *and* Aristotle, that the senses do not as such give us 'common sensibles.' Aristotle's followers themselves soon grew dissatisfied and imputed our apprehension of the *Koina* to intellect, or rational apprehension. Apart from muscular sense, they cannot be psychologically explained, and it was through neglecting this that the Scottish school fell back on common sense, belief, law of the conditioned and so forth.

Next[1] we have Aristotle's doctrine of reason ($νοῦς$), with the interpolated discussion of imagination or phantasy

[1] Book III, chh. iii.-viii. These should not only be read but *worried at*. Wallace's introduction is not very helpful.

(φαντασία). This, like perception, may be viewed either subjectively or on its physiological side. Aristotle considers both aspects, giving in the germ what in this century has been developed by Professor Bain, who uses 'idea' for 'image.' The subject is treated more fully in the treatise *De Memoria*, where memory is distinguished as imagination with a definite temporal reference (modern psychology can say little more), and where there are suggestions of laws of association—contiguity, similarity and contrast. Now Aristotle only notices association in connexion with reminiscence. This is a defect. Under association we simply refer to certain modes in the 'flow' of our images, whereas reminiscence is a complex intellectual function involving volition.

Why should there be so little here on imagination? Aristotle's whole doctrine of the psychology of representative intellection is very undeveloped, inasmuch as his discussion is rather epistemological than psychological, namely, on the relation of thought to its object; more, it is metaphysical or ontological, involving reference to an outer sphere of real being. And his metaphysic vitiates his psychology here even more than in his doctrine of sense. He asks whether images (φαντάσματα) are true or false; these are matters of opinion (δόξα), and opinion may be either. But this is not psychology. It is only in the *De Memoria* that in this connexion he is properly psychological.

Even there we find the assertion that *noûs* comes into man from without (θύραθεν). Aristotle could not in fact quite overcome the *Zeitgeist* of his age and his environment. Nor had he Plato's poetic mantle to throw around himself; he is nothing if not literal and prosaic. Grote's discursus at this stage (p. 480 et seq.), connecting the *noûs*-doctrine with Aristotle's physics and cosmogony is quite justified by that phrase 'from without.' Aristotle saw that knowledge was a philosophical question, yet he has not treated of it in the *Metaphysics*, where his theme is of 'being as being,' always excepting the first book, with its discussion of the principles of knowledge and their relation to sense. Yet here Aristotle had no idea of working out a theory of knowledge as a necessary introduction to a theory of being. For us, as we have seen (Lecture I), problems of being have since Kant come to be considered as subject to problems of knowledge. It is through the doctrine of knowledge that we approach ontological questions. Many a modern thinker has raised philosophical questions in his psychology, but Aristotle so rode off on them as to neglect the psychology of the intellect. Yet he did not neglect to point out that reason cannot work without images. Thought requires a basis of representative imagination. This is all that he does for the theory of thought as a mode of intellection.

Here note the remark in Grote (p. 484 and footnote *e*) on Aristotle's 'Nominalism'—good in substance, though the term is a misnomer, no reference having been made to language in the *De Anima*. Aristotle only said that we cannot conceive a general without a certain amount of particulars. The Nominalist says that we cannot think in general without the help of a name, that is, except by means of language. This at least is Hobbes's Nominalism. Berkeley's Nominalism holds that we cannot think without a form, that is, without reference to the particular. Thus Berkeley goes no farther than Aristotle. But there is no Nominalism in the *De Anima*. To this extent it is defective, that the relation of thought to language is passed over. Yet Aristotle did see that the two are connected, are practically the same thing on different sides. This we see in his Logic, where he always deals with judgments on the side of language, and with reasoning as expressed in arguments. And *suggestions* that he saw this are to be found up and down in the *De Anima*, yet they are barely to be so called. All is quite implicit.

If Aristotle had carefully worked out the psychological doctrine of thought, and considered the psychological function of language, he would have seen many of the difficulties of his *noûs* (so far as they were psychological) disappear without the need of reference to celestial bodies. For the question of thought suggests that of the *community* of knowledge, and it is this that troubles him—How is it that we all come to think alike? How have we a common consciousness? Imagination is of the individual consciousness, but that thought is common consciousness (cf. Reid's 'Common Sense') is inevitably begotten by a consideration of the psychology of thought. It is to explain this that he goes out to the Kosmos, to theories of the heavenly spheres, to an Eternal Noûs, who enters in and informs each of us, if not in full purity as with God, yet so as, by acting on our imaginations, to emerge in common consciousness. And all this to fill up the void left by ignoring language as a social act, a bond holding men together!

The relation of *noûs* to mind or soul generally, and of *noûs* as active and passive, has formed the battle-ground of Aristotelian commentators all along, opportunity being given by Aristotle's obscurities and deficiencies. For instance, while Grote very decisively negatives the view that Aristotle predicated immortality of the individual intellect, the mediæval commentators argue with equal decision for the opposite conclusion. I think that he is too positive as to what Aristotle's utterances may be held to warrant. Again, Grote speaks very clearly on the contrast between reason as active and reason as passive (νοῦς ποιητικός, νοῦς παθητικός, *De. An.* III, v). Wallace, too, among the liberties he now and then takes in text and translation, applies the former adjective to *noús* in his index. Yet nowhere does Aristotle himself call *noús* active (ποιητικός); he only suggests the term.

I hold that Aristotle was staggering on this doubtful ground, and that commentators have rushed in to wrangle where he feared to tread.

Once more, if Aristotle compared mind at birth to a blank writing tablet, he meant only that the *noús* was not a fixed body of innate principles, but something potential, which could grow and develop.

NOTE. I much regret that no notes are forthcoming on Aristotle's theory of conation (Book III, chh. ix-xi), with which the lecturer had announced the intention of dealing at the end of the course. For further discussion on emotion students were referred to Aristotle's *Rhetoric* and *Ethics.*—ED.

LECTURE XXII.

ON THE METHOD OF DESCARTES [1].

READING.—*Œuvres de Descartes*, ed. Jules Simon, 1844. 'Discours sur la Méthode.' *Œuvres choisies de Descartes*, ed. Garnier, 1876. 'Discours de la Méthode;' 'Règles pour la Direction de l'Esprit.' *The Method, Meditations, and Selections from the Principles of Descartes*, ed. J. Veitch, 1879. 'Discourse on Method.'

SUCH is the importance of Descartes in the history of modern philosophy that it behoves us to enter in some detail into the development of his thought. He, if any one, lets us know—especially in the *Discourse on Method* and the *Meditations*—what were the most intimate workings of his thought, what he started from, what he came to, and what he was aiming at. We must first see that we keep in mind the circumstances of his life.

Born 1596, of a noble family in, though not of, Touraine, René des Cartes went at eight years of age, a lad weakly in constitution but precocious, to the new and famous Jesuit school of La Flèche, the Jesuits having returned to France after the conversion of Henry IV. From the first the Jesuits have sought to attract men of the world to the Church by accommodating the Church to the world, chiefly by giving a highly efficient secular education to the young. They have always been well versed in the best thought of

[1] From lectures delivered April to June, 1880.

the country, and have bent that knowledge to the interests of the Church; but at the same time they have ever upheld and still uphold the Scholastic philosophy, especially as taught by Aquinas. Descartes' subsequent strictures on education did not include any reflexion on his own teachers, with whom he ever remained on friendly terms. Trained thoroughly in Scholastic traditions, he was also made proficient in mathematics. This had been neglected by the Schoolmen, but had revived at the Renaissance, when the work both of Euclid and of the Arabs (algebra) came to be known.

Bacon, who during Descartes' early youth was deep in politics, and in the publication of the *Advancement of Learning* and the *Novum Organon*, was almost absolutely ignorant of mathematics, and had no notion of its use in the study of nature. His Inductive Method has no place for it, and hence he does not properly head the modern scientific movement. To the extent that mathematics has rendered the latter possible, Descartes is the pioneer. Wolsey's chair of mathematics at Oxford was suspended after his fall for a century. Hobbes while at Oxford (1603–8) remained utterly ignorant of mathematics, and was over forty when he first saw a copy of Euclid's Elements, whereas Descartes was, like Pascal (his junior by twenty-seven years), a mathematical discoverer in his early youth.

Till he was twenty-three he studied mathematics, either exclusively and in seclusion, or in the intervals of military life. It was when he was serving under Tilly, at the opening of the Thirty Years' War, and was working still at mathematics in winter-quarters at Neuburg, that the crisis of his philosophic life occurred. He had been comparing the certainty of his mathematical results with the doubtfulness of all other knowledge, and this brought him to a state of despair. Tempted to resort anywhere for light, he turned to magic; then to inspiration from prayer, vowing a pilgrimage to Loretto if he could find peace of mind. Then came the day of seclusion, 'enfermé seul dans un poêle' (read the *Discours*, Part II). Mathematics, he saw, led to conclusions positively true. Could he not, by applying the method of mathematics to knowledge generally, get truth in other subjects as well?

After two more years of service and four of travel (including the pilgrimage), studying, as he said, the book of the world, he returned in 1625 to Paris, feeling that, if he had not yet got certainty, at least he had got on to the right track. There he alternately moved in scientific circles (no other city had a mathematical circle), and disappeared for months together. He would reappear ever riper in thought, and finally created great expectations among his friends. At length, after his return from studying siege-appliances at the siege of La Rochelle, 1628, he created a sensation at the house of Cardinal De Bagné, where he exposed the fallacies of Chandoux, a pretender to new science, by showing how it was possible, by using the current arguments of the day, to disprove anything claiming to be established truth, and to prove true anything apparently false. Cardinal Bérulle thereupon advised him to set forth a constructive philosophy. He *may* at this time have written the *Règles* (*Regulæ ad directionem ingenii*), but however that may be, he now removed to Holland, where society was quiet and liberal, and there he lived, off and on, for twenty years (1629–49), changing his residence twenty-four times, visiting England, Denmark and France, and finally returning to France. During that time all his chief works were written.

The publication of the *Discours de la Méthode* in 1637 at once attracted friends and foes. The *Meditationes de Prima*

Philosophia followed in 1641, the *Principia Philosophiæ* in 1644. The efforts of Dutch theologians to get him denounced and expelled, emanating from Utrecht and Leyden, kept him perpetually unsettled, and much controversial writing was drawn from him. He was invited to return to France, but neither there was it possible to live quietly, society being unsettled through the Fronde. Hence he accepted the invitation of Queen Christina of Sweden, a girl full of intellectual eagerness and his pupil already by correspondence, and went to Stockholm, 1649. To have to come to the palace to give instruction at five a.m. in the depth of winter affected his lungs and killed him, February 11, 1650.

The three works last mentioned and *Les Passions de l'Âme*, published just after his death, are those in which Descartes is most commonly studied. But much that we know of him is derived from his *Letters* edited by Clerselier (1665–7). Other works, e.g. the *Règles*, and the *Recherche de la Vérité par la Lumière naturelle*, were not published till 1701. After his death his MSS. were sent to Paris, but fell into the Seine, lay there three days, and were carelessly dried, so that there are flaws. The *Recherche*, though crude and incomplete, really gives the best exposition of his system as a method. Internal evidence shows it must have been written not later than 1629. The *Method* advocates the importance of acquiring a certain way of thinking before any philosophically valid results can be arrived at. With it, as a collection of Philosophical Essays, he published three applications of his method:—*Dioptrica* (on refraction, giving also a good account of sense), *Meteora*, and *Geometria*, the last setting out his special method as got from, rather than applied to, mathematics. Modern analytical geometry dates from this work. In the *Method* he hints at a greater work he was keeping back. He apparently thought it best to publish not a philosophy of mind, but a doctrine of nature, which was really the outcome of that philosophy. This standpoint marks him off from Galileo and Newton, who investigated on lines of positive science without having regard to mind. Accordingly, in 1630, he set himself to write the treatise *Le Monde, ou Traité de la Lumière*, at the end of which he brings in the philosophic principles which had been all along in his mind. This work, which was finished in 1633, he was about to publish, when Galileo was put on his trial before the Holy Inquisition on account of his Dialogue on the motion of the earth. The Copernican theory had not even then been accepted by the Church, although certain popes had been disposed in its favour. Galileo dared to expound it, but only as the hypothesis that best fitted the facts. Descartes had done the same in *Le Monde*, but as timid by nature, a sincere Catholic, and above all things preferring an undisturbed life to fame, he suppressed the work. What was later on published under this title was simply a section of the original work. The gist of the latter was actually given in the *Principia*, with the modified view that not the earth, but the medium in which the earth is, moves round the sun (Cf. *infra* p. 261). By 1637 his fears and scruples had given way, and in the *Method*, written in French, he refers to his *Monde*.

The Meditations, 'where are demonstrated the existence of God and the distinction of soul from body,' written in Latin, and appealing to the learned, were published in 1641-1642, together with the objections raised by certain critics who had read them in MS. The most important of these were Hobbes, Gassendi and Arnauld, the two former advancing Epicureanism and Sensationalism of a crude type.

Descartes after this took courage and set forth his whole philosophy in the *Principia*, in dogmatic form and not analytically as in the *Meditations*. The *Passions*, a psycho-physiological study of the relations of body to mind, was written in 1646 for his pupil Princess Elizabeth of Bohemia, grand-daughter of our James I.

An important minor work, entitled *Remarks by Descartes on a Certain Placard printed in the Netherlands*, was written in 1647 in opposition to the view of his ardent admirer Regius, or Leroy, a Utrecht professor, who had, professedly from the Cartesian point of view, transformed Dualism into something very like later Materialism, speaking of body as having two modes, thought and extension, and of knowledge as due to our sense-experience of body acting on body. The *Remarks* set out more clearly than elsewhere Descartes' view as to the relation between reason, innate ideas and experience. If elsewhere he is crude, here he is circumspect, agreeing with what Leibniz said later on of predispositions and aptitudes.

The *Recherche* adds nothing new, but shows him as having so mastered his philosophy that he undertakes to make it plain in dialogue to any intellect.

To understand how Descartes came to philosophise, let us begin with his doctrine of method as set out expressly, not in the *Method*, though in the four rules there given we have the sum and substance of it, but in the *Règles*[1]. His first point is that philosophy is *methodic thinking* as

---

[1] The *Règles* is incomplete, unfinished, tortuous and not clear; probably Descartes was striving to work his method out fully. Study especially Rule XII.

opposed to thinking received on authority or through custom, and is free from all trace of doubt. Erudition, conversance with opinions and facts, is not knowledge. True knowledge must have been individually thought over. Here he opposes both Scholasticism and the Renaissance. The philosopher's business is to arrive at *all* knowledge, for knowledge is one; until you know all you do not know at all. This was his attack on specialists. It is the business of philosophers to keep all knowledge together. This is harder now than then, yet there is now more need than ever to do so. Descartes, however, did not by universal science mean knowledge of everything, but that the way of arriving at truth, the method of discovery, is the same for all things. That is to say, you may be a specialist on the condition that you have had a philosophic training. A specialist should know something of the way of knowing truth generally.

All knowledge, he held, must begin with what can be clearly thought through and through. True knowledge he contrasts with vague opinion. We are now less inclined than Descartes to look askance at the probable. Descartes' certainty is found to be not so certain. There is even mathematical knowledge that is only probable. Nevertheless there is a great difference between what is well known and what is badly known. The opposition between truth and opinion does not lose its value, even when we are not so certain on some questions as he was.

To continue:—In order to arrive at perfect knowledge, at universal science, we must start from the simplest truths, from those we can most 'clearly' apprehend, namely, from *intuitions*, and proceed by synthesis to more complex ideas. If other relatively complex cognitions become as clear as those intuitions, we have then arrived at truth by *deduction*. But deduction, applied in any complex case, must begin with an enumeration or induction of all the points entering into the question to be set out—of all the conditions on which the solution depends. Thus the deductive act proper consists in passing progressively from condition to conditioned, and, if the way is long and the steps are many, in passing repeatedly up and down the same until all the elements are mastered, and the last and most complex, with all that it depends on, stands out with the same evidence as the first. The first conditions which are themselves not conditioned, and involve no conclusion, must have an immediate certainty and be intuitions, that is, directly known. For intuition, to start with, and deduction, as the way, are all that the human mind has to go upon for certainty. This is most plainly put in Règle V.

What we have to know indirectly we can know as certainty, as intuition, if we practise deduction in this way. And the method applies not only to all special questions, but also to problems of general knowledge. Descartes was a methodologist, but he had a philosophy to produce as well. To do this it seemed to him equally essential to go back to fundamental intuitions having reference to the fact of intelligence; indeed all knowledge of special questions comes for him to depend upon his philosophical proof of the possibility of knowledge generally. He insists in the *Règles* on the question of knowledge itself as preliminary to any solution of special questions of science[1]. He there strikes the note of the philosopher and not of the methodologist. We must know what the human mind can settle before we go in for any special study. The passages might have been written by Kant and may be compared with Locke's

[1] Cf. *Règles I* and *VIII*.

Introduction to his Essay. But of such we find no trace in Bacon.

The student may find Descartes' usage of the terms Deduction and Induction puzzling. He seems to waver in his choice and render satisfactory explanation by means of them impossible by employing them interchangeably, and in other senses than those of logic. According to his view of knowledge, there are some things we are sure of directly, or can by attention be brought to see that we really are sure of directly. These intuitions may assume the form of propositions, and as such they become useful in philosophy or science. In them our knowledge is reduced to its simplest terms, and we see between the terms of such propositions a necessary connexion. For example, 'body must be extended.' Whether the necessity be analytic or synthetic, he did not, like Kant, proceed to inquire.

Of other things we are not sure directly, but can become sure of by a process of thought connecting them with what we are directly sure of. And this process of becoming sure is what he calls deduction, or sometimes, when the steps are few, intuition[1]. But he would never have called a deduction an intuition if it were founded upon an induction or enumeration of conditions.

Now deduction, he declared, was a process that the commonest minds can perform. All men have direct intuition of some things, and cannot help having it; the final result of a deduction is also easily seen; thus logicians are unnecessary. Why then did he lay so much stress on method, and even on preliminary investigation? And what did he mean by contemning the old logic, a view shared for that matter by all the advancing minds of his time?

[1] Cf. *Règle XI*.

Descartes never completed his method. He broke down in the last rules when applying them to geometry. His slighting remarks on traditional logic are therefore possibly too hasty. But his opposition amounts to this, that he is less concerned about proof or exposition than he is about *discovery*. He wants not so much to set out what was already *got* as to find how to arrive at the unknown from the known. Yet his view was not that of J. S. Mill on real inference. Mill (in his *Logic*) was concerned about a theory of *proof*, of proof in general statements going beyond actual observation, and where formal proof was therefore impossible. Descartes wanted a theory of discovery. This is implied in his attempt, with the help of algebra, to systematise and extend the method of mathematical analysis, which was a method of actual discovery not unrelated to proof, yet different from the proving what has already been discovered[1]. Nevertheless, as we have seen, while decrying the old logic, he created difficulties by misusing terms borrowed therefrom. Instead of deduction and induction he ought to have used analysis and synthesis. He could then have used the former terms as well. For analysis assumes the form sometimes of induction, sometimes of deduction. Right procedure is analysis followed up by synthesis. There is no opposition between proof and discovery; they are complementary one of the other, and are both different aspects of the same process of knowing. Mark Descartes himself in Rule XII, where he says that knowledge is simple or composite, and considers the ways of knowing the composite through the example of the magnet. Some men set about investigating this with no method, turning away from the evident and looking to find something new in it by

---

[1] Vide my article 'Analysis,' *Encycl. Brit.*

chance. The scientific man, who knows the difference between the simple and the complex, musters all his particular observations of the magnet, and is thence able to deduce the nature of its composition, as far as experience can furnish the requisite data. This departs little from the best any man has ever said on the process of discovery. Mill strays into discovery from proof. Jevons divides the two. Nevertheless Descartes so mixes up his sound idea of discovery with the *terms* of proof that confusion results.

It should be borne in mind that up to Rule XII Descartes has been setting out general considerations on the problem of method. In XII itself he gives his theory of knowledge in a view of the knowing faculty, showing the relation of the intellect to sense, imagination and memory. Here is his first really philosophic point. We have to distinguish between ourselves as knowing and things known. The latter he deals with in the light of what we know of the knowing faculty. They are either simple or complex. The former he has disposed of already; we know them by intuition; composites we know by deduction. Into the latter he now goes more fully, dealing with them as Questions (*a*) perfectly comprehended; (*b*) imperfectly comprehended. (*a*) are questions of mathematics. Concerning (*b*) the twelve rules he was about to give are not given, but in the *Principia* we find the *results* of rules followed consciously or unconsciously.

Before leaving the *Method* let us glance at Bacon, Descartes' great predecessor in respect of method. We may easily draw a parallel between them. Both were men of their time, dissatisfied with the old ways; both were concerned about real knowledge and looked to method to bring it about. But here the parallel ceases. Bacon's point of view was objective. He always dealt with the external world as we find it in common life, with the ordinary idea of experience. He did not begin with a theory of knowledge as a ground for his method. He never philosophically inquired what is the relation of experience to knowledge. Yet it is remarkable how, from his unphilosophic point of view, Bacon does by induction virtually aim at explaining experience and comes round to Descartes' results. So far as nature is concerned, Descartes, no less than Bacon, regards extension and motion as the fundamentals upon which we can explain all our experience of the physical world. Bacon says constantly that, having got experience of a certain kind, we must get other similar experiences, mass them together, and so hope to find the 'forms' of things, or what we can make out by comparison of phenomena. Ultimately 'form' comes to be indistinguishable from 'sensible appearances' expressed in terms of motion. He shows, for example, that heat is motion.

But permanent differences remain. Descartes regarded all with a view to a general theory of knowledge. He proposed to deal with the whole realm of physical science in a certain definite and *progressive* way. Bacon had no idea of a general science except as a result of all special effort. Descartes gets his general principles by way of deduction, Bacon, by induction. Yet Descartes by no means makes light of experience and of experiment, but made a place for it in his scheme of knowledge. He says, for instance, that he could not proceed to medicine for want of experience and experiment. And in a letter he said that Bacon had so thoroughly treated of experimental knowledge in his *Novum Organon* that it was practically useless for any one to try to go ahead of him. But Bacon seemed to think that in a specific solution he had got all that the mind wants. Descartes thought that, having established experimentally, we could give a rational explanation deductively—which is the ideal of science.

Descartes prematurely and arbitrarily got deductions from general principles, and thus lost the full sense of contact with fact that exists in the properly scientific man. He attached more value to internal coherence and consistency than to the consistency of results with fact. He had not the sense of the duty of verification, which is now held as so important. This has come to us rather upon the line of Bacon's injunctions than of Descartes' practice.

LECTURE XXIII.

ON THE PHILOSOPHY OF DESCARTES.

READING.—The *Meditations*, i–v. (Simon, Garnier, or Veitch.)

IT will not be possible here to treat of Descartes' philosophy adequately in a general explication[1]. I shall therefore only single out special difficulties, and bring to bear upon them passages from other of Descartes' works than those prescribed for students' reading.

We have seen, in connexion with his Method, that if he is to have a philosophy, he needs an immediate certainty as a starting-point for all knowledge. In getting this for philosophy, he believed himself to have got a foundation for all physical science. The characteristic note of modern philosophy, the 'critical' point of view which has been accepted since Kant, is that before there can be anything worth calling science (in general), and especially any knowledge of things as they really are, there must be a theory of knowing—a discovery of what we *can* know and how we can know it, and of what we can *not* know. This, which became explicit in Kant, was anticipated implicitly in Locke. Descartes anticipated both. Kant arrived at his position by criticism; the English school tried to set it out by way of psychology; the same conception governs both, and it is at the bottom of Descartes' procedure.

[1] His philosophy is given in outline in Lect. VII; see also Lect. XI —ED.

We know that he found the certainty he sought in the intuition *Cogito ergo sum*, and on it he sought to build up his theory. *Does* he build it up on that one intuition? He really needed one more certainty, as we shall see.

Read how he arrived at his *Cogito* in the first Meditation:—*dubitandum est de omnibus*. The *omnibus* comes to be everything he had got from authority and tradition, all the opinions he had grown up with. In common life we feel sure on the testimony of sense. But sense is often illusion and never are we sure that it is not. We have not even a criterion to distinguish between dreaming and waking (this he modifies later on). Our very mathematical certainties may not represent reality. For our fundamental philosophic certainty we must get below all these.

Here note first that Descartes gives way to doubt, not for the pleasure of doubting, but only as a means to an end— only for the sake of getting to know. Compare his proviso in the *Method* (Parts II, III). He is not a sceptic. He has no wish to let practical life be affected by philosophic doubt. He simply means, 'You are not to be satisfied with things simply because they *are* in your mind.' All philosophers have meant as much, even if they have not expressed it as a principle. It is nothing more than putting one's self at the subjective point of view. All philosophers not only do so, but must do so. They have to interpret the things of experience in this new subjective light, and this involves doubting where there had hitherto been trusting. People would say, that pillar is white, and act upon this belief; physical science too would proceed upon it. But psychological analysis resolves this quality of the pillar into something less inherent than had seemed apparent.

Descartes then doubted in order to demonstrate. And, as

Leibniz wrote to Bernoulli, there is much difference between throwing doubt upon anything and seeking an ultimate demonstration of it. Nevertheless, he added, Descartes sinned doubly, first by doubting too much, then by getting away too easily from his doubts[1]. As for his doubting too much, it were more just to say, he doubted in too theatrical a way. It was a fault of manner; he lacked simplicity. Nevertheless everyone in passing over to the subjective point of view may, possibly must, undergo a struggle; and Descartes probably had real and great labour in getting away from the common conception of knowledge.

Now we have already seen how, when he had got to his *cogito*, or rather his *dubito*, he translated it, in the second *Meditation*, into *Ego sum res cogitans*—a thing that thinks, a mind, understanding, reason—that and *nothing but that*. All this, then, is implicit in the *Cogito*. From *I think*, and from nothing else, it follows that *I am*, that I am a *mind*. I am at bottom nothing but a thinking being, however I may come to see myself afterwards[2]. Note this and you will understand the objections to it. These were raised by critics to whom Descartes showed his *Meditations* in MS. Garnier's edition abridges them, missing many points in them. They are threefold:—

1. In *Cogito ergo sum*, the *ergo* introduces an inference, and thus implies a major premise—*Whatever thinks, is*. But this is a generalisation, not an intuition (Objection II). Descartes' reply (feebly abridged in Garnier) is that, in spite of the *ergo*, there is no inference, but a simple act of mental inspection. His meaning is 'I am *in that* I think.' 'My thinking implies my existence' *is* an intuition. More is the

[1] Cf. Erdmann, op. cit. p. 81.
[2] Compare *Meditation II*, with the last few pages of the *Recherche*.

pity then that *ergo*, indicating neither mediate nor immediate inference, should be there at all. In his reply to Hobbes, Descartes comes once upon the contrapositive:—If I were not I could not think. But enough of the *ergo*. The *Cogito* may be an intuition such as he wanted, but it is not the only one he uses.

2. To Hobbes's objections Descartes attached least importance. Hobbes, who was then (1640) fifty years old and had formed definite philosophic notions of his own, treated Descartes magisterially, and his criticisms are sometimes, though not always, trivial. He was unable to get at Descartes' point of view. Descartes replied:—To object that the inference 'I am,' or 'I am a thinking thing,' from 'I think,' is as weak as to argue that because 'I am walking,' therefore 'I am a walk,' is irrelevant. A walk is never taken to mean anything but the action, while thought is used indifferently for the action, for the faculty and for that in which the faculty resides. Thought is like no other process or thing, and to discern this is the first step in philosophy. Thought then may = thinking thing; and hereupon Descartes goes on to make a statement about substance, which is at variance with what he says elsewhere (*infra*, p. 256), namely, that we have no knowledge of substance except through its manifestations. As these are different, so do we infer different substance. Thinking, e. g. is different from extension; therefore thinking substance is different from extended substance. Substance—what it is in itself—was puzzling Descartes as it was to puzzle Locke.

3. Gassendi had no objection to the *Cogito*, but held that '*sum*' might be inferred as well from *ambulo* or any other action. No, rejoined Descartes, 'you can only say "you are," because you are *conscious* that you walk, that is, because you

think;' thus reaffirming the potency for philosophy of the subjective point of view. This shows how much Gassendi with his revived Epicureanism and Democritean Atomism stood outside philosophic thought. He is to Descartes what Democritus was to Socrates and Plato. Hobbes took the objective point of view as well as his friend Gassendi, but he had also a keen philosophic appreciation which places him nearer to modern thought. We now pass on.

The existence of self as a thinking being Descartes now regards as certain because, in the midst of all his doubts, he apprehends *with perfect clearness* that this is so. 'I know distinctly that I am, and distinctly what I am:' —a thinking being—and there is nothing else that I distinctly apprehend about myself. *I cannot get below thought.* Now if I can as clearly apprehend anything else, this too must be true. Else how should the *cogito* be true? Here he lays down his criterion of truth—Everything must be true which I perceive with perfect clearness and distinctness. Thought, when perfectly clear, portends reality. Why? Because this is the only ground that can be given in regard to self as a thinking being. Thus he has got his first certainty and his criterion.

But it is a criterion which takes no account of the *relative* character of anything that can be called truth or true knowledge. It fixes some things as final truths, which the mind rests in because they do not happen to have been resolved into higher or more general truths. And it denies that other things are in any sense truths, and that the mind for any purpose dare rest in them, because—they *do* happen to have been so resolved. For instance, the resolution of sense into an effect (in mind) of mechanical stimulation may be an important truth, but neither is that all that may be said scientifically or philosophically about sense, nor, when nothing of the kind is said, does sense cease to be some truth and become a mere source of error and deception.

His next step is variously stated. There are two kinds of considerations that seem to press on his mind at this stage. First, is there a certainty beyond self? Next, what are the circumstances under which his criterion, even when applied to self, can or cannot hold? He is not prepared to apply it straightway. He does discover another certainty which supplies the ground for the criterion itself, and this is the existence of God. Only as he has this is he sure about his criterion, and even about himself.

This seemed tortuous to objectors; nor did Descartes himself fail to see their point. In fact he gets to this second certainty, not from the first certainty (concerning self) by way of his criterion, or if from self then by way not of the criterion, but of a different principle— that of Causality, which for him assumed these forms:— Nothing can come from nothing; everything must have a cause; the more perfect cannot be a consequent of the less perfect; the cause must contain at least as much reality as the effect. If it contain more, it is a *causa eminenter*, just as the artist is more than his work; if it contain only as much, he called it *causa formaliter* [1], illustrating it by a die or seal and its imprint.

---

[1] The word 'formal' is in Descartes more obscure than the simpler term *eminenter*—standing out. It is really derived from the Aristotelian doctrine of action. Action with Aristotle always means 'forming'; hence Descartes takes formal to mean 'wrought by,' and *causa formaliter*, a working cause. But while this confuses the Aristotelian formal and efficient causes, Descartes induces further confusion by making formal reality synonymous with *actual* reality, and yet opposing it to what he calls *objective* reality (Veitch has good notes

This second principle, that of Causality, is so distinctly the means of his advancing in his system beyond self, that it has been well named his 'Archimedean fulcrum.' Spinoza saw as much when, in an early work, he set out an exposition of Descartes' philosophy in mathematical form. He said that unless this principle is assumed, away goes the *Cogito*. If out of nothing something *can* come, then I who think do not therefore necessarily exist. Descartes' own chosen principle of self-certainty is barren in his system compared with the principle of causality. The criterion of clearness and distinctness which he uses to establish his 'Ex nihilo nihil fit,' is *itself* not established beyond objection till God is proved to exist *from* that very 'Ex nihilo nihil fit.'

Ideas therefore, i.e. anything of which we are conscious, must like everything else have a cause. Now can any of the three possible kinds of ideas, innate, adventitious or fictitious, of which I am conscious, but the origin of which I do not know, carry me with the help of causality, beyond, out of, myself? 'Adventitious' ideas *seem* to come from external objects—can they?

All ideas are either of substances or modes of substance. The latter can be left aside as having less objective reality, i.e. as being less in thought than substances. Substances are fivefold:—bodies inanimate, animals, men, angels, God. These are all he has ever thought of. The second, third, and fourth he can drop out; for in having a certainty as to himself he can infer his equals, his inferiors, and beings

on this point). It should however be borne in mind that he uses 'objective' in the Scholastic sense. Subjective and objective have come to be used in precisely the opposite signification they bore for the Schoolmen. For Descartes too the objective meant *what exists as thought of*, mental representation. Subjective, on the other hand, referred to *what was placed under* in the way of substantial existence.

relatively superior to himself. As to bodies, there is nothing more in them than mind can account for. He can think of them, and think of them as sensibly perceived. A sensible perception is distinguished from other thoughts as being less *clear*, hence bodies cannot have more *reality* than mind. And—note this!—all that is really known of body is simply thought, is known only as he thinks, not as he is sensitive. That the body yonder is wax he knows only by thinking about it.

Now is it the same with the remaining substance, God? Here he finds a great difference, calling for special arguments. Read *Meditations III* and *V*, not *IV*.

He judges that he can explain body from himself; he can be the cause, even 'eminently' the cause of his idea of body. But of God he can have no idea from himself. He must find proofs of God's existence to make sure of the clearness of his thought. Grouping together all that is scattered through Descartes' works on this subject, we get as irreducible result three separate proofs put forward:—(1) The ontological, metaphysical, or *a priori* proof, viz. the existence of God is to be understood as given necessarily in the idea of God. (2) The having in my mind the idea of an infinite Being of which there is nothing in the finite nature of my mind to be the cause. (3) The fact of my existing (not thinking), and existing as imperfect. This can only be explained ultimately by the existence of God as a perfect Being. (2) and (3) may be called *a posteriori* proofs, or, according to Kuno Fischer, anthropological, being founded on a consideration not of the idea of God, but of the nature of man.

Now Descartes finds in the two last proofs sufficient ground to work on in the *Meditations*, since he does not bring in the first in Book III, where he gets to his real certainty, but only in Book V. Here then it is secondary. But in the more dogmatic *Principia* it is put *first*. Again, in the second response to the objections (end of *Meditations*), where he sets out his system in geometrical form—not that he held with this procedure, but merely to show, *if* he had chosen to do so, how he would have done it—he begins with proof (1). And this in demonstration is right, just as Euclid set out at first that which he arrived at last [1].

In proof (2) he applies the principle of causality to the ideas of which we are conscious. It is a positive idea—this of an infinite Being—not the result of abstraction, which would give us the Indefinite, not the Infinite. It is there, and, causality being true in the light of nature [2], it must be caused by a real infinite original. The idea of it is the mark of the artificer, and is Descartes' 'ideal' innate idea.

With regard to proof (1), compare the statement of it in the *Principia* (§ xiv.) with that in *Med. V* (Veitch, p. 148). The absolutely perfect must exist, since existence is a perfection. To this in the *Principia* is added that God's existence is not only possible but absolutely necessary and eternal. Wherefore these additions? To make his view more explicit, because he had been charged with merely dishing up a mediæval argument which had been repudiated by Aquinas, on the ground that we have no right to infer from essence to existence. Descartes pointed out his own opinion as divergent from this in Objection I. The argument is as old as Anselm, in whose time little of Aristotle was known and the schools were thoroughly Platonic. It ran thus:—God

[1] Veitch gives this exposition in an Appendix.

[2] Descartes uses 'light of nature' (1) in a depreciating sense, as what is common every-day experience, (2) as the whole collection of fundamental intuitions in any human mind.

is that than which nothing greater can be thought. But to be in intellect and in reality is greater than to be in intellect only; therefore God cannot be thought not to be. Some Schoolmen, and especially Aquinas, saw the error of making an inference from a definition. A definition is hypothetical. Reality must either be postulated or proved otherwise. Anselm's argument should properly have been '*If* God exists, He exists not only in intellect, but also in reality.' Kant, in the *Pure Reason*, shows the insufficiency of the ontological proof, as he called it. The proof, he said, supposes real existence to be an attribute which enters into a concept with other attributes, in which case the comprehension of a notion should be changed according as existence is or is not supposed. But one hundred real dollars *in thought* do not contain an atom more than one hundred possible dollars. Existence does not enter analytically into the conception of a thing. But Descartes did draw a distinction in his answer to Caterus, namely, between notions. In some, e.g. triangles, centaurs, essence does not involve existence, even though he can picture them most clearly. The notion of God however does include existence, and not only possible but also necessary existence. And accordingly in the second edition of the *Meditations* he added the word necessary. Kant, by implication, does not allow for this distinction, in which lies the whole force of Descartes' position. Whenever Descartes is pushed into a corner concerning this ontological proof, he always escapes on his fundamental argument that the idea (of God's existence) is one not so much of necessary existence as of necessary existence originally *in me*. Causality is for him at the bottom, and not the ontological proof, which usually fails to distinguish this between real existence and the conception of possible existence. '*I* am imperfect, and *I* have this idea of God or of perfection.' This of course is liable to the objection—'*You* have this idea of God; *I* have none.' And since Descartes' day speculation has (as with Kant) given place to *moral* argument, or the consciousness of 'moral sense.' Descartes himself suggests that his arguments have at least a *cumulative* value.

At all events he has got from doubt to certainty and a ground of universal knowledge. We have now to see what he means by truth and what is his doctrine of error. Notice first the two positions in the *Principia*, Book I. In § 30 the argument may be summarised thus:—God exists, and because He alone is perfect, He alone is perfectly independent; therefore all things depend upon Him, and therefore my ideas depend upon Him. My ideas must therefore be true because He is true. Again, the faculty of knowing which He has given us never apprehends any object which is not true as far as it apprehends it, that is to say, as far as it knows clearly and distinctly.

But in § xiii and in *Meditation V*, p. 148, the criterion is taken as certain in itself. Where it is directly applied Descartes does not doubt its power. But he admits there are cases where we say that we know, although it is by no means present to us that we clearly see what we say that we know; e.g. in the steps of a demonstration in Euclid, where we have possibly forgotten the first steps, forgotten, i.e. what we applied the criterion to, though we recollect we did apply it. God in this case guarantees the validity of our memory rather than that of the criterion itself. But if we know by the help of a perfect Being, how do we come to err?

Now turn to *Med. IV*. Error, he finds, is not in perception, but in judgment, where, that is, we turn what we perceive into an objective predicate[1]. But we may judge and yet withhold assent. When we do assent (or refuse), we exercise will in the sense of self-determination. Now the understanding is from God and errs not, nor does self-determination, by the power of which we come nearest to God. But the understanding is limited, the will is not. And whenever the will by its liberty of indifference either affirms or denies beyond the limit of the understanding's insight, then there is error, even if the judgment is a right one; and doubly so, if it is wrong. While if the will uses its liberty of indifference so as not to judge at all, we cannot err. That the will *can* refrain from judging renders God not chargeable for our errors.

If then we know self, God, and how to avoid error, what do we know beside, and how? This brings Descartes to the subject of bodies, or the external world. Read *Med. VI.* The existence of bodies cannot be concluded from the fact that we can imagine them. Imagination is not pure intellection or thought, as he explains later, but is a mode of our subjective life determined by the relation of mind to body. Being inferior to thought it may proceed from the thinking being.

Nor can the existence of bodies be proved from sensations. It is natural in us to refer the latter to outside bodies, but sensations themselves are no guarantee, as we know by the case, e. g. of an amputated arm, where some sensations are still referred to the lost limb, and by sensations affecting us in dreams, as in waking. Descartes' arguments here are very modern—but so also are Plato's in the *Theætetus*.

But my sensations of objects *must have a cause.* *I* am not

[1] Compare Kant's distinction between judgments of perception (e. g. if the sun shines the stone is warm) and judgments of experience (the sun warms the stone).

the cause. They result neither from my thought nor from my will. They must then be due to God as their cause *eminenter*, or conceivably to bodies as their cause *formaliter*. Which? To bodies, *else I am perpetually deceived*.

Note the difference between Descartes and Berkeley. The latter leaves off with the view that God is the *only* certainty, extirpating matter except as an idea coming from God. Descartes retained matter to exclude the charge of deception on the part of God[1].

To understand how speculative philosophy took the turn it did after Descartes, compare his dogmatic statements in the *Principia* (Part II) on matter, viz. bodies exist apart from mind as the real cause of our perception, and the mind perceives them as they are, in as far as it has clear and distinct knowledge. Mind, then, and body are alike substances, a substance being a thing that exists in such a way that it has no need but of itself for its existence. This is true of each substance with reference to other substances, yet obviously the determination cannot strictly hold for any finite mind or body, since all depend upon God. God therefore is the only true substance. Substance cannot be said univocally of God and of anything created. Here he seems to imply that we *have* immediate knowledge of substance, although he did not allow this in answering Hobbes. Mind and body, he had said, as substances essentially different and independent, were knowable only by their attributes, each having one principal attribute expressing its nature. Of these indefeasible attributes—thought, extension—all those modifications on the ground of which we speak

[1] In Hamilton's language he is a Hypothetical Realist, or, if an Idealist, then a Cosmothetic Idealist. However he strips bodies of all secondary qualities.

of substances having different *qualities* (not attributes) are by him called *modes*; such are figure (a mode of extension), imagination, feeling, willing (modes of thought)[1]. Modes are not found in Infinite Substance, for that is unchangeable.

In the *Principia* he proceeds to distinguish between attributes as essential and modes as accidental. Other qualities ascribed by us to bodies are really modes of our thought, as Number, and especially Time, also the five 'universals' or predicables[2]. Descartes was, in fact, no Realist in the old sense, but a Conceptualist—or a Nominalist as opposed not to Conceptualism, but to Realism. He comes here nearer to Kant. He held, it is true, that space was a mode of extension, something having objective reality, but time was a mode of thought—Kant would have said, of intuition, meaning of perception.

The modes of extension depend upon the movement of the parts into which matter is divided. Matter, i.e. is conceived by Descartes mathematically; there is ultimately nothing in it which cannot come under solid geometry. All changes in body are merely modes of motion. Towards this new conception other minds besides Descartes' were working. Bacon had made out that heat consists in an agitation of the minute particles of bodies. Compare too Hobbes's groping after a doctrine of motion[3]. Locke took over Descartes' distinction, and expressed it from his experiential standpoint as the distinction between Primary and Secondary Qualities.

---

[1] *Thought* (*pensée*) in Descartes is simply a name for all subjective experience, for whatever we are conscious of.

[2] Genus, species, differentia, property, accident.

[3] Vide *Hobbes* by G. C. Robertson (*Knight's Philosophical Classics*), pp. 33, 41-43, 93.—ED.

LECTURE XXIV.

ON THE PHILOSOPHY OF DESCARTES (*continued*).

READING.—*Meditation VI. Principia. Les Passions de l'Âme (Simon).*

WE pass lightly over Descartes' physical philosophy (which occupies the greater part of the *Principia*), but so as to note how it comes into his general scheme of philosophy. Beginning with man as pure intellect, he went on to the existence of the material world, and grasping this, came round again to deal fully with man and the 'Passions' of his nature.

We saw that, according to Descartes, body is extended, *and nothing else*, just as mind is a thinking thing only. Without extension we have no idea of body, or only a confused idea. Extension has length, breadth, depth, and there are no more ways of thinking of it; therefore body has these only.

Descartes is at some pains to defend his position that body *is* space (*Principia*, II. §§ 10–15), and it is interesting to note how he tries to show that there is nothing in his view at variance with ordinary notions. He further faces the question, which much occupied contemporary science, of condensation and rarefaction, and their action on the pores of bodies, trying to prove that a body remains the same, whether its pores expand or not. We see that he gets his notion of body by way of metaphysic, instead of positive science, and consequently has to defend himself against science. For instance, as space is essentially the mode of body, vacuum, as space empty of all body, is philosophically impossible; space cannot be free from all body. You may empty your bucket as you please, but you cannot empty space—and therefore body—till the sides collapse. What is nothing cannot have extension, and as space has extension, it always has body. And there never can be more or less body in space at one time than at another. Compare this treatment with Locke's on simple modes of space (*Essay*, ch. xiii). Locke's distinction between space and body is not got by way of metaphysic, but is accommodated to modern physics, and is a perfectly rational determination. We can distinguish between space which does not resist movement and space which does; and this difference can be psychologically grounded. His psychology is often crude, but here it stands firm.

Again, physics still assumes that there are such things as atoms—natural indivisible bodies. Nobody ever doubted that an atom, if extended, can be thought of as broken up, but that there are certain elements that can*not* physically be broken up is the basis of physical science. Descartes meets this by saying that atoms *cannot* exist, for space as always extended must always be divisible.

As to movement, Descartes laid stress on this, that it can be said only of a body with respect to what it is immediately in contact with. If a body does not change place with reference to what is around it, it can be said not to move. This, it may be, was said to justify his suppression of his own Galilean view sin the *Principia*. The theory, which we will not pause over longer, is another instance of the futility of solving such questions by metaphysic. Descartes ends by finding that movement was so different from extension that it must come from outside, from God, who created some bodies having motion, others having the, for Descartes, no less positive mode of rest. And it follows from the unchangeable nature of God that the quantity of motion and rest is invariable for ever. He is not content to put his conservation of movement as a hypothesis to be verified by results, but gives it as a certainty from first principles. He does not admit conservation of *energy*, nay, he abhors it. It was Leibniz who insisted on that notion. Descartes gives three fundamental laws of nature, i. e. of motion. Coming shortly after Galileo had enunciated three laws, and a generation before Newton gave them their final form, they are interesting (*Prin.* II, §§ 37-40). With the first two Newton practically agreed, but the third turned him from Descartes. His copy of the *Principia* at Cambridge bears the repeated marginal note 'error! error! error!' The law contains a denial of action and reaction in matter. Matter is the mere bearer of something communicated to it; it can have no energy.

In the second book, where he is determining different kinds of bodies, we come on his notion of fluid. Bodies are hard, i. e. resist separation, only in so far as they have 'rest' in them. Bodies which do not resist separation, have not rest but motion, and are fluid. This determination is made with a view to his explanation of the phenomena of the universe. His physics is an explanation of the universe on a hydro-dynamic basis. Given bodies that don't move and fluids that do, it follows that all change must come from interaction of particles that have been in motion from the beginning with those that have been at rest from the beginning. The smallest addition of motion in any direction is enough to set up *vortices*, that is, streams of motion by which bodies, the parts of which are not moved, may be borne along, going all through the universe. With this famous notion he goes on to attempt to set out a doctrine of the relation of the heavenly bodies, expressing all the results of the Copernican theory, yet so as not to run counter to the tenet of the Church that the earth stands still. Copernicus, in the face of Church doctrine, revived a notion started in the Greek period, but soon submerged. Then Tycho Brahe (1546–1601) accounted for the phenomena by the theory that the planets (not the earth) went round the sun, and the sun went round the earth. Descartes had a mind to be more careful than Copernicus, and to reason more truly than Brahe. His hypothesis is that the heavens as we behold them are fluid, that is, in motion. In them are streams, invisible through the rarefaction of matter, bearing the bodies along. The earth *reposes* in its heaven or vortex, while yet it is borne along with it.

He may have been quite sincere in this. By his definition of motion, if the earth remains always in contact with the same particles of its stream, *it is not moved*, however much it may change its relations to the planets. At any rate his theory got all the benefit of motion round the sun without the blame. 'I am much more circumspect than Copernicus,' he wrote. His hypothesis was accepted for some time, especially in France, but was dislodged by the Newtonian hypothesis of attraction. Not that physicists are even now agreed as to how action at a distance takes place. But when more accurate observations were made by Hooke and Newton's other predecessors, it was inevitably suggested to Newton, that action and reaction was a better hypothesis than bodies borne about in streams—a theory due not to observation but to general reasoning.

In the cosmogony too which follows (*Prin.* III. § 47)

the whole conception misses its point for want of true scientific method. It is interesting as speculation, as poetry, but it is not science.

We now come down to earth (*Prin.* IV). Materials and leisure did not suffice for him to write all he had schemed on Plants, Animals, Man (see Preface), hence he confines himself to objects as they affect our senses, leaving Plants out entirely, and dealing with Animals in the *Passions*, Book I, and in Part V of his earliest work on Method. Descartes experimented much in dissecting, but found nothing to modify his idea of animal, viz. that animals are simply material things more complex than the rest— are only machines of a more complicated kind—so complex indeed that we must call them automata, i.e. they have something within them that sets them moving. They are machines with hearts, the heart distilling the mechanical agent of 'vital spirits' into the blood, and this bearing them to the pineal gland in the brain, on which all external impressions finally impinge, and from which all outward movement issues. Animal life is the expression of the complexity of their mechanism. But animals have no self-consciousness and therefore no soul or mind; for without self-consciousness there is no thinking. Whereas, whatever sense may be, man *as man* is thought. Descartes conceives no middle ground between thinking and extended being. Man is both. Animals are only the latter.

Descartes' followers rigidly applied this theory, even to the length of treating animals with barbarity. Even the gentle and holy Malebranche, on being remonstrated with for mercilessly belabouring a friendly dog, replied, 'You don't suppose it feels?' Vivisection was largely practised by them, and regarded with as much indifference as the breaking up of a stone. Nevertheless Descartes himself often said, it were better, in the interests of moral training, to treat animals as though they did feel. He had no doubt at all that animals were pure automata, but he was not oblivious of the difficulties besetting his theory. Animals might act like men and show mind to some extent, nevertheless there was nothing in their ways that could not be interpreted as the action of a fine machine.

From animals to man the distance is great. Animals are only bodies; man is fundamentally not body. He is in the first instance 'I myself,' knowing myself as mind and body; and if I acquire the conviction that there are other men, of them also it may be said they are mind and body. What then is the relation between these two? What is the character of man as mind, and then as body?

Before Descartes had arrived in the *Principia* at his doctrine of nature he was disposed so to aggrandise the sphere of thinking as to regard all mental manifestations—feeling, willing, imagination, and even sense—as modes of thought. In the *Règles* (XII.) sense and imagination are names for nervous processes. At the same time he conceives a force, one with body, but yet spiritual, which acts and reacts upon them. He then goes on to include in that force itself sense, memory, imagination and thought proper—all being pure intellect acting under certain conditions. Yet again, he denies that memory is mental. If we do not remember our dream-consciousness, it is because memory, being bodily, is not able to rehearse the mental. Thought, for Descartes, implied an ever-present consciousness of thinking.

Life, for Descartes (cf. the beginning of the *Passions*), is not soul at a lower power, but is out of relation to it.

It is an affair simply of body, explicable in terms of physics only—not even of chemistry. Animals have life, but not soul (or mind)—a conception which is not borne out by observation, nor now maintained except by the incautious. In succeeding generations this materialism with regard to life was extended to mind. Evolution is entirely and utterly outside Descartes. Angels and God have no body; animals have no mind. Man alone has both—mutually interrelated. *How* this can be when they have been pronounced mutually exclusive and contradictory is a difficulty that does not escape him. He attempts to explain, but the difficulties cause him sometimes to shift his ground. In the *Meditations* and *Principia* he finds that this mutual interrelation of body to mind makes sense and imagination inferior to pure thinking. In the *Passions* his procedure is different. He is fearful of bringing animals into too close a relation to man, if he allows sense and imagination to be modes of thinking involving relation to matter. Else it might be said, Animals have sense, and thus mind of a low sort. He does not deny sensations and appetites in animals; they act as if they had these. But it is not sense-appetite or imagination either that he seeks to explain by reference to any conjunction between mind and body, but a set of proper mental states which cannot be assigned to animals—'passive mental states,' namely, which he opposes to the 'simple actions of the soul.' He does not abandon his view of imagination and the rest as modes of thought, but calls them, and also sensations and appetites, *passions* as regards the soul. It is not only to save the character of man that he lays stress on so-called passions; he desires to consider emotions proper with an ethical purpose, of which he has said little elsewhere. He has also a more explicit statement to make of the conditions of mind's relation to body. Sense, imagination, &c., are what they are because of that relation. And in this work we find the expression, turned to such account by Leibniz, of *confused and obscure perceptions*, arising from the mutually discrepant functioning of soul and body.

We come at length to the statement (Art. 30) 'that mind is united to all parts of the body conjointly,' the latter being in a way, i.e. as organ, indivisible. Thus he is forced to allow, in the human body at least, more than mere extension. Yet, he proceeds (Art. 31), notwithstanding this general connexion, there is a certain part where mind functions more particularly, and that is (not the heart but) the brain, and in that the only part not bilateral—the pineal gland. He had thus a sound idea of the importance of the nervous system as few had before him. But here the same difficulties meet him. For the pineal gland has two *sides*, has extension, while mind is unextended. He might just as well have taken the whole brain or the whole body. The gland (Art. 34) stands between body and soul, and transmits changes both ways by way of the fine matter (animal spirits) produced by the heart, transmitted by the nerves as through tubes, and stored in the so-called ventricles of the brain. The gland can be moved in as many ways as there are changes produced in the body from without. It can also be divinely moved by the soul. And there he leaves it—in the *Passions*.

Now he had said nothing can move of itself. Motion is a constant quantity, and must be transmitted. How does the immaterial soul move the extended gland? If his reply to the fourth objection (Arnauld's) in the *Meditations* be referred to (Jules Simon's ed. p. 233), it will be seen that the soul does not really set the body in motion, but can only *direct* (*déterminer*) the motion of the vital spirits. This idea of a directive power is worthier, and has of late years been urged by physicists. In it he found a distinction between animals and men. A man's actions on being struck are characterised by a more varied range than a dog's, because of his power to direct the vital spirits. Consciousness cannot give us the means of creating movement, but it can give a different *outcome*. Descartes' difficulties are really of his own making. The definition that he persists in giving of body and mind must entail perplexity as to their mutual relation; and it is these definitions that made Geulincx, Malebranche, and Leibniz differ so widely from their master.

Finally as to the 'Passions,' Descartes uses the word in a wider sense—passions of mind as opposed to actions of mind, thought including of course both—and in a narrower sense—all sorts of perceptions or 'knowledges' that do not arise through actions of the mind but are as the mind receives them. In other words, passions are all mental states except volitions. Of these there are three kinds. First—and there seems here a contradiction—some passions may arise from mind as the cause of the perceptions, as when we perceive that we will. He admits these are perhaps better called actions. Secondly, indirect affections, or sensations due to external bodies. Thirdly, direct affections, or appetites[1].

Thus he does not deny here that sensations and appetites, arising in the body, are of the mind, although he is more inclined to refer them all, as with animals, to the body. His judgment wavers. To him the emotions seemed, of all states due to the interaction of soul and body, far more impressive than imagination and sensation. Even when

[1] In Art. 23 he adds fortuitous representations.

not excited by sense—as, e. g. fear at sight of a tiger—an emotion has a confusing disturbing effect on the purely mental life. It may be said, appetites are powerful disturbers; but Descartes might have replied, they disturb us only as they rouse emotions that disturb us. And objects, he said, excite passions only by reason of the diverse ways in which they may hurt or profit us, or in general be important for us. It is *only* as objects can be thought of as beneficial or hurtful to the body that emotions can arise. Emotions, then, are the expression of a *value* for the individual. This is true and shows a sound grasp of the import of emotion.

He also orders the emotions well and scientifically, as primitive (or general), and secondary (particular), although general considerations, both ethical and logical, are mixed up with his exposition. The primitive emotions are wonder, love, hate, desire, joy, sorrow, his definition of emotion being however applicable to only five. In his striking doctrine of Wonder, where he shows great psychological acumen, he really has hold of the same element as Professor Bain has in *neutral* feelings, or emotions of relativity, which no thorough scientific analysis can ignore. He means that there is a certain emotional condition that is neutral in the sense of not being hurtful or beneficial. And while he thus places Wonder first, he assigns a special ethical importance to it at the end of his treatise, as that emotion by which the freely willing mind is able to subdue the other passions, *since it is subservient to the emotionally neutral function of knowing*.

The other five fall into three groups. Love and hate are the simplest expression of the mind as regards pleasure and pain. The good = the loved; the bad = the hated.

They are one emotion in different relations. Desire is the phase where good and evil are in the future. Joy and sorrow are passions in the actual presence of good and evil; and are dual like the former two. Why is Desire not dual? A man desiring has always hope and fear. Desire therefore *is* dual, but implicitly so. Wonder is not dual, for though it is a passion, it has no relation to good and evil, but arises simply from novelty. From these genera all other passions may be derived as specific or secondary.

From his definition of mind as thought, and emotions or passions as states where pure thinking is affected by body, it follows that in order to clear thinking the emotions must be kept down; nevertheless he well saw how much driving power there lies in passion properly directed. And of all the passions that one which makes for knowledge and may be made to support mind as thinking is wonder. The remedy for passion as disturbing mind is the free, voluntary activity of thought. To keep passions down, we must think clearly, know fully, under the guidance of wonder. Knowledge of the true value of things, of the true limits of our powers, of the unalterable laws of nature as it can be got by exciting wonder or curiosity, suffices to hold the other passions in subjection. The soul, by its power of thinking, can suppress one passion indirectly by dwelling on another. This is good psychology, whatever may be said of his physiology, namely, that the pineal gland diverts the course of the vital spirits. But, he held, this was a weak method; the better way is to live with firm and determinate judgments touching good and evil as attained by clear thinking.

Here his system properly ends, and it is in this connexion that he made the greatest advance on his predecessors in psychology. He was distinctly on the track of physiological psychology, though of course with deficient knowledge of the nervous system.

As to the merits of his system generally, it may be said (1) that in *reach* and *all-comprehensiveness* it stands perhaps unique in the history of human thought. (2) Note the *logical consequence* of it, onward from the methodology, in which this is made the first requisite, to the most detailed applications of its general principles, and into the heroic efforts made to grapple with the difficulties which it hardly pretended to surmount. I do not mean that everything in the system follows with perfect consequence, but this is certainly aimed at, and there is never any shifting of particular consequences. (3) Mark also its *originality*, which is attested at every step, notwithstanding the fact that in this or that point there had been ancient and scholastic anticipations (especially in Augustin)—some of them striking—of Descartes' doctrine. It constituted an almost incredible advance upon Scholasticism, especially in the apprehension or explanation of nature. And this may be claimed for it, even although it so often puts the material world out of sight when human mental conditions are considered. It put forward the sceptical subjective point of view as against the authoritative, traditional and formal dicta of Scholasticism, constituting, by virtue of its personal starting-point, a philosophy which, if it cannot be considered satisfactory, never can lose its meaning as Scholasticism, with its abstract generalities about things, has done.

LECTURE XXV.

ON CARTESIANISM [1].

It was in Holland and France, the land of his adoption and the land of his birth, that the effect of Descartes' philosophy was at once decisive and immediate. There it was both actively opposed and actively propagated and developed, unlike its fate in England and Germany, England particularly, where it was received without enthusiasm, and in neither was immediately—in England not at any time—carried further.

In Holland mere propagation (headed by Reneri and Regius) began to give place to transformation and development through Claubergius (a German in Holland) and others, till by Arnold Geulincx, a convert to Calvinistic Protestantism, Occasionalism was put forth as the legitimate interpretation of the master's thought. Violent religious hostility, from the time of Voetius at Utrecht, on the part of the orthodox clergy, caused the Cartesians to draw towards the dissenting theologians—the Arminians, &c.—with whom they were denounced as enemies, sometimes Jesuitical (!) enemies—to the faith.

In France the development of Cartesianism took place not in the Universities, which remained scholastic, and where (at least in Paris in 1671) it was formally proscribed, but

[1] Selected from the author's MSS. and from lectures delivered 1880, 1886, and 1891.

among the religious orders. Opposed by the Jesuits whom Descartes had been so eager to gain, but who stood to the Schoolmen or to Gassendi until the new empirical philosophy arose, the system was accepted by the Jansenists of Port Royal, the fathers of the Oratory, and other congregations. It was looked upon with favour by Fénelon, Bossuet, &c., propagated in private associations for science, and in society became a fashion. The most sympathetic critic and follower was Arnauld, whose criticisms Descartes treated with most respect. The most important was Nicole Malebranche, priest of the Oratory (founded by Descartes' patron Cardinal Bérulle, a free order for the advancement of theology). Malebranche was turned to the passionate study of philosophy by Descartes.

The thinkers who thus succeeded Descartes may be called Cartesians, not only because they were stirred up by him to thought and to the discovery of a way out of the contradictions in which he landed himself, but also because for all of them the refuge lies in the idea of the Infinite Substance, God. None of them are theological thinkers in the sense that the Schoolmen were. The starting-point with all is the human reason, and the goal is rational explanation. But the way lies through the (rational) idea of the Deity. They are Theistic thinkers, and are ultimately Pantheistic, perforce if not voluntarily, for the whole Cartesian movement tends to Pantheism.

Now Descartes' philosophy in its result is properly expressed by Kuno Fischer as a double Dualism, viz. of substances opposed and constituted by the opposition:— (1) of God (Infinite) and the World (finite), or all things created; (2) of Mind (thinking substance) and Body (extended substance). Descartes is seriously concerned to maintain that God exists apart from the world, and the world exists *per se*. And Mind, as part of the world, is, by its liability to err, and still more by its power to escape from error (free power of self-determination), regarded by him as having a substantial existence. Nevertheless by his own definition of substance, it is impossible for him to apply it univocally to God and anything created. Mind is dependent upon God for knowledge. Matter is entirely inert, and must be moved by God. And creatures are not only called into being by God, but need re-creating every moment. Existence is a continual creation.

With regard to the other dualism, however strongly he maintained the absolute independence of mind and body, we saw him in difficulties through the testimony of facts to the existence of a relation between them. He wavers between calling this a substantial union or a unity of composition only. He wavers as to sense and imagination. His chief merit is his courage and honesty in uttering his difficulties. His dualism he must be understood to maintain notwithstanding; and the contradictions are so many inconsistent and wavering concessions to facts which he cannot shut his eyes to. Or if at times he is upon a way to surmount the difficulties by aggrandising the theistic element, it is at the expense of his dualism.

The action of his school was determined by this position of the master, and had two courses open to it:—

1. To maintain the dualistic principles strictly—as strictly at least as possible—and by a definite line, instead of the master's wavering attitude, to explain away some, if not all, the difficulties, resigning if necessary the very idea of natural or philosophical explanation, the desire not to let go which was the occasion of his very hesitation and wavering.

2. To maintain the dualistic principles only in such a form as that the difficulties cease to be in the same way real, i.e. to give a natural or philosophical explanation of the difficulties, but in so doing to resign the dualism.

The first course is known as the theory of Occasionalism. The dualism of body and mind is strictly maintained; that of God and the world as far as possible, since it is the divine (personal) agency that is explicitly and uniformly recurred to for the solution of the difficulty as between body and mind. Occasionalism, in short, surmounts the difficulty of interaction of body and mind at the expense of natural or philosophical explanation, and by overlooking the difficulty between God and World:—uniformly at the expense of philosophical explanation; and if not by uniformly ignoring the difficulty between God and World, then with an explanation of this which tends towards the *second* course.

Now the difficulty of Body and Mind is twofold:—

(a) There is no doubt according to Descartes about the substantiality of both. Bodies in no respect need minds for their existence, nor do minds need bodies. But bodies and minds undoubtedly appear to be related to each other in two obvious ways:—mind is acted on through body, e.g. in sense; body is acted on by mind, e.g. in volition. Now how, if they are totally opposed substances, can mind move body, or body impress mind? Both Geulincx and Malebranche replied, by the action of the Deity upon *occasion* of the change in either, God alone being able to effect it. There is in reality *no* interaction between body and mind. By omnipotence God excites perception when he moves body. Hence it is not less wonderful for my tongue to move when I will to speak than that the globe should tremble.

(*b*) But mind and body have a more special relation:—mind knows body, body is known by mind. Then how can thinking substance know substance that does not think? How, being itself non-extended, can it have even an idea of Extension? Malebranche replied—Plato had inspired the thought—by having a vision of Extension (as of all things) not only through but 'in' God; for God can possess the idea of Extension, and ideas are not only divine, but are not to be detached from the nature of God. It is not we who know, but God who knows through us [1].

The second course is Spinozism [2].

This retains the dualism of body and mind only as an opposition of *attributes*, instead of substances, while the dualism of God and World wholly vanishes. *Deus sive Natura* is *one* substance, of which Thought and Extension are alike attributes, and minds and things passing modes. God therefore as single and solitary substance—thus was the theistic element in Descartes' system—which is theistic, if ever philosophy was—developed in and by Spinoza [3].

Manifestly the two directions of thought here outlined

---

[1] Note that whereas Malebranche explained knowledge by God, Berkeley explained God's existence from his theory of knowledge.

[2] READING.—*Spinoza*. By Principal Caird. (Knight's Philosophical Classics.) (Circumspect, exact, good generally, especially on the epistemology.) *Spinoza*. By Dr. Martineau. (Learned, eloquent, but too polemical for deepest insight.) *Spinoza*. By Sir F. Pollock. (Brilliant but inexact.) Kuno Fischer and Erdmann, in their histories of philosophy.

Of the translations—White's (Trübner) and Elwes's (Bohn series) are both very good, but should be read if possible with constant reference to the original (best edition, Vloten and Land, Hagae Comitum, 1892-3).

[3] In the *Ethica* Spinoza has attained to fully developed Monism; in the *Tractatus Brevis* he is still a half hearted Dualist.

are both Cartesian. Spinoza, as little as Geulincx or Malebranche, would have thought as he did but for Descartes. The two lines of thought are not however equally Cartesian. It is one thing to take for a principle the Dualism that Descartes tried to reach consistently, though he could not, and seek a means (philosophical or not) of resting there. It is another thing to take for a principle the Monism or Pantheism that Descartes could not avoid falling into and (although with the help of a dualism of Thought and Extension) to work out into its utmost details a system antagonistic to Descartes'. The difference is the difference between the action of disciples and the action of an original thinker who takes and hands on the torch in the philosophic race. That Spinoza, and not Geulincx or Malebranche, made a real advance, and the necessary advance in thought from the point to which Descartes had been carried, is clear from this, that neither of these two found it possible to save their master's Dualism, or to get out of the current that bore them towards Spinoza. If Spinoza himself succeeded as little in reaching a sure resting-place, that was not because his thought was not a distinct advance and a grand achievement, but because his principles, both his own and those he had from Descartes, were what they were.

Let us now look more closely at the second course (Spinozism) in its relation to Descartes.

It may seem strange to put forward Spinoza as the last great link in the Cartesian chain, seeing he began to philosophise hardly later than Geulincx, and had worked out the greater part of his extraordinary system before Malebranche knew a line of Descartes' writings. The last link he is, nevertheless, in respect of the logical import of his doctrine.

Even historically also, if we go upon the date of the publication of their most important works, Malebranche precedes Spinoza. Though he lived forty years longer than the latter, and began to think later, his chief work *Recherche de la Vérité* appeared three years before Spinoza's *Ethica*, and already in that work his involuntary Spinozism is clearly enough marked. The truth is, Malebranche drifted towards Spinoza before he knew of Spinoza's system, and when he did know it, spurned it and sought to steer away from it, he drifted as before. Malebranche's course was marked out for him in the principles he started from. So was Spinoza's. But the latter took it with such a will that he swiftly explored all that it led to—explored and died while Malebranche still was young. Even the next great thinker, Leibniz, forced by Spinoza into a new track, had time to live and shape the thought of the eighteenth century, before Malebranche died. So much is Malebranche outside the main course of European thought—so strongly did that current set from Descartes to Leibniz through Spinoza.

Baruch (Benedict) de Spinoza (or Despinoza) was born at Amsterdam, in 1632, of a Jewish family, emigrants from Portugal directly, but probably of Spanish origin, which had emigrated on account of the Inquisition. His principal teacher was the famous Talmudist, Rabbi Morteira, a philosopher after the Jewish-Scholastic manner of Maimonides (1135–1204). In the translations of his works named above his biography is given[1]. Persecuted in his lifetime and an object of the fiercest hate long after his death, he has within the last century, through Jacobi, Goethe, Schleiermacher and others, had justice done to the singular purity and nobleness of his solitary life, and perhaps rather more

[1] The Bohn Translation dates his birth wrongly.

than justice done to the philosophic value of his unique and imposing doctrine.

The extent to which Cartesianism was the moulding influence on that doctrine is a point on which there has been much discussion. On the one hand, to Spinoza's devotees—Dutch and Jewish investigators—his work appears not only one of the most remarkable, but the most remarkable achievement of the human mind. To them his philosophy is the crowning result of philosophic thought never to be surpassed. Their ecstatic admiration would not allow that the accident of Descartes' existence could have influenced him very greatly, and that he merely received the torch and handed it on to others. As if to atone for their forefathers' ill-treatment of him, many Jews within the last twenty years are proud to claim the great thinker as one of themselves. Sir F. Pollock, on the other hand, and Kuno Fischer exaggerate the influence of Descartes, the former asserting, not without reason, that the view which minimises it springs out of an insufficient study of Descartes' works in relation to those of Spinoza. The difference of view is due in part also to the different value attached to Spinoza's philosophy as a whole [1].

Dr. Joel and others [2] try to prove that Spinoza got his ideas not from Descartes but from his own people, especially from Maimonides and Crescas (fl. about 1400).

Spinoza often mentions Maimonides, but not in the *Ethica*. Maimonides was the greatest Jewish thinker of the Middle

---

[1] The controversy may be followed best in Professor Sorley's excellent article 'Jewish Mediaeval Philosophy and Spinoza,' *Mind*, 1880.

[2] Cf. Professor K. Pearson's article, 'Maimonides and Spinoza,' *Mind*, vi.

Ages. He did for the Jewish faith what was done by Arabian philosophers for Mohammedanism, and by Schoolmen like Aquinas for Christianity. Arabian, Jewish, and Christian thinkers were guided by the same principle, namely, that of rationalising religion, of harmonising it with philosophy. We do find traces of Jewish habits of thought in Spinoza, but no ground for asserting that there is in him any idea which, being a Jew, he could not have got without Maimonides.

Crescas headed the reaction against Maimonides, as William of Ockham did against Aquinas, holding that faith could not be rationalised, could not be expressed in terms of philosophy, but was there to be accepted intact. He denied the freedom of human will, affirming the necessity of human action. So did Spinoza, more than any one, unless we except Hobbes. But it is a long step to say that he got this from Crescas. I do not, I say, find anything in Spinoza which cannot be expressed by the fact that all three were Jews.

Spinoza was an original thinker if ever there was one, but he would not have thought as he did if Descartes had not thought before him. I do not deny the Jewish influence generally, but I hold that Spinoza is a logical development of Descartes.

Again, I can say no more for the alleged influence on Spinoza of Giordano Bruno[1]; there is no real ground for connecting them. But I do believe that Spinoza was far better informed in Christian Scholastic philosophy than is supposed. Spinoza's was no such wild-flower intellect. Modern philosophy, remember, was fighting its way into existence, and Scholastic philosophy, in resisting it, was

[1] Cf. Erdmann, II, § 272, 1.

itself vigorously issuing new text-books. Do not assume that Scholasticism had perished by 1700; it then held all the Universities; all the Catholic Universities it still holds, and it has in our day experienced a vigorous effective revival.

Spinoza certainly took up the problems that Descartes had left, and solved them to all intents and purposes in Cartesian terms, as he would not have done unless Descartes' results and methods had been there. If however Spinoza ever was a Cartesian, he consciously broke away from Descartes and made his fame thereby. His first work which appeared in 1663, on Descartes' *Principia* geometrically expounded, gave evidence at once of his dependence and his independence. But how far he was a Cartesian is best seen in the work of Arnauld, Geulincx, and Malebranche, who, professing themselves disciples of Descartes, and shrinking in horror from Spinoza's views, were hardly able to avoid coming to his conclusions. Spinoza ended by opposing Descartes, but he did so under Cartesian influence.

The relation of Spinoza to Descartes, as far as concerns the special difficulties arising from the dualism of Thought and Extension, has been already indicated. The difficulty as between God and the World Spinoza gets rid of by giving up the world—by denying to it any *substantial* character of its own, by making it, in all its variety, a mere mode of the Divine Existence, to which it never can assume an attitude of opposition. The difficulty as between Mind and Body he gets rid of by denying the substantial character of both, and allowing them only a modal opposition:— Mind is not Body, an Idea is not an Extended thing; they are opposed so as that the one never can be the other; but they are not only opposed, for they are united and held together in their mutual opposition, being only modes—

passing modes—of the one great Substance underlying them and all. Such opposition thus overcome means mutual correspondence, and here Spinoza must be called Occasionalist—Occasionalist at least as to the bond between the mental mode and the bodily mode, if not as to the bond between links in the mental chain and between links in the bodily chain. But it is not the Occasionalism of Geulincx and Malebranche with the problem—how do diverse substances come to be related?—and with the solution of a personal Deity intervening. The correspondence for Spinoza is Law of Nature, and *his* problem is—Given one substance, whence comes all the variety in Nature?

Such is the special relation between Descartes and Spinoza, but this far from exhausts the connexion between the two, as might be said of Descartes and Geulincx or Malebranche. Spinoza is so much the greater figure than either of them that the connexion is more worthy of being established. And he so distinctly by his originality stands between the next great figure, Leibniz, and Descartes, that his own dependence upon the inaugurator of modern speculation requires to be more fully set forth.

I find it in three particulars:—(1) in the prominence given to the notion of Substance, (2) in the idea of mathematical method to be applied to philosophy, and (3) in the exclusion of Final Causes from human science. All three particulars are characteristic elements of Descartes' thought. In Spinoza's they are derived from Descartes; only they are so transformed by the original power of the man that they come to be more strictly characteristic of his own.

(1) Whoso places this notion of Substance in the front of his thought stamps its character once and finally. He is a speculative Dogmatist. He speculates upon and with

the knowledge he has, instead of making it his first object, with Locke and others of the psychological school, to inquire how he came by that knowledge. He dogmatises upon things within and beyond experience with a perfect confidence in the ability of the human mind, instead of making it his first object, with Kant and the Critical school, and with the psychological school again, to inquire into the limits and the scope of the mind's power. Such a speculative Dogmatist was Descartes. But Spinoza was doubly so. Descartes, though he quickly enough dogmatised, had at least his preliminary doubt. Spinoza had none. Descartes, though he speculated freely enough as to the hidden nature of things, at least tried to recognise what he found, and fell into his inconsistencies because he would labour to reconcile undoubted facts and natural experience with his speculation. Spinoza speculated with a perfect disregard of natural experience, and, because he would not stoop to any such accommodation, *appears* less inconsistent with himself.

The *pantheistic* element in Descartes' thought, viz. the tendency to conceive the notion of substance in the truest sense as being only One, and the *naturalistic* element, viz. the tendency to conceive the One Substance or God as Order of Nature, were brought together and set in the front of Spinoza's thought as the mother-idea of it all. For this his thought must, as I have said, be regarded as the necessary logical development of the Cartesian system, as the last word that can and must be said about the universe upon Cartesian principles. And the rigid manner of the development, the spirit of philosophic calm in which that last word is uttered, are such—are, in spite of all criticism, which touches the conception far more than the execution, such—that Spinoza's philosophy remains as yet, and is likely to remain, the very type of a Naturalistic Pantheism.

Spinoza also inherits from Descartes the notions of 'attribute' and 'mode.'

Now, for Spinoza, mode gets into a direct relation with substance, as it does not for Descartes. For the latter modes are not things, while for the former they are the only explanation of *res particulares*, being the way in which the one substance expresses itself. Mode in Descartes is attribute specialised in a certain way, and is understood quite apart from the question of substantiality. That he had settled at the beginning by positing infinite substance and finite substance. Spinoza could not quite so easily accept Descartes' compromise. The business of philosophy being to account for our experience, i.e. for particular things, and Spinoza having undertaken to do so by Monism, he had to eliminate from 'mode' the notion of substantiality. No less has he to account for 'attributes,' such as thought, extension, &c. How far he has consistently fitted both terms into his system is a much controverted point[1]. To me it seems that he is not without inconsistencies to answer for in his usage of the terms, going, in language at least, straight from substance to mode (cf. *Eth*. I. Def. iv. and Props. iv.[2] and vi. Proof), and yet no less referring modes to attributes (cf. I. Prop. xxv. Cor.) His inconsistencies show (i) that he had *not* quite made up his mind in this

[1] See especially Martineau's *Spinoza* and Kuno Fischer's and Erdmann's Histories of Philosophy on this point. The lecturer (in 1891) entered in detail into the controversy, but space prevents me from reproducing.—ED.

[2] Do not take Spinoza too strictly here in his use of 'substance' in the plural.

connexion, (ii) that he felt the difficulties entailed by holding on to Descartes while being determined to arrive at a different conclusion, (iii) that he felt the difficulties inherent in Substantialism—difficulties which, in becoming by a later age fully realised, have altered the position of philosophy concerning that which was the ultimate viciousness in the attitude of the age.

(2) The method of mathematics is not the only speculative method in philosophy, but it is a speculative method. A thinker may reject it, like Hegel for his dialectic method, and still be intensely speculative, but the thinker must also be intensely speculative who accepts it: for the use of it commits him to the assertion that resort to specific experience is as unnecessary in metaphysics as in mathematics, that the most general truth about the nature of all things is already as well ascertained, or as ascertainable and ready to be formulated and fit to be applied in new cases, as the most general truth about number and form. A bold assertion! It was however a very common assertion in the seventeenth century, and one that men might be excused for at least desiring to be able to make. The certainty of mathematical truth, which Schoolmen had concerned themselves so little about, and the uncertainty of philosophical truth, which Schoolmen had been working at for centuries, could not fail to appear in somewhat disagreeable contrast, and the contrast in turn to excite boundless hopes if the method that led to uncertainty and dispute might be changed for the method that ended in certitude and unanimity. That the contrast should particularly strike and excite a born mathematical genius like Descartes—the first great mathematician since the Arabians—was only natural. It led him to what we know and have seen:—

the method of science is one, and is to be drawn and generalised from mathematics; is deductive from certain and fixed principles; passes from causes to effects; displays a must-be of things; works so certainly from principles so large that the only difficulty is in selecting from among the 'infinity of possible effects' those that correspond with the actual things and facts of this poor universe. Descartes has all this, and it is not little; but his mathematic is implicit; he does not go farther—not even in his systematic work—to evolve the results from his principles in regular geometrical form (except when expressly challenged in the 'Objections'). That was left to Spinoza. Definitions, Axioms, Theorems, Lemmas, Corollaries—Spinoza adopts the whole machinery—adopts or tries to adopt, and believes he sustains the whole responsibility of it. Descartes' *practical* departure from mathematical method and the abrupt collapse of his project in the *Règles* (never, though he had plenty of time, resumed), are explicable from his very mathematical power, or at least from his tact or common sense; he saw that the thing could not in fact, or should not, be done. Spinoza was kept back from attempt and achievement by no such superiority of scientific ability. And as an inferior mathematician he was pedantic in his use of the method. Leibniz, the next great mathematician and philosopher after Descartes, found fault after fault in Spinoza.

Spinoza however was so thoroughly a Dogmatist that he could not but work by this method. Kant rightly discerned that the dogmatist cannot proceed in philosophy by any other method[1]. With him, as with the mathe-

---

[1] V. *Kritik of Pure Reason* (Max Müller's translation), pp. 610 633: 'On the Discipline of Pure Reason in the Sphere of Dogmatism.' Students were emphatically referred to this passage.—Ed.

matician, first notions are *given*, not *sought*. The essence of Dogmatism is to be prepared from the first with an equation between thought and reality. If the day comes when we do discern the riddle of the universe and there is nothing more to know, then the method of setting it forth will be the mathematical method of philosophy. But I venture to predict that its matter and conclusions will be very different from Spinoza's. For us, working where we now stand, I have nothing but the strongest disapproval of the use of mathematics in philosophy.

For consider:—how is it that in geometry we are able to proceed from fixed principles to propositions that are necessary? Because we are here dealing with matter that we make, control, constitute. But this does not make the method valid in regard to nature. If it is applicable and in so far as it is applicable to nature, it is because all our sensations are, more or less, ordered in space. If then we can make out anything with regard to space, we can apply it to nature generally.

We perceive space by activity put forth. We make space in the knowing of it. We know it in the making of it. If this is the proper explanation of the mathematical method, the only question to be asked is, are we in philosophy occupied in the same way? Philosophy is the ultimate interpretation of experience. Is experience something that we make in the way that we make space?

Now experience is not something that we simply receive. It is in a manner, as Kant taught, a construction of ours. Our thoughts about things are our mental activity functioning in various ways. But there is a difference. Activity is involved in thinking, and therefore in experience. But there is also an element in experience that is given. That element may be greater or less, but experience is in any case reproductive and representative. We have to wait for what comes to us before we can know. In metaphysic therefore, as in physical science, definitions are statements of results arrived at, and not principles proceeded from. Our metaphysical notions—cause, substance, &c.—continually change as mathematical notions do not. And our notions of substance have changed since Spinoza. Hence he has not, as he implies, solved the riddle of the universe for all time. He meant to be strict, honest, exact, but he attempts the impossible. His work is a model of what *can* and of what can*not* be done on these lines.

LECTURE XXVI.

ON CARTESIANISM (*continued*).

(3) From the mathematical method, adopted by Descartes and his followers in the peculiar scientific conditions of the time, the exclusion of so-called Final Causes—of Aims or Ends—necessarily followed. A Schoolman, more theologian than philosopher, may read all great things in the world according to some religious idea of a divine purpose, and in his ignorance of natural causes may pretend to a science of smaller things in vain general statements about the ends that things serve. A thinker like Aristotle, casting the first scientific glance over the multiplicity of nature, may less vainly eke out his explanation in such a way; or labouring to comprehend in magnificent, if premature abstraction the first principles of being, may credit nature with an immanent τέλος, or End, of which all motion and mutation is the slow accomplishment. A thinker like Kant, seeing nothing in the realm of nature but a vast complex of phenomena linked each to each by the iron chains of cause and effect forged within the mind, may look beyond to a region of supra-sensible noümena, and conceive it as a Realm of Ends to get free play for that power of self-determination in moral beings which he will not resign.

But in proportion as any thinker takes the mathematical analogy and follows it out consistently in the whole field of knowledge, or of assumption, he must submerge the teleological view. It is not as the means to any end that the three angles of a triangle are equal to two right angles; the triangle, we say, 'makes' them so (and makes them so with a causation which anybody might call universal and necessary), but no purpose is served, no aim thereby promoted. This Descartes did not fail to see, and the idea guided much of his scientific action, guiding it well in physics away from the emptiness of Scholastic explanation. Spinoza saw it, and the idea guided his every thought as it never guided the thought of mortal man before or since.

The point is so important, so specially significant, as to require a more particular handling. Descartes' rejection of final causes is but partial compared with Spinoza's. It lies to hand to connect this with his less rigid employment of the deductive (geometrical) method. The main idea of the method Descartes doubtless has, but, beginning his metaphysics with a datum of the mature consciousness, and evolving from it and with it whatever it will give, he cannot be said to apply the method with any strictness at the first stage of his speculation. This he does rather in his Physics only. With his metaphysical notion of Body or Matter as extended and nothing more, and his assumption that all mutation, real or phenomenal, is mechanical, he does then rigidly enough proceed to construct and explain from fixed principles. Now it is precisely at this stage that he makes exclusion of final causes[1], and the exclusion, while it constitutes his advance upon those who went before, struck a right note for those who came after him in the history of science. But while the exclusion is limited—for, as we know, it is not by him extended in any sense to the greater

[1] Read *Principia*, iii. §§ 1-3.

world of mind, every mind according to him being absolutely self-determinant, and thought not being bound by a law of cause and effect—it is at the same time put upon grounds that betray a manifest unsteadiness of vision. Not because final causes would be unwarrantably foisted in by the mind upon a scene of mere mechanical action and reaction (as even Kant who accepts them elsewhere declared), but only because it is too great presumption for a human mind to measure the universe by human needs, or try to fathom the purposes of the Deity, does Descartes enter his protest against a teleological physics. That is a view, no doubt, but not the view (still less favourable to final causes), that depends upon the adoption of a peculiar method in philosophy. If we will see the method strictly adopted, and with singleness of mind carried out to its last conclusion in the direction we are now considering, we must look beyond Descartes to Spinoza.

Spinoza clearly is held back by no mental preoccupation from following wheresoever his method of philosophical inquiry leads him. If God and Nature to him are one, and if Nature is best exhibited as a system in which from the core outwards everything is as it cannot but be, he will not, like a Schoolman, embark on the search for divine ends, or, like Descartes, draw back from the search only because it is too high for man[1]. Nor, like Descartes again, can he allow any *such* difference between Mind and Body as would require the assumption of a different scientific procedure. Mind and Body are for him perfectly distinct. Not Descartes with his two opposed substances could draw the dividing line more strictly and hold it more unfailingly than does Spinoza, with his opposed attributes of Thought and Extension, pre-

[1] Read *Ethica*, i. Appendix.

serving their opposition into the most transient mode of each. But, opposed as they are, they, at every stage, high and low, are in correspondence. No mode of Thought without its parallel mode of Extension; no fact of body unaccompanied by some mode of thought (*Eth.* iii. 2. Schol.); and where there are two chains, in which link answers to link, although they are two, the links of the one for itself hold as rigidly together as the links of the other, because each is a chain. Thoughts in nature being thus not less bound together and mutually conditioned amongst themselves than are things, the necessities of science are in each case alike. A body in motion moves another, and the law of the movement, not the end or object of it, is the physical science of the case. A thought begets a thought, and not any free initiative of a mind creating its own purpose should be assumed, but the law of the production is all that should be sought.

Now Descartes, where he negatives Final Causes, namely, in his physical science, puts forward Efficient Causes; and this constitutes the great merit of it. Everywhere indeed in his philosophy, metaphysical as well as physical, this notion of Cause, meaning Efficient Cause, stands forward; and to him it is greatly due that in modern times we have so far left behind that vague Aristotelian notion of Cause, covering the four principles of things:—Material, Formal, Efficient or Movent, and Final—as to have come to associate the notion exclusively with the Efficient principle; and this not only in all science, but even in philosophical discussions about Causation (where, as in Hume, Hamilton, &c., the question is as to there being any potency and *virtus*, or only mere antecedents of a certain kind, in the cause which is efficient). The notion of Efficient Cause, embodied in the *Ex nihilo*, &c., is what carries Descartes, at his metaphysical stage, over the otherwise impassable gulf fixed *by himself* between his self-consciousness and objective reality; and his whole physical philosophy consists in nothing else but the attempt to show that everything in nature results from mechanical interaction of bodies—bodies in their character of being extended, taking and giving amongst themselves the unchanging quantum of movement once communicated to them by the Creator. So that, notwithstanding his references to mathematical method and the deductive cast of his intellect, Descartes' philosophical explanation is seldom a mere manipulation and explication of notions and abstract principles assumed.

But such it ought to be, if the full responsibility of the method is accepted; and such Spinoza aims at being.

For, as to the first point, it should be remarked, beyond what has already been said, that Final Causes are not more excluded from mathematical truth than is the notion of Efficient Causation. When, to use the former example, the triangle is said to *make* its angles equal to two right angles, it makes them in any properly causative sense as little as it makes them for any end or purpose. Even those who recognise a necessity of connexion between cause and effect will not, if like Kant they are wise, confound it with necessity of implication. The equality of the angles to two right angles follows from triangular nature quite otherwise than it follows that a body if let go will fall to the ground. What is contained in a notion follows from the notion, and comes within the mind's ken in one way; a thing that is caused in nature by another thing follows upon this, and is apprehended by the mind as following, in another way. A system of philosophy, if conceived and worked out on mathematical principles, will deal in notional connexions, not in causal relations. But if this could ever be said of a philosophic system, it is to be said of Spinoza's.

Let me not be misunderstood. Spinoza speaks often enough of cause, and even has the phrase *causa efficiens;* but where he speaks of efficient cause:—'Deum omnium rerum esse causam efficientem' (*Eth.* I. 16)—it is made clear that the efficiency is only inclusion in the definition, conclusion from the definition and, immediately afterwards (I. 18), that the cause is *immanent* and in no sense *transient*; whilst in speaking of cause simply, he either, if it is of modes, means it in a sense not ultimate, or when the sense is ultimate, means precisely this implication of all in the idea of the one Substance.

For Spinoza is pre-eminently the demonstrative thinker. He believes, if ever man did, and far more than Descartes ever did, that he has grasped the inner secret of the universe and can lay bare in the orderly evolution of thought the meaning of all that is. The demonstration he himself supposes to rest upon a few truths perfectly self-evident— at least when he sets them forth, for no man before him had the same insight into them—and to be the most irrefragable, clear, and final exposition of the whole system of things. Another might say that the principles upon which the demonstration is supposed to rest are neither truths nor at all self-evident, but only a rash, though striking abstraction from experience, and that the demonstration itself halts and is insufficient, or at the best is eked out by sidelong glances at the actual. But demonstration, and strict demonstration, is nevertheless what Spinoza aims at and believes he has achieved.

Here then we touch the true difference between Descartes

and Spinoza, and can apprehend the speculative stride taken by the younger thinker. It is not only that where the one gets rid of final causes in physical science, and upon grounds that may be called theological, the other bans them utterly from the universe upon the ground of strict philosophical principle, but it is that whereas Descartes deduces and constructs with a principle of Efficient Causation, Spinoza rejects, or tends to reject, also the notion of Efficient Cause, and, with perfect consistency, resolves, or fain would resolve, everything upon a principle of Necessity of Implication.

A word finally on Spinoza's psychology and epistemology. The latter is a very remarkable doctrine and very closely interwoven with his psychology and his metaphysic of mind and body, but always with an explicit ethical object (*Eth.* II. Pref.) In Parts I and II of the *Ethica* he is laying the foundations and preparing the materials for his doctrine of how man may be ethically perfect.

Special note should be taken of the seventh proposition, Part II [1]—a metaphysical assertion on which all his psychological observation is based. It is the first explicit utterance of the later doctrine of Parallelism. This is now always purely phenomenal in assertion [2], serving the purposes of psychological science without prejudicing ultimate hypotheses, being held by Dualists no less than by Monists of to-day. The doctrine of the latter both in its phenomenal and metaphysical aspects has great affinity with that of Spinoza, but has been got at differently, viz. by induction. The common result has brought Spinoza into vogue, so much so that

---

[1] 'The order and connexion of ideas is the same as the order and connexion of things.'

[2] Thus:—'With every psychosis is concomitant a neurosis.' (*Elements of Psychology*, Lect. VI.)—ED.

younger students need to be reminded that it is only lately he has been seriously considered as a thinker. Spinoza starts as a dogmatic metaphysician, thinking that by his definition of substance he can account for mind and body as they appear. In the end he practically abandons his first position and writes as a Phenomenalist. Law of Nature replaces Substance. Phenomenalism has got *up* to where he came *down*. His dogmatic Substantialism is overlooked.

There was nothing new in Spinoza's Parallelism. Aristotle was a Parallelist, dogmatic also in his procedure. Descartes and the Occasionalists are so also. Leibniz in his Monadism was a Parallelist. My emphasis is due to the attitude of modern Parallelists, who write as if they were first in the field —even inventing the term Automatism—or at most connecting themselves with Descartes only. Everything modern on body and mind is in Spinoza *in principle*, and is also much more clearly thought out than it is by many, his detail being often remarkable, e. g. when dealing with Perception, Conception, Memory, &c. Hence Spinoza is in the front and will remain there.

No part of him should be more studied than the latter half of Part II giving his epistemology [1]. Nor should Part III be slurred over, with its psycho-physical doctrine, systematic beyond anything of the kind previously attempted. Note (i) in the definition of emotion how the subjective and the bodily side are both brought forward, and (ii) that the forty-eight definitions are, as in all natural science, statements of *results*. Note also (iii) the distinction between active emotions and passions, these being a measure, an indication of human bondage, i. e. of mind as limited, as confused in its

[1] Note especially Prop. XL. Note II, containing his expression of thorough-going Realism (Platonic) and of Nominalism.

representations (Props. 58, 59). By connecting 'affect' and self-consciousness with activity[1], he prepares the way for his solution of the ethical question in Part V, where he transforms the notion of knowledge into emotion. Before our knowledge is effective for purposes of life it must be 'touched with emotion.' Morality for Spinoza is knowledge emotionally transformed. Thus while he begins as a bare formalist, he ends by being a rapt mystic. Through the stiff crust of his form he palpitates with intense emotion if not with passion.

Leibniz.

In such a system as Spinoza's there was so much to shock the prevailing ideas and feelings of men, that those who were least opposed to the philosophic method of it were driven by its results to seek other principles for their speculation; and if Spinoza's principles could be shown as following from Descartes', then other principles than Descartes'. With that, however, there was an end to the direct Cartesian influence, an end to the Cartesian school. Though the next thinker might represent the same general direction of thought, though he certainly was stirred up to think by the Cartesian ideas, the conditions had become so much changed that we have in him a new philosophical era. This era is associated with the name of Leibniz.

To understand all that went to the making of Leibniz's

---

[1] The emotions are shown by Spinoza (III. Props. 59, 57 and 6) as making for self-conservation. In the more general statement (Prop. 6) he gives things an individuality, a *vis* of their own, which is not as if they were mere shadowy 'modes.' This hangs together with his theory of *motus et quies* (II. 13, Axioms), which is interesting as coming between Descartes' Extension and the modern dynamic conception of things.

thought is no easy matter. He was a man that united in himself so much, in fact both ancient and Scholastic thought, while he stood in conscious opposition to the thought both of Bacon and Locke. Here I am mainly concerned with his relation to Spinoza and Descartes.

Leibniz's doctrine of substance was expounded in conscious opposition to Spinoza's, but was not arrived at in mere immediate revulsion from the latter, but as if Leibniz had had to pass through the *stage* of Spinoza's doctrine, in support or in opposition, before he could arrive at his own view. Rather, of himself Leibniz was able to see that Descartes' philosophy did indeed lead to conclusions such as those that Spinoza rested in[1], and without Spinoza was moved to reject them and set up new principles instead. But doubtless he was confirmed in his course as he came to know Spinoza's works.

Like both Descartes and Spinoza a speculative dogmatist, like both he put forward as the central idea of his philosophy a conception of substance, but a conception different from either of theirs. Struck out in ultimate revulsion from Spinoza's unity of substance, it was other than that conception of Descartes in which there lay wrapt up Spinoza's. Leibniz saw that the individual, or particular substance— sacrificed wholly by Spinoza, or emerging at the end of his system in spite of his principles—that individual substances, for that is the point, must on philosophical or other grounds be conceded; and that, for this, substance must be con-

---

[1] Cf. *Théodicée*, Pt. III. 'Qu'on prenne garde qu'en confondant les substances avec les accidents en ôtant l'action aux substances créées on ne tombe dans le spinosisme, qui est un cartésianisme outré. Ce qui n'agit point ne mérite point le nom de substance,' &c. *Œuvres*, ed. Paul Janet, t. i, p. 393.

ceived so as not, with Descartes, to render particular substances in the last resort impossible. The new philosophical era, then, is Individualistic, instead of Pantheistic.

Leibniz is no less dogmatic than Descartes and Spinoza in *assuming* thought to be fully representative of reality. But he went beyond Descartes' Dualism and Spinoza's Monism in his Monadology, positing a multiplex gradation of substances, each a monad simple, unextended, with active force for its essence. He starts however in his philosophy, first and last, from the fact of Body. The explanation of this, or what is required for its explanation, leads him on to all the rest[1]. More, he was, among *metaphysicians*, the first who makes an approach to comprehension of the vast complexity of nature. But Body, he held, must be thought as Force. And Force, as an indivisible and so immaterial, simple, original being, must be thought as Substance. Force-substance is ever active, and, being the source of its own activity, is a self-active being, individual or monad. But with self-action goes self-distinction—absolute difference—and thus there is an absolute multiplicity of monads. The essence of an individual consists in self-formed peculiarity, which could not be except in its being distinguished from other peculiar beings.

Every monad, then, is a singular substance, an individual force, and therefore at once limited and independent, passive force and active force. That is to say, all substances save one are not, with Leibniz, as with Descartes and the Occasionalists,

---

[1] Cf. e.g. 'Le corps est un agrégé de substances, et ce n'est pas une substance à proprement parler. Il faut, par conséquent, que partout dans le corps il se trouve des substances indivisibles.' Lettre à Arnauld (1690). 'Et il faut, qu'il y ait des substances simples, puisqu'il y a des composées.' *Monadol.* § 2 (1714).

devoid of true independence, powerless, passive: they are independent, active, instinct with power. They are not, in their dependence, either merely extended or merely thinking: their independence, one and all, consists in their being each a Force—each a force for itself, one among many, each not another, simple and indivisible, a monad.

How should there not be substances many, and each indivisible, when there are substances composite like bodies? How should the character of substance not consist in being Force, when bodies are not lifeless extension, but quivering with inherent energies, and when minds are forces likewise? Passive force is the principle of matter, active force the principle of form. Passive force manifests itself as body, active force manifests itself as soul. But soul and body (Form and Matter) are conceived to be the two forces making the nature of every body. Every monad is therefore an animated body. Every body is a mechanical, and every soul a living, being; and thus every animated body is a living machine. In the machine there are only motive or mechanical forces; the vital powers are formative and work towards an end. Every living machine is therefore a body moved according to ends, or a system of purposive motions.

Since then bodies work mechanically according to Efficient Causation, and souls work vitally according to Final Causation, Leibniz, in the conception of the monad, unites the two principles of Causality and Teleology which had divided all previous systems. For final causes are related to efficient causes as purposive to mechanical force, as life to machine (mechanism), as soul to body, soul and body being not different beings but the two primordial forces of every monad. Now as soul and body make a natural unity or individual, there are not two distinct worlds of souls and bodies, but one universe, and for the explanation of that universe the teleological and mechanical principles must be combined. But they are not for Leibniz combined as in Spinoza's *ordo idearum idem est ac ordo rerum*, which rested upon an assumption of causality as being the same in thought and in extension, and which reduced the difference of these in the unity of substance. Soul proceeds teleologically only, body mechanically only; but soul, for its own ends, also infolds body.

Soul and body, then, though both original 'moments' in the monad, are not on equal footing: they remain as active and passive force: they are as end and means. Unlike works of human art, however, there is in them no separation between end and means[1].

This conception of force is in harmony with the increase of physical knowledge at the end of the century. Leibniz as much as Newton had got an idea of matter as not barely extended, with so much movement put into it, as Descartes had said. He saw the necessity of transforming the concept of matter from the philosophical point of view just when Newton was seeing that it was necessary to do so from the point of view of positive science.

How an aggregate of simple unextended substances becomes phenomenally extended, Leibniz explains from the confused perception of the percipient monad or mind. While human minds are self-active monads, bodies are each a multiplicity of monads in reality, only *appearing* as continuous and extended to the mind through the

[1] 'Les machines de la nature, c'est-à-dire les corps vivants, sont encore machines dans leurs moindres parties jusqu'à l'infini.' *Monadol.* § 64.

confusion of sense. *All* living monads have inner states, which in some are developed as perceptions, representations, but these are of different degrees of clearness in different monads. Perceptions are *clear* when their objects are marked off from others; *distinct*, when the parts of the objects can be distinguished; *adequate*, when this distinctness extends to the absolutely simple elements of the objects. Human soul differs, for example, from animal soul not only in dominating over a body more highly organised, but also, and this more, in having distinct perceptions, distinguishable from one another and from the mind itself; in fact, in having reflective consciousness, and being to itself what the other monads are to the eye that observes them. By this reflective activity the individual becomes Person, Self, Ego; the creature becomes a member of the moral world; soul becomes mind; representation or perception becomes apperception, thought, knowledge; appetite becomes will.

There is however no cleft between perception in animals and in men.

The perceptions of the monad in part clear are in all the rest confused. Now 'action,' Leibniz said in the *Monadologie*, 'is ascribed to the monad in as far as it has distinct perceptions, and passion in as far as it has confused perceptions' (§ 49). Thus for Leibniz the unconscious or sub-conscious, infinitely small or obscure perceptions out of which consciousness arises, establish a harmony between the material and the moral world—the kingdom 'of Nature' and that 'of Grace'—for by conceiving monads as perceptive forces the elements of the material world are spiritualised; and on the other hand by its obscure perceptions the mind is connected with the material world. Thus the two are continuous.

This obscure side of the soul, moreover (like the passive moment in the human soul-monad), is the ground of all individuality—what Leibniz calls the 'je ne sçais quoi'—whereby each is naturally determined to a special line.

The monad by virtue of its perceptive power is microcosm [1], but each monad, as individual, reflects the universe from its individual point of view, most clearly those parts in closest relation with it. Being thus limited, its representation of the All is necessarily confused. All things being microcosms, there follow three laws making the order of the universe:—the laws of Analogy, of Continuity, of Harmony. Are all beings microcosms or representations of the same universe, they must be analogous. Are they analogous, they must also be different, gradually different, forming an ascending series of beings. Is there an endless plenum of microcosms, there must be a difference at an infinite number of stages; the gradual differences must be infinitely small, and the gradation of things be perfect or continuous.

And thus the monads must form a steady succession of homogeneous substances; they must therefore exhibit the greatest variety amid the greatest uniformity, and so form a harmonious world-order;—God, the original monad, with perfectly adequate perceptions, and all other monads as effulgurations of his nature. Amongst such we distinguish (*a*) spirits or thinking monads, like men, able to have clear and distinct perceptions, some of them even adequate, and to have consciousness of self and of God; (*b*) animals, or monads having sense and memory; (*c*) plants and minerals, sleeping monads with unconscious perceptions, these being

---

[1] 'Perceptio nihil aliud . . . quam multorum in uno expressio' (Ep. 2 ad De Bosses); and again :—'Perceptio nihil aliud est quam illa ipsa repraesentatio variationis externae in interna.'

vital forces in plants. To the human mind the order of monads appears in sense as the order of things in time and space.

The flow of perceptions *in* each monad depends upon an internal immanent causality; monads, in Leibniz's phrase, having no windows at which to take in from without. The change in the relations of monads, on the other hand, their movement, junction and separation, rest on merely mechanical causality. Between this flow of perceptions or internal states and these movements there subsists a pre-established harmony, pre-established by God. In man, body and soul correspond as two clocks of the same rate of speed, set together. This system of pre-established harmony, referring all things ultimately to the Deity, requires a moral explanation of the world from God as its source. But then God also must be justified out of the order of things; hence Leibniz's choice of the word Theodicy, a word he first used in a letter to Magliabecchi in 1697.

In conclusion we may briefly summarise the position of Leibniz in relation to other thinkers, ancient and modern. Agreeing with Spinoza and Descartes that the nature of things is to be expressed by a conception of substance, he is against Spinoza in conceiving substance as self-active force, stirring not in a single being, but in an endless number of substances; and against Descartes in conceiving substance as self-active force, not as in two kinds of substance, but alike in all things. Thus as against them *both*, he is for *homogeneous* atoms with the Atomists. But he takes his atoms, against Atomists ancient and modern, not as bodies, but as forces, as eternal forms, 'substantial forms.' Here he agrees with the Schoolmen and the Greeks, especially with Plato. Nevertheless he is against Plato and with Aristotle in conceiving his forms not as ideal, general types, but as natural forces, independent individuals, each an 'entelechy.'

If we call upon fancy for help to get the fitting schemata to underlie the purely logical complex, and think that in the whole world there is nothing else but merely simple, constant, unchangeable, substantial, subjective, force-exerting, self-acting, representative entelechies or monads, with varying intensity of activity—these numberless entelechies or monads placed in pre-established harmony with each other by a Monad of monads, so that every monad, in spite of its inability to be really influenced by the others, yet constantly represents to itself with more or less distinctness the activities of all other monads and harmonises with this to one common end:—we shall truly conceive the universe according to Leibniz.

LECTURE XXVII.

ON KANT'S CRITICAL PHILOSOPHY [1].

READING.—*The Kritik of Pure Reason* (transl. by Max Müller or by J. P. Mahaffy), and *The Prolegomena* (transl. by J. P. Mahaffy). London: Macmillan.

I. *Kant's Importance in the Present State of English Thought.*

KANT thought more deeply than any man in his generation —the last of the eighteenth century—and for a time reigned supreme over the intellect of his own country, so that there all thinking in the following generation was coloured by, and even had shape from, that which his had been.

The like has not seldom happened in the history of human thought. Is then our interest in the nature of his opinions merely historic? There are great philosophic names, later as well as earlier, of whom that would have to be said, but it cannot be said of Kant. His is a power that has survived, or, if it ever died, it has had its resurrection. That it lives and works is manifest whether we look abroad, or watch what is stirring in our midst at home. In Germany, all through the great period of scientific work which has

---

[1] Selected from a course of four lectures delivered at the Royal Institution, January, February, 1874.

supervened on that time of speculative fever in the early years of this century, unparalleled in the history of any age or country, nothing is more remarkable than the sway of Kantian ideas over the minds of the true leaders from Johannes Müller to Helmholtz. It is not that such men have been in any sense professed followers of the philosopher —Helmholtz especially, in those excursions into the philosophical region by which he has signalised himself among men of science, as often as not crosses swords with the great thinker who himself was a man of science—but they have seen and avowed that here was one whose thought could grasp the principles of scientific inquiry and even forecast some of its issues. Such efforts too as those later years have brought forth to think out a philosophic conception of things in the light of new positive knowledge have borne a reference to the sober work of Kant, with relatively little regard to the more daring pretensions of his philosophical successors. Earlier thinkers are allowed importance according as they lead up to him, and he—hardly any other—is held to have found a sure footing among shifting sands.

In France—to speak of France with a single word in passing—the influence of Cousin after long wavering came at least to be exerted in favour of a doctrine which is only a modification of Kant's, while a thinker so different as Comte also became in time not insensible to his power. And at the present day a school of active thinkers is firmly organised who pay their first allegiance to the founder of Critical Philosophy.

In our own country an interest in Kant is one of the most striking features of the philosophical movement now in full course. How this has come to be a few indications must suffice. As early as 1794 a young German, Nitsch by name, began to lecture in London upon the new system of thought then at the height of its repute in the land of its origin, and he seems to have found for a time not a few hearers. Before the end of the century also more than one statement appeared in print of the main principles of Kant's philosophy, and some of his minor works even were translated. Small, however, must have been the impression made when young Thomas Brown, himself destined to do some work in philosophy, could have the face to draw entirely from a French exposition the matter for his boyish ridicule expended on the great thinker in the second number of the *Edinburgh Review*. Not mirth but helpless bewilderment was begotten in the mind of Dugald Stewart, the philosophical light of the day, when a little later he tried to gain a notion from one quarter or another of the new portent in the sphere of thought. It was only outside the professional circle that any real knowledge of Kant could then be found. Among the pupils of Nitsch was one, Thomas Wirgman by name, who spent years in the study of Kant at the original sources, and then laboured by every device of exposition to unfold the pure doctrine to his countrymen. In Wilkes's *Encyclopaedia Londinensis*—one of the many universal repositories of knowledge provided for that age—there appeared in the years from 1813 to 1823 some very long articles by Wirgman, which left unexplored little of all Kant's work that has even yet become known to English readers. The ardent man as good as translated whole works of the master whom he worshipped, distilled the whole Critical Philosophy into short sayings, set it out in parti-coloured diagrams, defended it often with telling point, taught it and made it quite plain (so he avers) even to his boys. It was all in vain. Oblivion covered him and his labours, and it was left for others of greater name to bring forward Kant far less thoroughly to a later and more open-minded generation. Sir William Hamilton did something, and his follower Dr. Mansel did something more. Dr. Whewell also laid hold of some of Kant's conceptions and turned them to good account in the interpretation of the historic growth of the sciences. Gradually, by various channels, certain main principles and results of the system became familiar to the English mind, and began to challenge the attention of the inquirers working on steadily in the old English vein of positive psychological research. Kant's chief work, the *Kritik of Pure Reason*, and the greater part of his ethical writings meanwhile had found translators; and now the last few years have seen the efforts of a knot of workers in Trinity College, Dublin, to expound the Kantian doctrine in a coherent form and set it over in opposition to the latest developments of home-grown thought. The efforts of these workers, chief among them Mr. Mahaffy, are worthy of all praise, despite some traces of a disposition to assume that now for the first time anywhere Kant has got his chance of true interpretation. However that may be, Mr. Mahaffy is laying English readers under a permanent debt of gratitude. There will never, I fear, be any acknowledgement of poor Wirgman's due.

Now there is one reason, or rather there are two reasons, easily understood, for the importance of Kant at the present time—for his unique importance in comparison with any of the thinkers, earlier or later, who are commonly classed with him as speculative philosophers. Kant is not a speculative philosopher, however it may be common to class him; and he is a philosopher who, whatever the province he claimed for philosophy, left, nay vindicated, to the positive sciences a domain of their own, whence they cannot be dislodged.

Supposing him at the same time a thinker of unsurpassed reach and power, nothing else seems wanted to explain his pre-eminence in an age devoted above all to the pursuit of scientific inquiry.

There were philosophers before Kant who took up that attitude towards the sciences—English philosophers chiefly, with Bacon as their forerunner. Locke, the first who made systematic inquiry as to the possibilities and limits of human knowledge, tracking it from its sources, found, as his main result, a justification of the mode of research then being practised by one whom he calls 'the incomparable Mr. Newton.' Berkeley was not an idealist who would hear nothing of experimental investigation of nature: he understood and approved of it thoroughly in principle, however much he wished the common scientific conception of nature to be supplemented by a philosophic view. Nor was Hume such a sceptic that he derided—he rather lauded and spurred on to—positive inquiry on the basis of experience. By the side of these, however, there were in Europe, from about the middle of the seventeenth century, or a little earlier, thinkers of a different cast; whose philosophy was no sober inquiry into the conditions of human knowledge joined to the practice or recommendation of experimental research, but a succession of bold attempts to reason out the All— modern only in the conception that external nature, instead of being shut out of view, as in the thought of the Middle Age, was brought expressly and even predominantly within the sweep of the speculative effort. Nor is any abatement to be made from this description because Descartes, the first of these thinkers, and Leibniz, his intellectual peer, did much to perfect the mathematical instruments necessary for carrying farther the scientific investigation of nature. They neither practised nor enjoined—at least not consistently—the method of inquiry common to Galileo and Newton. In their view the various positive sciences, beginning to rear their heads by the side of philosophy, had no legitimate standing. There was nothing to be known that could not be rationally evolved from within the mind, or what could not thus be reasoned out was of no importance. Not indeed that this was expressly declared, but the speculative philosophers worked on as if it were so. Facts of experience were made no subject of systematic concern, and drew notice only when they seemed, on the whole rather unexpectedly than otherwise, to lend a kind of confirmation to the grand theory.

But if the three last centuries are a new intellectual era in the history of the human mind, because philosophy has reverted—and not least through the efforts of these thinkers —to its original and proper function of carrying disinterested inquiry, high and low, near and far, to the uttermost limit of human conceiving, they are a new era not less in that, in the way of positive science, inquiry has started from the solid ground of experience, and, however free its flight, has always come back again to rest upon the solid ground. The natural sciences have grown up, and are indefinitely growing, as a legitimate and fruitful system of search into the different aspects or departments of nature—proceeding upon experience and having no higher object than to explain and control experience. Thereby is altered the position of philosophy. Though philosophy may have continued to be the rational guide and director of human conduct, and may claim to retain hold upon fields where positive inquiry has not been able to gain a footing, it has to reckon with rivals upon what was once an undisputed part of its domain. The rivals have established themselves on their chosen ground by accomplishing what philosophy tried but failed to accomplish there, and, so far as that ground is concerned, the changed position of philosophy is that it retains the function only of understanding and prescribing the general limits of what the sciences may there attempt. This was what the English thinkers saw and kept always in view in their philosophy, each in his own way. It was what Descartes and the other speculative philosophers did not see or would not allow. As we judge now, the English thinkers better understood the task which their age required of them. Kant likewise understood it, and thus is for ever to be distinguished from the school or schools of speculative metaphysicians. He is one of those philosophical inquirers who make no pretence of stemming the resistless tide of scientific research—whose thought is rather bent towards guiding it into effective channels.

Regarded as a mental philosopher, however, there is a side of Kant on which he holds with the Rationalists (as they may be called), and takes ground against the English thinkers; whence his own claim, and also his repute, to have united the different streams of thought that were before him in a doctrine embodying all the truth of either. The English thinkers sought to explain all knowledge as developed out of particular experiences, and it was from this point of view that they could so easily make allowance for natural science by the side of their philosophy; this being but an application to the general question of human knowledge of the same habit of thought or method of inquiry exercised in the upcoming sciences. Kant on the other hand denied that knowledge, as actually had, could ever be developed from such experiences as the English inquirers adduced, and made it a great part of all his philosophic task to explain from the native constitution of the mind how experience, truly so to be called, could come to pass. Nor can it be doubted that in the execution of that task he displayed a depth of insight and width of intellectual grasp never before shown; so that, man for man, he must be pronounced a far greater thinker than any of his English predecessors. It only does not therefore follow that he was on the right track, and they were on the wrong. There have been thinkers hardly inferior to himself, upon some lines perhaps superior, who were on a wrong track, when he was on the right. A cause is after all something greater than any of its upholders—greater, that is, than their particular conceptions of it. It is so in the sciences, which take to themselves the best results that all workers bring, and often are advanced by inferior men when greater ones have strayed. One thing at least is certain, that Kant, in as far as he sided with the Rationalists, claimed a finality for his philosophical position which did exclude the notion of farther inquiry as touching that. And in view of the course of human thought in modern days, before or since Kant, that is a claim that must be regarded with some suspicion.

For it is possible to look upon the course of modern thought as one long struggle waged between the rival principles of inquiry, for which there are no more expressive names than Reason and Experience—a struggle in which the cause of Experience evidently makes way, though Reason does not retire except to renew the encounter from fresh positions, and Experience does not advance except by multiplying its forces and ever reorganising them in face of the adversary. As regards the investigation of nature we have already remarked that science, instead of reasoning out from within how things could or should be, as of old, now seeks to interpret the universe simply as found—its parts in the light of one another. But it should be added that positive investigation, in advancing to occupy ever new fields, has not thus broadened its scope without also acquiring depth. There has been forced upon it the necessity of satisfying, as far as may be, that instinct of coherent vision which prompted the earlier speculative efforts; and the word Experience to a scientific mind has come to have a significance which it needs an education to understand. Similar is the result, or tendency, visible in the progress of the attempt to account for the fact or facts of human knowledge. That is the central question which philosophy at all times has had to consider, and it is the question which modern philosophy, as differing from the sciences, claims specially for its own. It is so expressly in Locke and in Kant; it is so implicitly in the other thinkers who disregard or disavow the restriction. In Descartes' theory of knowledge speculative Reason has the form of pure intellectualism; to him sense-experience is sheer and incurable delusion, while truth and certainty appertain only to knowledge that is supposed born with or innate to the mind. It is a naïve conception, and facing it, in like manner, Experience stands at first in the form of the crude sensationalism of Hobbes—crude and hardly making pretence to afford a full explanation. Comes Locke, however, with his systematic inquiry into the origin and limits of knowledge, and the philosophical standard of Experience is definitively raised: it is proclaimed that all knowledge originally comes by the way of experience in the individual, and that by a reference to the sources of psychological experience the import of aught claiming to be knowledge must be judged. On the other side, Leibniz abandons the Cartesian position, and it is with a very much deeper conception of knowledge as the development of potentialities lying in mind, or, again, as the interpretation of experience according to native mental predispositions, that he sallies forth by way of Reason to explain the All. Confidently his disciples, Wolff the chief, build up a huge dogmatic system out of his large ideas; the while Berkeley and Hume push farther along the line of positive inquiry opened by Locke, and find a derivation in psychological experience for much reckoned hitherto simple in consciousness. At the same time there is in both, as compared with Locke, a deepened sense of the limitation put upon knowledge by experience, whatever different expression it has in each; Berkeley rejoicing to be able thus to annihilate the bugbear of unintelligent matter with all its soul-debasing influences, while Hume finds his pleasure in calmly pricking the bubbles blown by the vanity of human reason.

What neither seriously attempts beyond Locke is to find a full and systematic explanation of human knowledge and science as existing in fact. This is the task reserved for Kant. As little disposed as they to make light of experience, and more than they concerned to justify the standing of modern science, he is with them the sworn foe of metaphysical speculation. No innate ideas, ousting experience, as for Descartes—no predeterminations to think, making experience superfluous, as for Leibniz—can for him explain the facts of real objective knowledge. But neither can he accept the position of the English Experientialists, working without system where they are in the right vein, and without discernment of the true issues to be met. Hence his new manner of inquiry, named Critical, into the foundations of human knowledge, resulting in the detection of a variety of rational elements or conditions to be necessarily assumed as prior to experience, and with the complement of experience—by no means without experience—making real knowledge possible.

It looks like the reconciliation of all differences which it is meant for. But is there an end of conflict—Reason satisfied with such a justification or excuse for its old pretensions, Experience contented with this frank and decisive recognition of its claim to be considered? By no means. After Kant, in Germany speculation returns to the onset with a vehemence never known before, and in the end sinks exhausted rather than is overcome. In England the cause of Experience finds new upholders, who bend their energies in good earnest to the development of a theory of scientific evidence, also to the pursuit of psychological research as the only positive foundation for a philosophy—a philosophy not to be thought of as other than progressive while psychology in relation with the sciences generally makes progress. And in such a sense, the principle of Experience, more or less profoundly conceived, does in fact at the present time dominate the field of philosophic thought, not here only but also in the land of Kant.

Will it continue dominant? And what then of Kant? Experientialism, amongst ourselves, has made its last great advance with so little reference to the import of Kant's doctrine as a whole, that its real conflict, where it is at variance with that, may be said to be still to come. Perhaps it is not altogether a matter of regret that the English philosophical inquirers of this century—I exclude those of the younger generation now rising up—have not gone to school, as they might have done, under Kant. Working upon the line of the old tradition of English thought, they have done their best with their own principle of inquiry, and the result is there to be judged. Nor is it a result, in one or other of the present or newly-departed leaders on the field of thought, to be lightly spoken of. In logical theory and psychological science it is not to be denied that English inquirers of the last two generations have made signal progress: the fame of their work is spread abroad. Addressing themselves, without special regard to Kant, to the questions concerning human knowledge which the philosopher has to consider, they have sought an experiential solution of difficulties which made him desert their position, after he had been in it. Their solution has found a large measure of acceptance, falling in as it does with the general scientific tendency of the time, and Kant's solution of such questions, as, for instance, the necessary character of mathematical truth, physical causation and the like, has been set aside, when not neglected. But nothing strikes the attentive reader of Kant more than his anticipation, already then, of the kind of solution which Experientialism would give, and has in fact given. One sees that he did not forsake the experiential position without a very hard struggle to remain there, and that he did forsake it only because of the impossibility, as he ultimately deemed, of explaining from it the actual facts of human knowledge. Now that he did right to abandon it, I do not say; the progress of inquiry since then has done much to justify the faith of those who have clung to the position. But we may be sure they were no common difficulties that urged him to enter upon the thorny path of his critical inquiry: and the full force of these difficulties has still to be apprehended within the English school. Nay, I venture to think that until the dominant Experientialism, even as transformed in the system of Mr. Spencer, has come face to face with Kant's doctrine, not at this point or at that, but at all points, and has stood the encounter, it has not secured its future. Kant's Critical Philosophy, if it did nothing else, raised deeper, yet at the same time more determinate, questions than any philosophy before, and though his own way of answer be not final, the questions abide. It concerns English thought at the present day to mark them well, and that is the reason of Kant's special importance now.

LECTURE XXVIII.

ON KANT'S CRITICAL PHILOSOPHY (*continued*).

II. *General View of the* Kritik *and the* Prolegomena.

THE *Kritik of Pure Reason*, in the shape that it finally received from Kant, dates from the year 1787. It first saw the light in 1781, after those eleven years of close and sustained thinking that supervened in his life upon the long period during which he slowly grasped the issues of other men's thoughts, and came at last to conceive the idea of an inquiry to be driven down deep beneath them all. The second edition of the *Kritik*, appearing in 1787, was considerably changed from the first—changed in the expression, Kant himself declares, at important points to make his thoughts clearer; changed in the conception, others declare, to make it less abhorrent to the prejudices of the vulgar. It is easier to repel the insinuation than to allow the improvement. However well-meant, the change in expression clouds the sense not seldom instead of clearing. What is called the change in conception, while it can in no case have sprung from the baseness of compromise in one of the most fearless of thinkers, is no more than an effort, only partially successful, towards a greater consistency than was possible, or at least was attained, in the first execution of so stupendous a work.

At all events the position in which Kant rested from 1787

was already taken in 1783. Two years after the appearance of the *Kritik*, when it was beginning to draw public notice, but hardly yet had been grasped in its full scope by any readers, while it was grievously misapprehended by some, Kant wrote a short and simpler treatise to bring out the main principles and results of his investigation, without the elaborate system of its supports. The *Prolegomena to any Future Metaphysic*, very serviceable as an introduction to the severity of the method of the *Kritik*, is conceived in the same key as the second edition of the latter.

The *Kritik* contains the systematic exposition of Kant's thought, so widely conceived, so laboriously worked out. When his mind, in full maturity, originated the great purpose, part of it seemed to be achieved as with a spring, but it was by no means so with the whole, and the years as they passed saw him groping about for a path and baffled long before he found one. The traces of the internal struggle, wherever it was severe, are only too apparent in the exposition, though this was far from designed. Kant did not write out his work till he had succeeded in thinking it out—the mere writing out took, it is said, but five months after so many years of mental effort—and the greater difficulty in the exposition at some places represented in his own view only the greater complexity of subject there. For it was a system of philosophical thought fully and equally developed in all its parts, and no mere essay towards a philosophical view, that Kant put forward in the *Kritik of Pure Reason*. Nor was it less a systematic whole, because it did not attempt over again the task of past metaphysical systems—because it even stopped short of the soberer positive doctrine which it held out in prospect as the true substitute for these. 'The inventory of all our possessions through pure Reason, systematically disposed'—such is Kant's own description of his work. A mere inventory, and not the rational possessions themselves; yet withal one systematic and complete.

Reason: it dealt with knowing—the mind's faculty of knowledge; not with Being, as dogmatic metaphysic had done.

Pure Reason: it dealt with knowledge as dependent only on the mind, or with faculty before and apart from all experience; not with the variety of the sources or channels of experience, as Locke's inquiry had done. *Kritik* of Pure Reason: it was an exhaustively reasoned search for the conditions of such knowledge, which, well or ill grounded, could not, Kant held, be denied in fact; not an exercise of dialectical ingenuity, irregularly pursued and bent to mere negation, as Hume's scrutiny had been.

Finding, then, in the result, the general cognitive faculty to be twofold—a faculty of Sense and a faculty of Thought—and that each had fixed and native conditions of exercise, Kant made a corresponding division of his systematic work, and set forth, with full detail of grounds and consequences, the doctrine of Sense and doctrine of Thought thus critically evolved. This doctrine he called Transcendental because treating of the conditions of knowledge prior to experience.

The subsidiary work, the *Prolegomena*, is cast in quite a different mould. It is not so much that it is short and summary where the *Kritik* is elaborate to painfulness, and that in particular it does not exhibit the most characteristic side of Kant—his determination to slur over no difficulties in his path—but rather that it has, by the side of the *Kritik*, the distinctive character of disclosing the route by which he began to work down to that resolution of the problem of knowledge in general which the systematic work gives in full.

As Kant himself technically expresses the difference, the *Prolegomena* proceeds analytically while the *Kritik* is synthetic; and though the resolution in the one case is far from being as exhaustively pursued as is the composition in the other, the insight, nevertheless, given into the working of his mind cannot be too highly valued. The *Prolegomena* shows us the very questions that broke Kant's rest till he found answers for them, and, if it does not give the complete answers as they may be extracted from the *Kritik*, it gives in each case what he is most disposed to lay stress upon.

We have seen what was the school of dogmatic metaphysic in which Kant had his philosophical nurture. Wolff's system of metaphysic began with a general doctrine of pure Being, or Ontology, and then broke up into three parts dealing with the special kinds of being, namely, World or Cosmos, Soul, God. By pure reasoning Wolff sought to determine the character of all these, and there could be nothing but Reason to determine them by. He had indeed his empirical physics and empirical psychology, but these were subordinate to the rational doctrine of World and Soul, more especially as far as concerned their ultimate essence or inner substance, of which there was no experience. Of the World as a harmonious whole of real beings appearing, as far as they appeared to our sense at all, in the guise of external nature, or, again, of the Soul as that permanent substance or force, the spring of all our conscious life, there could be no experience; still less could there be any experience of the Infinite Being, the Being of Beings. Yet into all these supernatural entities and pure Being itself Wolff claimed to have rational insight; nay the more, the farther they were removed above experience.

A fine prospect surely, that philosophic reason should be

able to determine all that was best worth knowing—determine it fully, and (what was of as much account) determine it all from within. Nor could there be any doubt that it was by an unconquerable impulse that the human mind was ever being driven forth beyond its experience to find a realm of the purely intelligible, when system after system of metaphysic had been appearing since the dawn of reflexion. But was it not a strange and suspicious circumstance that system after system as regularly disappeared, even though it were only to appear over again in some new shape; nothing here being fixed, while other sciences were making steady progress? The prospect, however fine, somehow remained prospect always. And now here was Hume, with cool steady hand drawing a veil that shut out all such prospect for ever; nay, as the result of his dialectic, leaving it doubtful whether even on the field of experience any one thing could be brought into fixed and certain connexion with anything else. It was time indeed that metaphysic should be called on to establish its pretensions—to establish them, or failing that, to abandon them. Such was the form in which it first became a question with Kant to inquire into the nature and capabilities of Pure Reason. Metaphysic as dealing with the supernatural, was a creation of Pure Reason: Was such a science possible? The *Prolegomena* is mainly an answer to the question in that form. It is answered by implication and with much more circumstance in the *Kritik* in this other form:—*Is knowledge possible through pure Reason, apart from all or any experience, and transcending experience?*

Whether Hume was right or not as regards knowledge of the supernatural, Kant came in time to be convinced, as he had from the first suspected, that the general question of knowledge was tried upon far too limited an issue by his acute predecessor. In particular was it not a fact that sciences existed, pure in respect of having their origin not in experience and being freely extended without reference to actual experience, yet real in having an indubitable application to the realm of experience? What of Mathematics, the very type of exact knowledge, carried so far by the continuous labour of many generations? And what of that body of laws or principles (in which the law of causation was but one), which men had ready to employ for the interpretation of their natural experience, and which taken altogether formed a general Science of Nature? Related to Metaphysic in respect of their method, so that any settlement of its fate must needs reflect upon them, they had all the character of universal recognition and progressive development so notoriously wanting to it. Why then not judge of its pretensions or claims in the light of their achievements? Let it be discovered how *they* could be what in fact they were, and so it might be clearly seen whether *it* could be what in fact it yet was not. A critical search for their conditions would at the same time show what conditions should be required of it. Therefore the *Prolegomena*, for the sake of the main question, seeks first to answer two others: *How is pure Mathematics possible? How is pure Science of Nature possible?* Both are answered by implication and more exhaustively in the *Kritik* in another form: *How is knowledge possible through pure Reason, which shall hold for experience received by Sense and fashioned by Thought?*

If this makes clear the relation of the two works, it will be possible without misunderstanding to pass from the one to the other, where need is. There remains, however, one mode of statement which not only may be adopted from the point of view of either, but has the advantage of bringing the whole inquiry into the compass of a single question. *How are synthetic judgments a priori possible?* Till the critical question is made to assume this general form, it does not admit of a general solution. The solution in full is to be looked for only in the *Kritik*, or rather the *Kritik* is the solution. But first the statement of the question itself needs some explanation [1].

III. *Mathematical Necessity and Muscular Sense.*

Reverting to the first special question in its most general form: How is the pure science of Mathematics possible? or rather, How is pure geometry possible?—for it is practically to geometry that Kant limits the inquiry—there can be little doubt that it was through this question that he first got beyond Hume, when already by the year 1770 he is seen with his doctrine of space wrought out. It took a much longer time before he was equally sure of having surmounted Hume's doctrine of physical experience. The reason for this was not only because the second question was one more difficult in itself: Hume did not grapple with the first in that portion of his work known to Kant [2]. Neither had Locke done much more to explain the true import of mathematical science, though to attempt it lay still more in his way than in Hume's, bent as he was on giving a positive account of the variety of human knowledge from the ground of experience. Before Kant's time the Rationalists also had failed to

---

[1] The student should here refer to *supra*, Lect. XIII, and study the 'Transcendental Aesthetic' in the *Kritik*.—ED.

[2] Hume's *Inquiry concerning Human Understanding* was translated into German in 1765; the *Treatise* (in which he does deal with the question of mathematical truth) was not translated till 1793. Kant, when he wrote the *Kritik*, knew the former work only.

account for the nature of the science of mathematics. Splendid mathematician as Leibniz was, he did not in his philosophy distinguish between the logical necessity of analytic judgment and the necessity that might be claimed, which he was foremost to claim, for judgments that were really synthetic. Kant just did that, and so put the question as to mathematical truth in train for settlement! It may be said that on all hands before Kant the necessity of geometry was saved at the expense of its character as a real objective science.

The answer of the *Prolegomena* to the question, How can geometry be at once a science of pure intuition and objectively valid? if not in these words, may be thus stated:— Geometry can make universal and necessary determinations, if it makes them concerning that which is not got by way of experience, but is furnished forth from within the mind; and these determinations are objectively valid of sensible things, if sense-experience cannot be had by the mind except under conditions of that which is thus supplied by the mind. Geometry deals with space and is valid for objects as filling space. If space is not got through sense, but is given with the sensibility—is presupposed before sensations—then whatever is determined regarding it is necessarily determined for all that cannot be received except as falling within it.

But this is only half the battle. We are not told how the determination of space is made. Granted that, being made, it is made also necessarily for all that in any case it may enfold, the real difficulty is as to the making of it. Space taken merely as a Form of Sensibility—a sort of indispensable frame within which sensations are received—is something inert and barren, explaining nothing. That the mind should be so constituted as to receive sense-impressions only in a fixed way is one thing: it is another that the mind should be able, as regards this fixed way of receiving, to make all kinds of *a priori* determination of it—to make it the subject of an endless variety of pure intuitions. Or let the difficulty be put thus: Geometry in its intuitive judgments brings together into synthetic unity different aspects of space. Where does the combining power come in?

The *Kritik*, within its wide scope, does not fail to meet and resolve this difficulty. It draws a distinction, which we shall dwell upon more fully at a later stage, between receptivity of sense and spontaneity of knowledge through understanding. The mind is not only liable to be affected, but is capable of acting in the one case, as in the other, in a determinate manner prescribed by its constitution. Its action is what is called thinking, and how Thought must operate to become Knowledge proper may be called the central question in the whole critical inquiry. Geometrical science, being knowledge—knowledge indeed of the most perfect sort—involves thinking or the spontaneous activity of mind; but, as its judgments were said to be intuitive, depending upon no generalised experience—nay, for that matter, upon no experience at all—the mental action takes place in a manner peculiar. What the mind spontaneously brings before itself to be regarded intuitively, for example a line, is something singular, as much singular as in the empirical intuition of sensation. Without having an object actually before the senses it is as if an object were there. That condition, with reference to anything that we have had sensible experience of, is called Representative or Reproductive Imagination. The geometrical figure is also had in Imagination, but not representatively, because there never was any experience of it. The mental act by which it is called into being is an act of Productive Imagination. When we think of a line or circle we draw it in thought by a motion which, says Kant, is an act of pure subject. Drawing it so, we in the very act or fact accomplish a synthesis of the successive stages. Such is the agency through which it comes to pass that within space, as the pure Form of Sensibility, particular determinations can be made and particular conjunctions be established. The space of the geometer, had by pure intuition, is therefore something very different from space as the mere form of Sensibility. Were space not such a form, no pure intuition would be possible, or at least none having any reference or application to sensible objects. But for the pure intuition to take place, constructive action is necessary, and this, according to Kant, is the work of the faculty called Productive Imagination.

Between Kant and modern Experientialism the question as to geometry still remains under dispute. I say geometry, because that is the particular exact science as regards which Kant fully defined his position; but, of course, it is not only geometry that is involved. Modern Experientialism has generalised the inquiry, and has found its profit in so doing. But what is this Experientialism? Under that common banner are ranged inquiries of very different kinds. When Kant, defining the exact character of the pure science of geometry upon the side where its demonstrative certainty had been confounded with mere logical necessity, declared that it could never be explained if its subject were held to be given in or through any experience, he was reckoning only with psychologists like Locke and Berkeley, and with these when they had implied rather than asserted—certainly not when they had ever tried to show—that the science had an experiential origin. Professional mathematicians—except Leibniz, and he rather in his other capacity as a speculative philosopher— had not reflected upon the theory of their practice. But, since the time of Kant, and more or less in the light of his *Criticism*, mathematicians have been forward to probe the secret of their methods and sound the foundations of their science. Logicians also, or general theorists upon Method, have considered the case of mathematics in relation to that of the positive sciences generally. And psychologists, concerned to trace the development of human knowledge, have brought to light sources of experience and determined the character of intellectual processes of special import to the theory of mathematics. As regards the professional mathematicians, I take it to be a mere statement of fact to say that their late researches and their present outlook do not tend to make them rest content with Kant's resolution of his first problem. I refrain, however, from the presumption of offering a lay opinion upon the attitude now taken by the leaders on this line of special inquiry. Neither is the opportunity suitable for resuming and estimating such a general theory of science, inclusive of mathematics, as, in this country, J. S. Mill especially has wrought out from the ground of Experience. But as Kant based his theory of geometry upon a doctrine of Sense—his Transcendental doctrine, devised to explain what he denied was or could be explicable through psychological experience—there is forced upon us the consideration whether psychology can better now than then meet the requirements of the case.

In investigating the conditions of geometry Kant laid stress on the two facts that it dealt with a subject of which there was direct intuition, and that it accomplished its synthesis by actual construction. In both respects he must be held to have judged rightly, and shown great insight beyond his predecessors. The psychology of that day—whether that of Berkeley, which was the most advanced as regards sense-perception, or any that Kant himself wrought out before he entered upon the line of critical inquiry which raised him, as he thought, above the field of psychological research—took no account of any intuition but that of sensation in which the mind remained wholly passive. Hence it became necessary for Kant, as we shall see, to ascribe all mental activity to the faculty of understanding or intellect; and having to provide for the construction of figures *a priori*, he did, as we have already seen, call into play the intellectual faculty working as Productive Imagination.

But modern psychology has shown that empirical intuition is by no means confined to sensation in which the mind's state is to be described, with Kant, as *receptivity*, and in which the bodily organs of sense are also passively affected or acted upon. There is a direct intuitive consciousness when the muscular organs are thrown into action from the brain outwards, and in such circumstances the mental state can only be described as spontaneity or activity. Intellectual action there is as little in this latter as in the former mode of intuition, or, if the view be so taken, it is present as much in the first as in the second.

Why then, for the sake of the construction necessary in geometry, resort to the recondite agency of Productive Imagination? When we think of a line, says Kant, we draw it in thought by a motion which is an act of pure subject. Be it so; but to have intuition of a line we can also draw it, and do first draw it, by a motion which is an act of muscle with a peculiar state of consciousness attached.

Mere empirical intuition this, it will be said, and incapable of being made the ground of judgments holding necessarily and universally. True, it is empirical; but that it is incapable of being made the ground of all that geometry in fact is, is not so clear. It is empirical after a fashion of its own — a fashion very different from that of sensation proper. Sensations, as it were, come or happen to us; are had under certain circumstances over which we may not have the least control, and in the absence of those circumstances are not had. That is the true note of what Experience, in the despised sense of the word, is. How different our experience of muscular activity! We can have it when we like, for as long as we like, as varied as we like; and when we like, we can cease to have it. What more does Kant get from the Productive Imagination in the way of intuition *a priori*?

Then it is an experience which enfolds and circumscribes our experiences of sensation proper. When Kant declares Space to be the Form of all External Sense he says more than the truth; for there are sensations received by some of the external senses without any reference to space; or, at all events, there are among the so-called external sensations great differences in this respect, some being referred altogether away into objects as qualities thereof, others being referred not beyond our own organs, and so forth. But precisely in as far as any sensations have a reference to space, in so far are they subject to modification through muscular movements of which we are conscious; and if they have a definite setting in space, they are sensations which movements of ours may bring on, and which movements of ours may limit.

It is now a psychological commonplace to say that we apprehend objects as spread out in space through conscious movements of our members, and such experience renders account of their extension as much as our sensation renders account of their sensible qualities. We may think away, says Kant, all the sensible qualities of a body, but not extension. If he means its determinate extension of which we had experience by particular conscious muscular movements, the statement is not true: we can think that away as well as the rest. If he means space generally or space altogether, the statement is irrelevant; no Experientialist would pretend to think that away, in thinking away anything belonging to a particular body. Space in general or space altogether, supposing it developed by experience, was assuredly not got with the experience of any particular body.

Upon what varied and protracted experience it may be supposed to be developed, there is no time now to consider. Suffice it only to say or to repeat that the experience is such, in comparison with the experience had through the senses proper, that the difference of result—I mean between the appearance *of* space and appearance *in* space—is not at all surprising. And scientific determinations made of it, though they need not have that absolute character ascribed to them which Kant claims for geometrical propositions, must still be allowed a character of relative generality and priority in comparison with the propositions of physical science.

It is enough if the remarks just made have indicated that Kant's theory of Space and Geometry, however it rose high above any that had been thought out before, is now put on its defence and has a hard task to maintain itself. Yet no theory that may take its place can do so without well regarding all that it involves. Of such importance the part of Kant's critical doctrine which we have now considered can never be robbed.

IV. *On the Nature and Conditions of Intellectual Synthesis.*

WE now come to the most difficult part of Kant's critical doctrine—the part at least that has commonly been found most difficult, and of which even the general import has mostly remained sealed to the English thinkers who have touched it in going about their own business. In the *Kritik* it is the subject of a very long and crooked exposition, enough to daunt the resolution of many who are not weak. Kant himself found it the hardest part of all his task to think out, and was after all so little satisfied with his first exposition of it, that he must needs, at the most important stage, make another attempt in his second edition—an attempt ending in a result which not the most devoted adherent can pronounce a uniform improvement. It is the part of his doctrine where we seem to have most reason to be thankful for having the *Prolegomena* to bring out into relief the points of greatest importance from the surrounding mass of subsidiary argument; and we shall accordingly begin with the questions as there put and answered. But here, even more than before, it is impossible to confine the view to the minor work. Unless resort is had to the *Kritik* itself, the strength of Kant's position, with its elaborate system of defences, must remain unknown. Its weak points also, if we can discover such, must then become more apparent when he is seen wrestling with the difficulties which he was too acute not to apprehend, and too honest to glide over.

The general question as put in the *Prolegomena* is in this form: *How is pure Science of Nature possible?* which, as we must now understand, is the same as asking, How is it possible for the mind to determine anything necessarily about Nature? The mind does so, for example, when it declares that every event must have a cause; also in mathematical physics, or the application of mathematics to nature, the determinations made are necessary. About the fact, in Kant's opinion, there can be no doubt, and we may at once have before us his general answer to the question. Nature could never become the subject of synthetic judgment *a priori* if for our knowledge we were dependent on mere experience that comes to us; in other words, if Nature had an existence quite independent of the mind. It can be known as it is known only if the mind, which so judges *a priori*, itself constitutes or makes Nature.

The strain of this answer is manifestly similar to that of the solution given to the question about pure Geometry. But it is not less clear that the circumstances of the two questions are very different. The mind in making determinations of space by intuition *a priori* is, in Kant's view, in no respect dependent on experience. True, the determinations when made are valid for sensible objects; but this fact, which makes geometry a real objective science and has to be explained, does nothing to impair its purity as regards experience. On the other hand, Nature is the world of Experience—the complex of all the objects of Experience, as Kant himself calls it. How then can the mind make or constitute that which confessedly it has to acquire? Or how can that be experience which the mind, in order to know anything about it *a priori*, must constitute?

Kant meets this difficulty also by a further application of the distinction of Form and Matter before employed to account for *Intuition a priori* of Space and Time. Such intuition was possible because it bore altogether upon the mere form of sensibility, which is innate, to the exclusion of the matter of sensation, which is received or acquired.

In like manner *a priori* determination of experience will be possible, if it bears altogether upon the mere form of experience to the exclusion of its matter. The matter of experience is the variety of phenomena constituted of sensations received in Space and Time, and this matter cannot but be empirically got; but Nature is more than a variety of phenomena. We have just spoken of Nature as a *complex* of objects, meaning that the objects are in fixed relations with one another—are connected—bound up together. Otherwise expressed, Nature is the complex of the objects of experience constituted through or according to fixed laws. Formally, it is the system of laws. These laws in so far as necessary—which is to say, the form of experience—cannot be acquired as matter of experience is. The only alternative is that the form must be innate—that the necessary laws of experience spring from the mind; and that experience, in the full and effective sense that is meant when we speak of Nature, is constituted by the mind imposing laws upon phenomena.

. . . . . .

Now the *Prolegomena* says shortly that judgments of perception or merely subjective associations (e.g. 'when the sun shines on the stone it grows warm') are turned into judgments of experience or objective conjunctions holding necessarily for all (e.g. 'the sun warms the stone') by the addition of concepts having their origin *a priori* in the understanding. This is fully explained only in the *Kritik*[1].

The truly fundamental question at this stage with Kant is as to the nature and conditions of intellectual synthes.s—

---

[1] Read *Transcendental Logic*, first division; especially Book I of *Transcendental Analytic*. Cf supra, Lect XIII.—ED.

at all stages indeed, but more especially now at this. The general problem of the Critical Philosophy, How are synthetic judgments *a priori* possible? showed it to be so everywhere. In the *Prolegomena* the first special inquiry, How is pure mathematics possible? raised a question of synthesis. The second special inquiry, as to Science of Nature, raises it again. In the first part of the *Kritik* (the Transcendental Aesthetic) the question was submerged, only to come forth expressly now. What was the result of the Transcendental Aesthetic? That all sensations are received by the mind in the form of Time, and external sensations farther in the form of Space. In Sense the mind is passively affected, and not less so, because the affection takes place under conditions that are fixed in its nature. There is, in Kant's view, no synthesis in the faculty, or, as we should more properly call it, the capacity, of Sense. Synthesis means activity—Spontaneity as opposed to Receptivity—and in Sense the mind is not active at all. But the mind can act—can combine; manifests another faculty truly to be called such—the faculty, namely, of Thought or Understanding. That faculty also will have its fixed conditions, as the other had. The mind will think in a determinate way, as it was shown to be in a determinate way liable to be sensibly affected, and by reason of its native constitution in the one case as in the other. To discover the *a priori* conditions under which the mind thinks or performs synthesis—that is the second part of the critical task.

. . . . . .

Kant wrought out the theory with infinite pains in revulsion from the scepticism of Hume. The force of all that Hume had urged as to the impossibility of finding outside the mind a ground of order and connexion among things he was constrained to allow; but while Hume was content to rest all upon mere subjective custom—a tendency to imagine upon the strength of past experience—Kant's interest in science of nature, if nothing else, impelled him to find some surer foundation. Nothing besides was more obvious than that Hume, in his dialectical handling of Cause in Nature, was touching but one side of a much greater question—the question of objective knowledge generally; and no less a question than this, in all its aspects, could Kant stop short of raising and trying to settle. The world had never seen the attempt made with such consciousness of its full import before.

It was made by Kant upon assumptions both as to fact and principle that drew a clear line of separation between him and Experientialism, which had spent itself for the time in the scepticism of Hume. But Experientialism girt itself again to the task of positive explanation, and stands now in a very different position from where it stood when Kant sought to take away the very ground from beneath its feet. What is known as the Associationist school in psychology—which connects itself, doubtless, through Hume with Berkeley and Locke, but which made, as it were, a new start after Hume in Hartley and the elder Mill—has expressly aimed in this generation at rendering an account of Objective Experience. And in particular the theory of scientific knowledge of nature, which was Kant's first care, has found among Experientialists in the younger Mill one who made it his chief object of philosophic concern. Mill's *System of Logic* indeed, however different its aspect first and last, does attempt from its own point of view a task corresponding with that of Kant's *Transcendental Logic*. Through Mill the conception of a Real or Material Logic as opposed to one purely Formal, has become familiar to English minds; and a Real or Material Logic is what, from his own principles, Kant gave in his *Transcendental Analytic*. Let this be well understood, that with its own lights, and in the light moreover of advancing science, the present English school has made it its object to give all that satisfaction which Kant failed to find in the thought of the English school before his day, and set himself to supply upon a different line of investigation. With what present success, and yet with what remaining obligation to ponder now, since it did not ponder earlier, Kant's extraordinary work, I have already tried to suggest. I have greatly failed if I have not conveyed such a notion of the reach and profundity of that work as to make the obligation apparent. Quite apart from the validity of Kant's principles or assumptions, there is, in his appreciation of the problems to be grappled with for the explanation of objective knowledge, a depth of insight which later inquirers might have profited, and still have to profit, by.

The side of Kant's doctrine now before us on which it is most open to remark or exception, is where he distinguishes the two faculties of Sense and Thought. Nothing could more cast suspicion upon the distinction—amounting to opposition—as he puts it, than the heroic nature of the effort necessary to bring the two again together. That the two should be brought together was of the very essence of his general doctrine: this we have seen already, and it will still more decisively be seen another time in his criticism of metaphysic as the science of the supernatural, or his criticism of the rational faculty claiming to think without reference to empirical intuition. His determination to bring them together marks him as much off from the Rationalists, as, upon the other side, his manner of distinguishing them separated him from the Experientialists. But what is the result of the effort? An opposition like that between Sense, in which the mind is merely receptive, and Thought, in which the mind is all active, cannot be got rid of by placing Imagination between the two, and declaring that on the one side it partakes of the character of the one, and that on the other side it partakes of the character of the other. Or if it can be so got rid of and there is no contradiction in the union of such characters, then the two extreme faculties have been unwarrantably thrust apart, and there is no occasion for spending so much pains to bring them together. Either way there is something wrong with the theory.

The pure faculty of Imagination, with Kant, does in truth everything for knowledge. Wherever synthesis has to be operated—and knowledge is a synthesis—forth steps the ready-witted agent to do the work, and never in vain. With its two faces—one towards Sense, the other towards Thought— it has the survey of all and acts accordingly. Nor was it in Kant, compared with his predecessors of any school, a small achievement to have thus set knowledge going as from one mainspring. He did set it going. He did not only say:— 'In knowledge there is this and this, as is plainly to be seen,' but he showed how it might come to be, and proceed. It is another question whether he succeeded in finding the truest expression of the process when he called it an act of pure subject. Let me recall what I have said or suggested on a former occasion as to the now extended view of the sources of psychological experience, particularly as to our direct consciousness of muscular movement. That has a bearing upon the development of our physical experience not less than upon that of our apprehension of space and form. We cannot move without having passive sensations along with our consciousness of the movement; we cannot receive passively the sensations that enter into our apprehension of objects without executing actual movements. Is not the beginning of synthesis to be sought here? To justify the answer 'Yes,' a far more elaborate argument is necessary than any experiential psychologist has yet attempted to work out, but it is one for which the psychology of the present time is preparing. When it is made, the attempt will have the better chance of being successful, if Kant's profound explanation of objective experience is at no point ignored.

LECTURE XXIX.

ON KANT'S CRITICAL PHILOSOPHY (*continued*).

V. *The Ideas of Pure Reason.*

THE general result of Kant's *Transcendental Analytic*, so far as it is negative, has been sufficiently caught, and been passed on as a commonplace, in later English philosophy, agreeing, as it practically does, with the result attained in their own way by the English inquirers themselves. But the result of Kant's thought, so far as it is positive—his explanation, namely, of objective experience with the consequences flowing therefrom as to the character of Science of Nature—has been only imperfectly apprehended, for want of the patience requisite to follow the threads of an investigation which the nature of the subject more than any fault of his renders extremely complex. In that positive doctrine of pure knowledge by way of understanding, however, lies Kant's highest claim to philosophical importance.

It is, however, in as far as it is negative that we are now to be concerned about the general result. Let it be remembered that the object of the whole critical inquiry was to test the pretensions of Metaphysic to be a science of the supernatural; or, in the other language employed by Kant, to discover whether by pure Reason anything can be determined regarding that of which there can be no experience.

We have seen how, in Kant's view, there is a wholly pure or rational science of mathematics, applicable to the world of experience; also, to certain lengths, a pure or rational science of nature, which is the realm of ordered experience. What then of metaphysic which professedly deals with all that transcends experience? Can pure Reason determine anything synthetically in that region—speak positively and at the same time with a real meaning there? The mere want of experience would not seem to be a bar against such knowledge of the supernatural. Mathematics, in which Reason proceeds by way of pure intuition, depends upon no experience—is not knowledge of anything given in experience. Yes, but mark the difference. Mathematical science, while it is intuitive, extends only to the form of things, and determines nothing as to their real nature. For the knowledge of that we are dependent upon sensible experience, so that our knowing consists farther only in the interpreting and ordering of this under certain pure concepts which are expressions for the varied functions of the mind's synthetic activity.

Now, unless it is asserted that we have pure intuitive knowledge of things metaphysical—which can only mean that we have the power constructively to generate them, in other words, to create them, as is the case with mathematical figures—and this nobody maintains, it is clear that our knowledge of these also must proceed by way of general thinking or comprehension; and then it does become important whether we have hold of anything to think about. In physical knowledge or common objective experience we have matter for thought in the affections of sense which we receive, and when this is elaborated through the action of understanding the result is knowledge. Is metaphysic in like manner, or in any corresponding manner, knowledge, or is it only mere thinking?

It is, then, with physical knowledge or knowledge of Nature —not mathematics—that Metaphysic must be compared. Physical knowledge is a knowledge of things or objects: but objects of what sort? Let us see, working backwards from the position we have reached. Objects were constituted such in relation to pure self-consciousness—under pure concepts of the understanding—within schemata developed by the pure faculty of imagination; and what were they else, that is to say, previous to being so constituted? A variety of sensations, which are subjective affections, received within the subjective forms of Space and Time. We see that even when the part of intellect or understanding is left out of account, the matter of knowledge is purely subjective—is something which *appears* to the senses—is *Phenomenon*. Knowledge must thus be declared to be of phenomena only. Outside of this subjective circle we cannot get. However, then, we may be able to make universal and necessary determinations about phenomena—and that we can do so is the positive result of Kant's investigation so far—we make them about nothing but phenomena. This is the general result on its negative side. How should we be able to pass outside the circle of sensible appearances? We may, indeed, says Kant, be quite sure that the sensible appearances portend somewhat else; we may have most sufficient reasons for denying that the phenomena are mere illusion and show— Kant, as was said before, vehemently resents the imputation that he could suppose them such; we may—nay, we must— conceive of Things-in-themselves as the real ground of things as they appear to our sensibility, and because they are conceived call them *Noümena* by opposition to *Phenomena*.

It matters not, so far as knowledge of ours is concerned: at least it matters not, so far as any knowledge is concerned that goes beyond mere conviction *that* they are. *What* Things-in-themselves are, we cannot know. We can know them only as they sensibly affect us, and then they are no longer Things-in-themselves. We do, however, know something of what they are not. They are not in Space or Time; for Space and Time are mere subjective forms of our sensibility and contain sensations only. Neither have the Categories any application to them; for the Categories have application through the transcendental scheme only to what is given in Time. Thus the conception of Things-in-themselves is one wholly devoid of positive meaning; and knowledge is confined to that of which there is experience, actual or possible. On the one hand we have sensible experience to be knit up into knowledge through the Categories, and we have no other matter of experience to be knit up. On the other hand the Categories are there as pure forms, empty till there comes matter to fill them—bare functions effecting nothing till sense gives them that upon which they may set to work.

Metaphysic as a general science of the supernatural, of things whereof there can be no experience—general because it employs concepts—is upon that showing impossible.

But, however it may be with metaphysic as a *science* of the supernatural, if there is one thing clearer than another, it is that men will not, and even cannot, rest shut up within the circle of actual or possible experience; they will put out from their island, as Kant calls it, for a land—a very different land—beyond the sea. That region, which they cannot find, they will conceive of as they can, peopling it with thoughts and fancies to stand for objects or real beings there. In other words Metaphysic is a natural and ineradicable tendency of human reason. No conviction as to the limits of knowledge, founded upon such an inquiry as has now been carried through, can avail to prevent it. Nor can any critical inquiry, even when directed to Metaphysic itself, avail to stem it. But direct criticism may, notwithstanding, be of use to expose once for all the true character of the tendency and to call off the mind to other pursuits, this one being seen to be vain. Therefore Kant proceeds to subject to the closest scrutiny the metaphysical dogmas set out by previous thinkers, especially those of Wolff, the most systematic dogmatist of all. In one sense, as has already been more than once observed, this part of the critical doctrine is his crowning labour. Equally, however, may it be urged that such scrutiny is entered on as affording the best test of his positive theory of objective knowledge wrought out before. At one stage in particular this will be seen to be the uppermost thought on Kant's mind—namely, in the famous doctrine of the Antinomies.

In the *Kritik*, the question now presents itself in this shape :—*Is Thought by itself knowledge?* Can we by pure thinking, without reference to matter of intuition, make synthetic determination *a priori?* The part of Transcendental Logic which expounds the elements of pure knowledge by way of thinking, is called by Kant Transcendental Analytic, and is a Logic of Truth. When, without regard to the material element of Intuition, the mere form of Thought is made to give an illusion or show of knowledge, Transcendental Logic becomes what Kant calls *dialectical*. The critical scrutiny of such dialectical illusion is the second part of this Logic, and gets the name of Transcendental Dialectic. It is in the main a critical inquiry into the faculty of Reason, taken in the special sense in which it is opposed to the faculty of Understanding. Both are included under the general faculty of Thought, or intellectual combination through general notions, but they differ as regards the notions they employ [1].

The function of Reason as a natural faculty of mind, has reference to all such knowledge as the Understanding is competent to attain to. The knowledge that we have through Understanding operating on the manifold of sensations is Ordered Experience—a knowledge that is limited every way. The experiences limit or condition one another, and hence the need arises to have them brought to a higher intellectual unity. In the processes of thought as exhibited in Formal Logic Reasoning or Syllogism has the function with reference to bare judgment, that it brings a conditioned under its condition. And in like manner, argues Kant, Reason as a synthetic faculty has laid upon it the obligation of bringing together under the higher conditions, or rather under the highest possible condition, the varied knowledge operated through Understanding. Short of the condition which is itself unconditioned there is no halting-place; for anything less only leaves occasion for the same work of rational interpretation to be repeated. Now, seeing that with everything given as conditioned all its conditions must at the same time be supposed given, Reason is moved to conceive of the whole sum of conditions as unconditioned

---

[1] By 'faculty of Reason' Kant does not mean that which he calls 'Pure Reason' (in the title of his work), and which is his name for the general faculty of knowledge *a priori*. This, in the result, is shown to include a faculty of Pure Intuition, and a faculty of Understanding through pure concepts. It does not include, or it includes only upon an altogether different footing, the faculty specially called Reason in contradistinction to Understanding.

ground that is wanted for ultimate intellectual satisfaction. But in the clear impossibility that there is of mustering and keeping hold in thought such an endless series of conditions, what Reason actually does is to make an object out of its mere notion or idea of the Unconditioned; and then, treating this as if it were an actual object of which we could have experience, Reason would make use of it to give the ultimate theoretic explanation of all that Experience does in fact bring to view. Such, in the most condensed form, is a representation of Kant's view of the function and procedure of the faculty of Reason with regard to human knowledge in general. It may now be understood how the Criticism in detail will consist in the exposure of a tendency which, however natural, gives a mere pretence of real knowledge.

Kant, by a new stroke of subtle refining, seeks to show that just because there are three and only three forms of syllogistic reasoning in pure logic, so the faculty of Reason, in its synthetic operation upon the knowledge got by understanding, develops three pure concepts or—as he prefers, in view of their peculiar nature and use, to call them—Ideas as functions of unity. Commentators have often and justly remarked that this exercise of his subtlety, if open to no other exception, is thrown away. In truth he had Wolff's system of dogmatic Metaphysic before him, and there within the general doctrine of pure Being or Ontology he found wrought out a rational doctrine of Soul or Psychology, of the World or Cosmology, and of God or Theology. Being, with Wolff, was either Matter or Spirit, and Spirit was either finite like the human soul or infinite as God. Then Wolff only set out systematically the subjects that all metaphysicians had been confidently reasoning about; and Kant, for his task of criticism, had here no need of other clue to guide him. Was the question one as to Metaphysic claiming to be a science of all that was most truly real? The World as macrocosm, the Soul as microcosm, and the Deity as ground of both, were by universal acknowledgment the unseen and deeper realities whose nature was to be rationally expressed. Was the question as to the faculty of Reason working to interpret by its Ideas, or from out its Ideas to develop, all lower knowledge related to experience? These and no others in their rational expression were the parent-conceptions of all.

The Rational Psychology of Wolff and other metaphysicians, when it seeks to determine the essential nature of the Soul or thinking principle, and thence to afford the explanation of all mental experience, involves, according to Kant, in every one of its affirmations a Paralogism or Fallacy of Pure Reason. The doctrine asserts (1) that the Soul is a thinking or immaterial *Substance*; (2) that it is a *Simple* Substance, and so not liable to dissolution; (3) that it is a substance always *identical* with itself, in other words, a *Person*; (4) that it has an existence apart from other things, though able to enter into relation with Body. In the case of every one of those assertions the fallacy consists in the Reason making a real thing or entity out of that pure consciousness of self which, for him, was involved in every act of thinking.

Logically regarded, self is the subject to which all thinking is referred, but logical subject is not the same as real substance. So, in thinking, self is undoubtedly to be regarded as simple with reference to the manifold which is bound together; again, as one and the same while the manifold varies; once more, as distinct from all else which comes before it. But, argues Kant, all this proves nothing whatever as to the real nature of the soul. Accordingly all speculations based upon the metaphysical assertions thus shown to be false conclusions from the facts and conditions of phenomenal consciousness have no warrant. Immortality, for example, cannot be established by any effort of Speculative Reason. As little, however, can any assertions running counter to the foregoing be upheld. Materialism in its principles, and in its conclusion against immortality, can by no possibility be proved. As regards immortality upon which interest is here centred, the result of the critical inquiry is that no valid reason of the theoretic sort can be given either for or against it; and as there can be none against it, it is open to be proved upon other grounds.

When Reason, acting upon its general idea of the Unconditioned, proceeds next to interpret the phenomena of Nature or the mind's Objective Experience, it involves itself in difficulties of quite another cast. Taking phenomena on the side of their conditions, and impelled to conceive of these in their totality or completeness, it goes beyond experience and thinks a world or cosmos as a separate whole. The start here is from experience, but in every way the extension made is such that experience can never come up with it. So, under the four heads of Categories through which experience is constituted, absolute determination is made of the world in four ways. It is asserted (1) to have absolute beginning in Time and bounds in Space; (2) to be compounded, in respect of its sensible reality, of parts absolutely simple; (3) to involve causes which act with absolute freedom in no necessary dependence upon one another; (4) to imply the existence of an absolutely necessary Being as either part or cause.

But however cogent be the reasons that are assigned for these assertions from the point of view of pure dogmatism whence they are made, the strange fact presents itself that, from another point of view, precisely opposite assertions can be made and upon grounds of reason not a whit less strong. (1) The world is as to Time and Space infinite; (2) there is nothing simple, but everything without exception is composite; (3) there is no freedom, but everything happens according to natural law; (4) nothing exists that is absolutely necessary.

On the one hand, in the series of conditions, a first is taken as itself unconditioned and made the absolute ground of the series; on the other hand, it is the series itself that is taken as unconditioned. Either course may be justified equally and developed to its consequences.

Such is a brief representation of what Kant calls the Antinomy of Pure Reason, and nothing, he declares, is so much calculated to pull it up in its headlong course of speculative interpretation. Once give Reason way, and it cannot help becoming thus divided against itself. Criticism is the only means of filling up the breach—of composing the strife. To be able so to do is, with Kant, the true test of any philosophical theory of knowledge, and none but his own can withstand it. As thus:—The Antinomies fall into two classes—the first two to be called Mathematical, the other two Dynamical, in the same sense as that in which those terms were used to distinguish the Principles of Pure Understanding. In the Mathematical Antinomies the unconditioned in either form of it is homogeneous with the conditioned which it is set up to explain; thus in the first Antinomy, the world, whether taken as infinite or absolutely bounded in space, is conceived after the fashion of things which we have sensible experience of in space. In the other class of Antinomies the unconditioned and conditioned need not be thus homogeneous; a cause may be of a nature quite different from that of its effect. Now where the unconditioned and conditioned are alike, the two opposed assertions in the Antinomy are contradictory and exclude one another; not one only, however, but both must be held false. For, as we know that it is only phenomena that are in Space and Time, and these pure forms of our sensibility have no application to things in themselves, the world of Reason, which is not the world of Experience, cannot possibly have ascribed to it either infinity or absolute limitation in the one or the other form.

The second Antinomy is to be resolved likewise. Division in space has application only to phenomena of which there is experience, and takes place as there is experience of it: the opposite views err alike in misconceiving the world of sensible experience for a world of things-in-themselves, or in applying to the latter language which has a meaning only in relation to the former. Different is the resolution to be made of the Antinomies of the other class. Here the counter-assertions are verbally opposed, but may both be true in a different application. It is quite possible that all phenomena may be connected with other phenomena as their cause, and so the chain of cause and effect in nature be unbroken, and yet that they should depend on causes working freely in the intelligible world of Noümena or things-in-themselves. So, again, it may well be that there is nothing within the realm of phenomena that is not subject in every way to conditions, and yet there may exist intelligibly an absolutely necessary being—the unconditional ground of all that appears.

Kant's conclusion, then, is that, if not sought within the sphere of phenomena, free agency or freedom of will is possible, also that no argument from experience can exclude the possibility of an absolute being—the supernatural cause of Nature. But he proceeds to show that, when Speculative Reason, planting itself wholly outside of Experience, seeks to determine Being in general, and turns its subjective Ideal of Being brought to highest unity into an objective existence, including all reality and perfection, moreover conceived as a person, the step, regarded from the critical point of view, is wholly inadmissible. As if conscious of the uncertainty of the step, Reason, in the way of Speculative Theology, has sought to justify it by a variety of arguments; and Kant accordingly subjects these, known as the proofs of the existence of Deity, to a scrutiny which remains for ever memorable.

The proofs commonly given are brought to three—(1) the *a priori* or ontological argument, from the very nature of the concept or idea of Deity; (2) the cosmological argument, from the contingent existence of things actual to the existence of a necessary being as their ground; (3) the physico-theological, also called the teleological, argument, from the evidences of design in nature to an intelligent First Cause or Creator.

In the last resort, according to Kant, all depends on the validity of the *a priori* or ontological proof. The argument from Design, however striking and forcible, does not take us beyond Nature, or, even supposing it to do so, cannot prove the supernatural cause to be one and absolute. At least it cannot do this of itself without the help of the second or cosmological argument from contingent to necessary existence; while that in turn labours under the defect that the necessary existence has still to be proved the Being inclusive of all reality and perfection. Does then the conception of a Being as most real and perfect prove the existence thereof? Yes, it is argued, because it would be contradictory to suppose such a Being non-existent, or, again, to suppose a Being most perfect, if the attribute of existence be wanting. But just there, Kant urges, lies the error. Existence is no attribute to be added to or taken from a concept: the content of a notion remains the same, whether reality is ascribed to it or not. Real existence is a synthetic, not an analytic predicate, the ground of which for phenomena is sensible experience received by us. In default of such experience, impossible in the case of a being not phenomenal, thought cannot make the necessary synthesis. The existence can neither be begged nor proved.

The general conclusion, then, to which Kant is brought is that the Ideas of Pure Reason are in no respect principles *constitutive* of a knowledge beyond experience, as the Categories are principles or rules constitutive of experience. Through the Categories objects are constituted or made, and they may be drawn out into synthetic propositions *a priori* valid for all experience. The Ideas, transcending all experience, constitute nothing objectively for want of appropriate matter, such as sense supplies to the Categories; and drawn out into such synthetic propositions *a priori* as make the burden of metaphysical systems, they give a mere pretence of knowledge. Yet are they not, therefore, of no account for our cognition? Applied to experience constituted through the Categories or pure Concepts of Understanding they have a *regulative* function of the highest importance. They are constantly directing that knowledge had through understanding be brought, as far as may be, to unity and system.

They are, then, so many problems to be solved, and not less effective for direction or regulation, because of the insight which criticism gives into the theoretic insolubility. For example, however impotent Speculative Reason may be to establish an absolute First Cause, what more promotive of systematic scientific knowledge than the view that the world is one and the work of a Supreme Reason?

The Kritik of Pure Reason, in disallowing a science of speculative metaphysic, after explaining and justifying the pure science of mathematics and physics, leaves wholly problematical the immortality of the soul, free-will, and the existence of God, to demonstrate which was the metaphysician's highest aim. Often Kant has been understood to demolish all three assertions as pure figments, and it has been charged against him as inconsistency and weakness that he forthwith proceeded upon other grounds to set up again what no one so triumphantly as he had overthrown. But this is altogether to misconceive the man and his work. We see him in his earliest period of speculative confidence concerned above all to affirm and maintain the existence of Deity, and again years after Hume had destroyed his faith in reason at all other points, it still asserts itself in him with regard to this central position of all. By-and-by, indeed, when embarked on his own critical inquiry, he recovers his faith in reason at other points, only to lose it here; but there is sufficient evidence in his work and otherwise that, however the fearless honesty of his intellect drove him to resign what most he had cherished, in his heart he cherished it still. He leaves this question and the others, as I said, problematical; which means, indeed, that the answer is uncertain theoretically, but that an answer is required. And if an answer in the affirmative is uncertain, he takes quite special care to show that a negative answer is theoretically no more certain either. The field is open then for argument other than of the theoretic sort.

It must suffice here to give the merest indication of the way in which Kant was able to attain to the measure of certainty which he found needful. The supernatural shown by the *Kritik of Pure Reason* to be closed against man's speculative insight, is disclosed by a *Kritik of Practical Reason* as the necessary condition of man's moral action. There is in human consciousness a law of duty, categorically imperative: Act so that the maxim of thy will may at all times become a universal law for all. The law is there, but how can man so act? He can because he ought: in having the duty he has the power: he must have the power. Freewill is the first postulate of moral action. Now, of a truth, it is not as man is a natural being having a place in the world of phenomena that he can thus act freely: in the realm of phenomena everything takes place according to a necessary law of causality. But speculative reason was good for this at least that it pointed to a realm of intelligible existence, of which it could be said affirmatively that it did exist and negatively that it was not subject to the law of phenomena in space and time. The *Kritik of Pure Reason* farther solved the third antinomy by showing that it could well be that human actions should be determined in the way of natural causation by phenomenal circumstances, and yet that they should be at every stage determined quite otherwise across from the supernatural sphere in which a law of freedom—of pure self-determination—might reign. What thus theoretically was possible, the fact of Duty turns into necessary assumption. Man must be free as an intelligible being or Noümenon; and it is upon man as Phenomenon that the law of Duty is imposed. Freedom of Will is thus the great postulate of the Practical Reason. But the Practical Reason, besides enjoining a law of Duty, provides also a final end of action in the idea of an unconditioned Supreme Good; and man being a sentient as well as a rational being, Happiness as well as Perfect Virtue or Moral Perfection must be involved therein. Now since there is no necessary conjunction of the two in nature, it must be sought otherwise. It is found in postulating Immortality and God. Immortality is required to render possible the attainment of moral perfection. Virtue from respect for law, with a constant tendency to fall away, is all that is attainable by man in this life. Moral Perfection, or complete accommodation of the Will to the Moral Law, can be attained to only in the course of an infinite progression, which means personal immortality. God must farther be postulated as the ground of the required conjunction of Happiness with Moral Perfection. Happiness is the condition of the rational being in whose whole existence all goes according to wish and will; which is not the condition of man, for in him observance of the Moral Law is not conjoined with any power of disposal over the laws of Nature. But as Practical Reason demands the conjunction, it is to be found only in a Being, the author at once of Nature and of the Moral Law; and this is God.

This part of Kant's doctrine has, as usual with him, its two aspects. There is the denial of any speculative knowledge of the supernatural, and there is—prepared in the *Kritik of Pure Reason* and consummated in the *Kritik of Practical Reason*—the assertion that there are grounds for the strongest practical conviction of it.

It is easy now, as Kant's contemporaries found it easy then, to lay the finger upon the weak place in this two-sided theory. The Noümenon or Thing-in-itself, the unknowable ground of what appears, which notwithstanding from the very first proves to be so far knowable and known that its existence is most positively declared, ends by having much else positively affirmed concerning it. It is namely somewhat in its nature higher and better than the phenomenon; for in man it has the right to impose on his phenomenal being an imperative law of action. It also is a cause with reference to the phenomenon: Kant's whole theory of sense as a receptivity rests upon this basis, and his postulate of human freedom under his solution of the Third Antinomy demands it. But surely here transcendent application is made of a category whose proper sphere of application, in Kant's own view, is experience. It was not to be expected that thinkers should rest in such a conception of the Noümenon as unknowable. Either it had to become fully known and so be got rid of, or it had to be got rid of by being discounted. Speculative Reason had to find a means of surmounting the barriers which Kant had set, or need was that human inquiry should withdraw therefrom and frankly resign itself to the phenomenal. Kant's speculative successors from Fichte to Hegel spent themselves in the former task, and their efforts left little, if anything, to be ever after attempted in that direction. In various ways—by the pursuit of positive science and the resort to psychological inquiry —others have taken the alternative course—a course that from the nature of it is in no danger of being too speedily run.

Kant in his *Kritik* decided for ever—if it had been left, which practically it was not, to be so decided—that verifiable knowledge is confined to the region of phenomenal experience. Practically it was not left to be so decided, for already the positive sciences had advanced too far to be stayed by any philosophic theory. Not the less, however, was such a comprehensive theory as his a great and opportune work in the interest of the sciences themselves. It is not all scientific men that are aware, even as regards their own special science, by what right of tenure it is held; and even superior scientific men have been known, off the line of their own special science, to have curious ideas as to the possibilities of human knowledge, from which a course of the Critical Philosophy, better than anything else, would have saved them. Kant, by his profound analysis of the conditions of knowledge, established once for all in what directions and within what limits it could be had. Nor, because he thought it possible to determine *a priori* the general principles of physical science, were these principles of aught but phenomenal experience. Besides, it was the science of external nature only that he thus made bold to forecast. His Metaphysic of Nature made no profession to cover the field of mind. A pure science of psychology, even as phenomenal, was no part of his projected philosophical system. In his view there could be merely an empirical science of mind. All the more significant is it, then, that in later days those who are least disposed to underrate the importance of his philosophical labours turn to psychology for the means of resolving the difficulties as to human knowledge which his critical inquiry, if it did not succeed in resolving them, must always have the credit of first bringing to light. That philosophy must be based on a science of psychology, involving the best attainable knowledge concerning the growth and development of mental life, remains, after all the thought of the past, the dominant idea in the thought of the present. It is an idea altogether in keeping with the general intellectual tendency of the century. After much thinking about things as they are found, men have learned to look for a truer comprehension of them through an inquiry how they have come to be. We seek now to understand things in the light of their development and such conception as can be had of their origin. It is so in all matters of scientific interest—in things natural, whether animate or inanimate, also in things or institutions that have come into being through human action or effort. Why not also mind—more especially as mind has its evolution, not in the individual only, but also in the race? Yet, though insight may be had in this way not to be had otherwise, there is in such method itself no safeguard against superficiality of treatment. In regard to things not in our power it is easy to fancy that we are working out a continuous representation of their development, when the representation is anything but continuous, and when we have got but little hold of that which has truly to be traced. Therefore must analysis of the actual be never intermitted but carried deep, to make known what it is of which the origin has to be sought. I believe that Kant's critical inquiry into the human faculty of knowledge was an analysis that disclosed elements in it, the import of which has not yet been fully apprehended, and raised questions most real and pressing which yet await their answer from psychology. And I end as I began, by asserting that it greatly concerns the English psychology of the present day to give heed to them.

APPENDIX.

Note to Lecture XVIII, p. 183.

From *Elements of General Psychology*, Lecture II.

Scheme of Fundamental Sciences.

Objective.	Subjective.
[Logic]	
1. Mathematics.	Psychology.
2. Physics.	
3. Chemistry.	
4. Biology.	
5. Psychology.	
6. Sociology.	

$\left[\begin{array}{l}\textit{Regulative doctrines or disciplines (not sciences) dependent upon Psychology.}\end{array}\right\}\begin{array}{l}\textit{Logic.}\\ \textit{Æsthetics.}\\ \textit{Ethics.}\end{array}$

INDEX.

Abelard, 49, 50.
Abstraction, 70, 79, 80.
Academics, 29, 35.
Action, 86 et seq., 144, 194.
Active sense, 171.
Activity, 179, 285, 328.
Adamson, 13.
Altruism, 197.
Æsthetics, a department of philosophy, 2, 181.
Analysis, 21, 207, 216, 240, 357.
Analytic propositions, 127.
Anaxagoras, 31, 33, 218.
Animals, in Cartesianism, 262.
Animism, 173, 218.
Anselm, 49, 50, 252.
Antinomies, 343 et seq.
A posteriori. See Knowledge.
A priori. See Knowledge.
Aquinas, 42, 48–50, 53, 232, 253–278.
Arabian philosophy, 26, 36, 42, 44, 278.
Archimedes, 28, 36, 54.
Aristotle, his so-called 'metaphysic,' 7, 8, 18 ; his influence, 26, 35, 43–46, 48–50, 52 ; on nature, 29 ; his *Categories*, 43, 69 ; works translated, 43, 69 ; his Realism, 47, 72–74 ; as conciliator, 101 ; on cause, 136, 141 ; on common sensibles, 156 ; on Plato, 211 ; his logic, 214 ; his psychology, 214 et seq.

Arnauld, 59, 60, 62, 235, 271.
Art, 186.
Association, 114, 115.
Associationism, 65, 112, 116, 131, 335.
Astronomy, 35, 210.
Atomism, 27, 302.
Augustin, 37 et seq.
Authority and philosophy, 37, 39, 51.

Bacon, Francis, 57, 58, 64, 102, 232, 241.
Bacon, Roger, 50, 54.
Bain, mixes up psychology and philosophy, 2 ; discounts ontology, 8 ; on muscular sense, 67, 133 ; a Nominalist, 79 ; on belief, 86 ; his philosophical position, 117 ; on matter, 169 ; on freewill, 196 ; on heat, 257 ; on neutral feelings, 267.
Belief, philosophical import of, 16 ; psychological analysis of, 86 ; philosophy of, 91 ; *b.* and knowledge, 86 ; complexity of, 89 ; *b.* and opinion, 208.
Berkeley, 23 ; his Experientialism, 64–66; his Nominalism, 78, 79 ; on cause, 140 ; *B.* and Locke, 113, 156 ; theory of matter, 154 et seq. ; *B.* and Descartes, 256.
Body and mind, 177, 255 et seq., 271.

Boethius, 43.
Boyle, 54.
British philosophy, 22, 52, 215, 244.
Brown, 67, 116, 306.
Bruno, 52, 278.
Burnet, 31 *n*.
Butler, 155, 191.

Calvin, 193.
Carlyle, 75.
Cartesianism, 270 et seq.
Cartesians, 56-60, 270 et seq.
Categories, of Aristotle, 43; of the understanding. *See* Understanding.
Causality, 122, 135, 249, 298.
Causation, 135 et seq.
Cause, 100; notion of, 135; in science, 139; in Cartesianism, 141; final, 287, 298; efficient, 290.
Charlemagne, 41.
Chemistry, 21.
Christian philosophy, 24, 25, 37 et seq., 199, 219.
Church, 37 et seq., 261.
Cicero, 35.
Claubergius, 270.
Clerselier, 234.
Cogito ergo sum, 61, 245 et seq.
Cognition, 15, 16, 67.
Coleridge, 101.
Common sense, philosophy of, 63, 118, 122, 165, 226.
Common sensibles, 156, 224.
Communication, 81, 148.
Comte, 6, 18, 141, 149, 209, 305.
Conation, 86, 191.
Concept, import of, 69; variety in 79, 82.
Conception, 67, 68.
Conceptualism, Socratic, 34, 70; mediaeval, 72-84.
Condillac, 67, 82, 206.
Conditioned, principle of the, 122, 138, 195.
Consciousness, circle of, 168, 341.

Conservative faculty, 120.
Consistency, 188.
Constantinople, fall of, 44, 50.
Contiguity, law of, 114.
Continuity. *See* Leibniz.
Co-ordination of sciences, 18-20.
Copernicus, 51, 55, 261.
Cosmology, 27, 32, 33, 345.
Cosmothetic Idealism, 166, 256.
Cousin, 305.
Crescas, 277.
Criterion, of good, 185; of truth, 248 et seq.
Critical philosophy, 57, 63, 124, 244, 304 et seq.
Custom, 114, 335.
Cynics, 30.
Cyrenaics, 30.

Dark ages, 24, 37-42.
Darwin, 148.
Deduction, 93, 238, 242.
Democritus, 27, 28, 30-32, 216.
Descartes, birth, 52, 231; scientific discoverer, 54; founder of modern philosophy, 57, 61, 62; his philosophic position, 61, 102; life, 231; method, 231 et seq.; philosophy, 244 et seq.; his criterion of truth, 248; as dualist, 62, 155, 271; on the self, 248; on substance, 247, 256; as Conceptualist, 257; on space, 258; on the soul, 264.
Destutt de Tracy, 67, 116.
Determinism, 192.
Dialectic, 208, 216, 343.
Ding an sich. *See* Noümenon.
Disbelief, 90.
Discovery, 240.
Discursive faculty, 120.
Doctors of the Church, 37, 41 et seq.
Dogmatism, 280; metaphysical, 56-59.
Doubt, 90.
Dualism, 40, 61, 62, 164, 271.
Duns Scotus, 50.

Index.

Eastern Church, 42.
Ecclesiastical philosophy, 24, 25, 37 et seq.
Eclectic, 35.
Education, in Plato, 209.
Effect, 137.
Effective thought, 24, 42.
Ego, 161. *See* Descartes, Soul.
Elaborative faculty, 120, 137.
Emerson, his aphasia, 80.
Empedocles, 217.
Empiricism, 57.
Ends, 185, 220, 287.
Entelechy, 217, 303.
Epictetus, 30, 35, 40.
Epicureans, 27, 29, 35, 39.
Epicurus, 29, 30, 219.
Epistemology and logic, 4, 13; *e.*, philosophy as, 5, 9, 10 et seq.; *e.* and psychology, 11, 12; beginnings of, 23. *See* Plato, Spinoza.
Erigena, 42, 46, 47.
Error, 254.
Ethical standard, 198.
Ethics, a department of philosophy, 2, 181; as a science, 184; *e.* and psychology, 191; *e.* and politics, 198; *e.* and Christianity, 199; *e.* and theology, 199.
Euclid, 36, 209.
Evolution, 147, 264, 357.
Experience, 58, 94, 148, 285, 311, 339; *e.* and reason, 23, 58, 64, 71, 242.
Experientialism, 58, 112, 138, 145, 152, 315, 326, 335.
Experientialists, 64.

Faculty—psychology, 119.
Faith and philosophy, 38, 40; *f.* and reason, 48–50.
Fatalism, 193.
Fathers, Christian, 41.
Ferrier, 165.
Fichte, 63, 355.
Final cause, 287.
Fischer, Kuno, 56, 251, 271, 277.

Forms of intention, 126, 324 et seq.
Freewill, 136, 192 et seq., 352.
Fröbel, 190.

Galileo, 54, 55, 210, 235.
Galton, F., 81.
Gassendi, 235, 247.
General philosophy, 1, 2.
Generalisation, 68, 137, 143.
Generic images, 80, 81.
Geulincx, 59, 60, 62, 141, 266, 270, 273.
God, idea of, 103, 249 et seq., 345, 350-354.
Good, idea of the, 206.
Greek philosophy, historical sketch of, 24 et seq.; under Scholasticism, 39.
Green, on method, 3, 159.
Grote, 101, 203, 219, 224-229.

Hamilton, confuses psychology and philosophy, 2, 120; his classification of philosophers, 23; his philosophic position, 63, 78; on faculty, 119; on cause, 137; on matter, 163; on freewill, 195; on Aristotle, 225.
Harmony, pre-established, 302.
Hartley, 65, 66, 115, 335.
Harvey, 54.
Hegel, 13, 63, 149, 212, 283, 355.
Heraclitus, 31, 32, 48.
Heredity, 147.
Hipparchus, 35.
Hippocrates, 35, 223.
History, 19; in philosophy and in science, 20, 22; of Western philosophy in outline, 23 et seq.; of psychology, 214.
Hobbes, 57, 64, 78, 232, 235, 247, 257.
Homo mensura, 34, 205, 222.
Hooke, 261.
Hume, his scepticism, 57, 59, 63, 115; his Experientialism, 65, 113; his Nominalism, 78; on associa-

tion, 114; on cause, 114, 137, 140; his theory of matter, 160; and Protagoras, 205; and Kant, 313, 319, 321, 323, 334, 352.

Idea, in Plato, 71; in Descartes, 104; in Hume, 104, 114; in Kant, 128, 162, 339 et seq.
Ideal, 185.
Idealism, 28, 56, 71, 72, 212.
Imagination, 9, 227, 337.
Imitation, 150.
Immaterialism, in Plato, 31; in Berkeley, 157.
Immortality, 352–354.
Import, 15, 22, 66.
Indeterminism, 192.
Individualism, 115, 149.
Induction, 94, 137, 143, 239, 242.
Inductive logic, 189.
Inductive method, 75.
Innate ideas, 99, 103, 250.
Instinct, 103.
Intellection, 2, 15, 67, 75.
Intuition, 103, 237, 327, 340.
Italian nature-philosophers, 52.

James, on belief, 84.
Jesuits, 231, 271.
Jevons, 117, 125, 189, 241.
Jewish philosophy, 36, 59, 219, 278.
Joel, Dr., 277.
Judgments, 127, 138, 255, 333.
Justinian, emperor, 26.

Kant, 9; his division of philosophy, 56; his philosophic position, 58, 63, 67, 124 et seq., 244, 304; influenced by Hume, 59, 65, 321, 323, 334; his theory of space, 129, 324 et seq.; his influence, 63, 65; on experience, 125; his Idealism, 161; his Realism, 162; on self, 162; on proof, 253; on intellectual synthesis, 331; on pure reason, 339; on soul, 346.

Knowledge, its philosophical import, 14, 15, 69, 341; theory of, *see* Epistemology; *kn.* and belief, 16, 86; universality in, 21, 68, 126; nature of, 23, 57, 85; discussed by Plato, 31, 204 et seq; as relative, 33; objectivity of, 97, 116, 154; *a posteriori* and *a priori*, 125, 332; necessity in, 126, 130.
Kritik of Pure Reason, 124, 317.

Lange, 32.
Language and universals, 78–83, 150.
Laura Bridgman, 83.
Law in science, 136; as norm, 182; moral, 354.
Laws, by Plato, 202.
Leibniz, a scientific discoverer, 54; a Cartesian, 59–65; a Rationalist, 107; *L.* and Locke, 108; on Descartes, 246; on necessary truth, 109, 324; on continuity, 260, 300; on substance, 296; on soul, 298.
Lewes, 149.
Leucippus, 31.
Locke, his Experientialism, 57, 64–66, 105; Nominalist and Conceptualist, 78; his influence, 110; *L.* and Berkeley, 113; his doctrine of matter, 155; on space, 259.
Logic, a department of (practical) philosophy, 2, 3, 181; as science, 3, 183; *l.* and epistemology, 4; *l.* and psychology, 186; departments of, 189.
Lucretius, 30, 35.

Mahaffy, 307.
Maimonides, 276.
Malebranche, 59, 60, 62, 142, 262, 266, 271, 274, 276.
Man, the measure of all things, 32 et seq.
Mansel, 82, 144.

Index. 363

Marcus Aurelius Antoninus, 35, 40.
Martineau, 141.
Materialialism, 32, 113, 170, 236, 347.
Mathematics, 209, 232, 283, 322 et seq., 340.
Mechanical philosophy, 27, 31.
Mediaeval philosophy, 24, 37 et seq.
Memory, 227, 263.
Metaphysic, 5, 7, 321 et seq., 339 et seq.
Mill, James, 8, 66, 78, 335.
Mill, John S., confuses psychology and philosophy, 2; rejects ontology, 8; confuses logic and epistemology, 13; his philosophical position, 66, 67, 116; on Realism, 75; a Nominalist, 78; on uniformity of nature, 95; as a logician, 117, 187, 240; on cause, 142; on external world, 172, 335.
Mind, philosophy of, 1; *m.* and world, 22, 27, 28; and body, 177, 271.
Modern philosophy, 53, 56 et seq.
Modern scientific movement, 54, 55.
Modes, 256 et seq., 274, 282.
Monadology, 108, 180, 300.
Monads, 108, 180, 300.
Monism, 274.
Morality, 184, 199, 295.
Morteira, 276.
Motive, 194 et seq.
Muscular sense, 67, 132, 171, 226, 328, 337.

Nature and mind, 8, 27, 28; philosophy of, 51; *n.* and experience, 332; uniformity of, 95, 136; *n.* and God, 274, 289.
Necessity. *See* Knowledge, Organism, Freewill.
Neo-Platonism, 35, 43, 47.
Newton, 54, 67, 260, 299, 308.

Nominalism, extreme, 49, 80; mediaeval, 72-84; in Aristotle, 228.
Nominalists, 64, 150.
Nomology, 3, 122, 182.
Norm, 182.
Noümenon, 162, 341, 355.
Noûs, 33, 101, 208, 217.

Object, 166, 189, 221.
Objective, in philosophy, 250.
Objectivity of knowledge, 97, 116, 154.
Occasionalism, 62, 141, 270.
Ontology, 5, 7, 11, 320.
Opinion, 206.
Organism, as predetermined, 133.
Origen, 39.

Pantheism, 75, 142, 271.
Papal supremacy, 48.
Parallelism, 293.
Paralogism, 161, 346 et seq.
Parmenides, 31, 32, 48.
Parmenides, 202, 204, 211.
Pascal, 54.
Passions, 262 et seq., 294.
Patristic philosophy, 37 et seq.
Pearson, Prof. Karl, 277.
Perception, philosophical aspect of, 4, 14, 70; in Plato, 71; and belief, 93; of external world, 154 et seq., 169; confused, 265, 300.
Peripatetics, 29.
Personality, 173.
Phædo, 204, 210, 213.
Philebus, 202, 204, 211.
Philosophy, psychological basis of, 1, 2. 356; confused with psychology, 2, 16; its meaning and history, 5, 6; *ph.* and conduct, 6, 17, 182; *ph.* and science, 6, 17 et seq., 54, 74-76; aspects of, 10; *ph.* and insight, 17; Greek, 24-36; mediæval, 37-53; modern, 56 et seq.; and mathematics, 283, 322-330.

Phenomenalism, 160, 294.
Phenomenology, 4, 11, 122, 182, 341.
Philolaus, 30, 31.
Physics, 7, 11, 210.
Plato, his use of terms, 5; his influence, 26, 35, 50; his Idealism, 28, 35; his theory of ideas, 34, 99, 210; his Realism, 46, 68-71; on pre-existence, 71, 148; his epistemology, 201 et seq.; his life, 201; his psychology, 205.
Platonism, 73.
Plotinus, 30, 36, 40.
Pollock, Sir F., 274, 277.
Porphyry, 30, 43, 46, 67.
Predestination, 193.
Predisposition, 105, 118, 147.
Pre-existence, 71, 148, 213.
Presentative consciousness, 121.
Pre-Socratics, 31 et seq., 202.
Probability, 88, 237.
Proclus, 30, 40.
Productive Imagination, 326-329.
Prolegomena, Kant's, 317 et seq.
Proof and discovery, 240; of God's existence in Descartes, 250; in Kant, 253.
Protagoras, 31 et seq., 205, 222, 225.
Psychological philosophy, 65.
Psychology, as basis of philosophy, 1, 2; as distinct from philosophy, 2, 16, 182; and from epistemology in particular, 11, 12; history of, 214; rational, 345-346.
Ptolemy, 35.
Pure reason, 125, 317.
Pythagoras, 31.

Qualities, doctrine of, 155, 171, 222, 257.

Rationalism, 58, 59.
Realism, 47 et seq., 56, 70-76, 164.

Reality, 4, 14, 15, 17, 62, 91, 175, 253.
Reason, 22, 49, 58, 64, 68, 122, 162, 311, 340, 344.
Reasoning, 186.
Reflexion, 109.
Regius, 236, 270.
Regulative doctrine, 3, 4, 181 et seq., 351.
Regulative faculty, 120, 137.
Reid, 23, 57, 63, 79, 118, 163, 191.
Relativity of knowledge, 10, 165, 173; in Plato, 205.
Renaissance, 52 et seq.
Reneri, 270.
Representative imagination, 120, 325.
Representationism, 164.
Reproductive faculty, 120.
Republic, 202 et seq.
Res, 77.
Roscellin, 49, 81.
Ruskin, 75.

Sayce, 81 *n*., 83.
Scepticism, 57. *See* Hume.
Schelling, 63.
Scholasticism, 24, 25, 37 et seq., 102, 232, 250, 269, 278; limitations of, 44; the case for, 45; Realism in, 47 et seq.; divisions of, 48.
Schwegler, 56.
Science, and philosophy, 6, 17, 74; history of, 20; modern, 54, 55; *s.* and language, 82, 83; causation in, 139; classification of, 209, 358; of nature, 322, 331, 341.
Scottish school, 63, 78. *See* Common Sense.
Sensationalism, 33, 67, 82, 99.
Sense, in Plato; in Kant, 336. *See* Active, Experience, Muscular.
Shelley, 70.
Sidgwick, 191.
Sight, 92.

Simplicius, 37.
Social factor, 149, 199.
Sociology, 184.
Socrates, 27 et seq., 70, 202, 218.
Solidarity, 149.
Solipsism, 179.
Sophistes, 202.
Sophists, 28 et seq., 222.
Soul, Aristotle's definition of, 173, 215; Plato on the, 221; immortality of, 352–354. *See* Animism, Descartes, Kant, Leibniz.
Space, 126 et seq., 285, 323 et seq., 341 et seq.
Speech. *See* Language.
Spencer, mixes up psychology and philosophy, 2; his philosophical position, 67, 215; on heredity, 148; his Realism, 166; on ethics, 184.
Spinoza, 59–63; life of, 276; on Descartes, 250, 280 et seq.; as Cartesian, 274 et seq.; as Monist, 279; as Occasionalist, 280; his psychology, 293; his epistemology, 294.
Spinozism, 274 et seq.
Standard, ethical, 198.
Stephen, Leslie, 184.
Stewart, Dugald, 63, 79, 118, 306.
Stoics, 29, 34, 35.
Subject, 166, 189, 221.
Subjectivity, 175, 217.
Substance, 61, 62, 73, 175, 250, 280.
Substantialism, 61.
Synthesis, 240, 331 et seq.
Synthetic propositions, 127, 323, 334, 351.

Tabula rasa, 102, 106, 147, 230.
Taine, on the concept, 79.
Teleology, 32, 220, 298.

Telesius, 52.
Tertullian, 39.
Theætetus, 35, 202 et seq.
Thales, 24, 26, 218.
Theodicy, 302.
Theory of Knowledge. *See* Epistemology.
Thought, 120, 186, 336, 343.
Timæus, 43, 202, 212.
Time, 126 et seq., 332, 341.
Touch, 92, 222.
Transition to modern thought, 51–53.
Truth, 187.
Tycho Brahe, 261.

Ultimate inquiry, 4.
Unconditioned, 345, 349.
Understanding, 121, 187, 208, 344; categories of the, 128, 334, 342.
Uniformity of nature, 95.
Universalia, Universals, 23, 47, 56, 68–84.
Universality, in philosophy, 21, 22; in knowledge, 21, 68, 126.

Validity, 15.
Verification, 17, 29, 95, 185.
Voetius, 270.
Voltaire, 67.

Wallace, Edwin, 214 et seq.
Whewell, 307.
Will, 86, 192, 255, 353. *See* Freewill.
William of Ockham, 37, 50, 51, 74.
Wirgman, 306.
Wisdom, 6, 183.
Wolff, 56, 59, 313, 320, 345.
World, as external, 23, 27, 154 et seq.

Zeno, 29, 30.

THE END.

The University Series

A NEW SERIES OF
USEFUL AND IMPORTANT BOOKS

EDITED BY PROFESSOR WM. KNIGHT

CHARLES SCRIBNER'S SONS, Publishers

THIS Series, published by John Murray in England and Charles·Scribner's Sons in America, is designed to supply the need so widely felt of authorized books for study and reference both by students and by the general public.

The aim of these Manuals is to educate rather than to inform. In their preparation, details have been avoided except when they illustrate the working of general laws and the development of principles; while the historical evolution of both the literary and scientific subjects, as well as their philosophical significance, has been kept in view.

The remarkable success which has attended the Series has been largely due to the union of scientific with popular treatment, and of simplicity with thoroughness; qualities that win the general reader everywhere, and that in America make several of the Manuals highly useful as text-books.

OUTLINES OF ENGLISH LITERATURE

By WILLIAM RENTON, Lecturer to the Scottish Universities. 12mo, with Diagrams, $1.00 *net*.

CONTENTS: First Period [600-1600], pages 9-112: I. The Old English Metric and Chronicle [600-1350], *a*. Anglo-Saxon; *b*. Anglo-Norman—II. The Renascence [1350-1500]—III. The Reformation [1550-1600]—IV. The Romantic Drama [1550-1650]. Second Period [1600-1900], pages 132-232—V. The Serious Age [1600-1700]—VI. The Age of Gaiety [1650-1750]—VII. The Sententious Age [1700-1800]—VIII. The Sympathetic Age [1800-1900]—Appendix: Literature of America [1600-1900]—Index: Conspectus of British and American Poetry.

The general arrangement of the book and valuable diagrams showing the division of literature according to ages and characteristics combine to make this manual especially fitted to use in the class-room.

Criticism is supplemented by exposition, with extracts to exhibit the fashion of a period, or the style of a master. The number of authors indicates the importance of a period, and intrinsic power the importance of an author. American literature is considered as a part of the whole, but a brief summary of its history and general characteristics is also given.

THE PHILOSOPHY OF THE BEAUTIFUL

By WILLIAM KNIGHT, Professor of Philosophy in the University of St. Andrews. In two parts. 12mo, each $1.00 *net*.

(Part I. ITS HISTORY.) CONTENTS: Introductory—Prehistoric Origins—Oriental Art and Speculation—The Philosophy of Greece—The Neoplatonists—The Græco-Roman Period—Mediævalism—The Philosophy of Germany—of France—of Italy—of Holland—of Britain—of America.

(Part II. ITS THEORY AND ITS RELATION TO THE ARTS.) CONTENTS: I. Prolegomena—II. The Nature of Beauty—III. The Ideal and the Real—IV. Inadequate or Partial Theories of Beauty—V. Suggestions towards a more Complete Theory of Beauty—VI. Art, Its Nature and Functions—VII. The Correlation of the Arts—VIII. Poetry, *a*. Definitions and Distinctions ; *b*. Theories of Poetry ; *c*. A Suggestion ; *d*. The Origin of Poetry—IX. Music, *a*. Its Nature and Essence ; *b*. The Alliance of Music with Poetry and the other Arts ; *c*. The Origin of Music—X. Architecture—XI. Sculpture—XII. Painting—XIII. Dancing—Appendix A: Russian Aesthetic—Appendix B: Danish Aesthetic.

THE USE AND ABUSE OF MONEY

By Dr. W. CUNNINGHAM, Cambridge. 12mo, $1.00 *net*.

A popular treatise, and the headings, Social Problems, Practical Questions, and Personal Duty, give a broad view of the scope of the book. The subject is Capital in its relation to Social Progress, and personal responsibility enters into the questions raised. The volume contains a syllabus of subjects and a list of books for reference.

THE PHYSIOLOGY OF THE SENSES

By JOHN McKENDRICK, Professor of Physiology in the University of Glasgow, and Dr. SNODGRASS, Physiological Laboratory, Glasgow. 127 Illustrations. 12mo, 340 pages, $1.50 *net*.

The aim of this book is to give an account of the functions of the organs of sense as found in man and the higher animals. Simple experiments are suggested by which any one may test the statements for himself, and the book has been so written as to be readily understood by those who have not made physiology a special study. It will be found a suitable preparation for entering upon the questions that underlie physiological psychology. Excellent illustrations abound.

ENGLISH COLONIZATION AND EMPIRE

By ALFRED CALDECOTT, St. John's College, Cambridge. 12mo, with Maps and Diagrams, $1.00 *net*.

The diffusion of European, and, more particularly, of English, civilization is the subject of this book. The treatment of this great theme covers the origin and the historical, political, economical and ethnological development of the English colonies. There is thus spread before the reader a bird's-eye view of the colonies, great and small, from their origin until the present time, with a summary of the wars and other great events which have occurred in the progress of this colonizing work, and with a careful examination of some of the most important questions, economical, commercial, and political, which now affect the relation of the colonies and the parent nation.

THE JACOBEAN POETS

By EDMUND GOSSE, Hon. M.A., Trinity College, Cambridge. 12mo, $1.00 *net*.

This little volume is an attempt to direct critical attention to all that was notable in English poetry from 1603–1625. It is the first book to concentrate attention on the poetry produced during the reign of James I. Many writers appear here for the first time in a book of this nature. The aim has been to find unfamiliar beauties rather than to reprint for the thousandth time what is already familiar.

THE FINE ARTS

By G. BALDWIN BROWN, Professor of Fine Arts in the University of Edinburgh. 12mo, with Illustrations, $1.00 *net*.

CONTENTS: Part I.— Art as the Expression of Popular Feelings and Ideals:—The Beginnings of Art—The Festival in its Relation to the Form and Spirit of Classical Art—Mediæval Florence and her Painters. Part II.—The Formal Conditions of Artistic Expression:—Some Elements of Effect in the Arts of Form—The Work of Art as Significant—The Work of Art as Beautiful. Part III.—The Arts of Form:—Architectural Beauty in Relation to Construction—The Conventions of Sculpture—Painting Old and New.

YALE ART SCHOOL, NEW HAVEN, CONN.

MESSRS. CHARLES SCRIBNER'S SONS,

Gentlemen:—As a text-book for the study of the "Fine Arts," there is nothing in the literature of the subject that answers the requirements as this little book.

The originality of Professor Brown's work is apparent. Out of a wide familiarity with the classical literature of the subject he has sifted the essential truths. And of the modern writers on æsthetics he knows and digests everything from Winkelmann to Whistler. But what distinguishes this book from others and gives it a special value is the treatment of the "Fine Arts" from their technical side. This is especially evident in his chapter on painting, which contains many suggestions of value to the young artist and amateur.

Respectfully yours, JOHN H. NIEMEYER.

THE LITERATURE OF FRANCE

By H. G. KEENE, Hon. M.A. Oxon. 12mo, $1.00 *net*.

CONTENTS: Introduction—The Age of Infancy (*a.* Birth)—The Age of Infancy (*b.* Growth)—The Age of Adolescence (Sixteenth Century)—The Age of Glory, Part I. Poetry, etc.—The Age of Glory, Part II. Prose—The Age of Reason, Part I.—The Age of Reason, Part II.—The Age of "Nature"—Sources of Modern French Literary Art: Poetry—Sources of Prose Fiction—Appendix—Index.

EDWARD S. JOYNES, *Professor of Modern Languages, South Carolina College.*—"My first impressions are fully confirmed. The book is interesting and able. It would be difficult to compress into equal compass a more satisfactory or suggestive view of so great a subject. As an introductory text for schools and colleges or private readers I have seen nothing so good. The book deserves, and I hope will receive, a wide welcome."

THE REALM OF NATURE

An Outline of Physiography. By HUGH ROBERT MILL, D.Sc. Edin.; Fellow of the Royal Society of Edinburgh; Oxford Lecturer. Maps and 68 Illustrations. 12mo, $1.50 *net*.

CONTENTS: Story of Nature—Substance of Nature—Power of Nature—The Earth a Spinning Ball—The Earth a Planet—The Solar System and Universe—The Atmosphere—Atmospheric Phenomena—Climates—The Hydrosphere—Bed of the Oceans—Crust of the Earth—Action of Water on Land—Record of the Rocks—Continental Area—Life and Living Creatures—Man in Nature—Appendices—Index.

Prof. W. M. DAVIS, *of Harvard.*—"An excellent book, clear, comprehensive, and remarkably accurate. . . . One who reaches a good understanding of the book may regard himself as having made a real advance in his education towards an appreciation of nature."

Prof. JAMES D. DANA, *Yale.*—"Evidently prepared by one who understood his subject."

JOURNAL OF EDUCATION.—"It should not only be read, but owned by every teacher."

THE ELEMENTS OF ETHICS

An Introduction to Moral Philosophy. By J. H. MUIRHEAD, M.A., Royal Holloway College, England. 12mo, $1.00 *net*.

CONTENTS: Book I. The Science of Ethics: Problems of, Can there be a Science of, Scope of the Science—Book II. Moral Judgment: Object of, Standard of, Moral Law—Book III. Theories of the End: As Pleasure, as Self-sacrifice, Evolutionary Hedonism—Book IV. The End as Good: As Common Good, Forms of the Good—Book V. Moral Progress: Standard as Relative, as Progressive, as Ideal—Bibliography.

THE ACADEMY, *London.*—"There is no other introduction which can be recommended."

Prof. J. A. QUARLES, *Washington and Lee University.*—"I am pleased with Muirhead's 'Elements of Ethics.' It seems fresh, bright, thoughtful, stimulating. I shall use it probably next year."

Prof. J. STEARNS, *University of Wisconsin.*—"An admirably clear presentation and criticism of the teachings of the chief schools of thought upon the leading points of ethical theory."

Prof. GEORGE S. FULLERTON, *University of Penn.*—"I find the book very clear, simple, and forcible, and I shall take pleasure in recommending it to my students."

THE STUDY OF ANIMAL LIFE

By J. Arthur Thomson, M.A., F.R.S.E., University of Edinburgh. 12mo, Illustrated, $1.50 *net*.

Contents: Part I. The Everyday Life of Animals. The Wealth of Life—The Webb of Life—The Struggle—Shifts for a Living—Social Life—Domestic Life—Industries. Part II. The Powers of Life. Vitality—The Divided Labors of the Body—Instinct. Part III. The Forms of Animal Life. Elements of Structure—Life History—Past History—The Simplest Animals—Backboneless Animals—Backboned Animals. Part IV. The Evolution of Animal Life. Evidences of Evolution—Evolution Theories—Habits and Surroundings—Heredity. Appendix I. Animal Life and Ours. Appendix II. "Best Books" on Animal Life.

Prof. J. H. Comstock, *Leland Stanford, Junior, University*.—"I have read it with great delight. It is an admirable work, giving a true view of the existing state and tendencies of zoology; and it possesses the rare merit of being an elementary work, written from the standpoint of the most advanced thought, and in a manner to be understood by the beginning student."

THE FRENCH REVOLUTION

By Charles E. Mallet, Balliol College, Oxford. 12mo, $1.00 *net*.

This book has a special value to students and readers who do not own the great works of such writers as De Tocqueville, Taine, Michelet, and Von Sybel. Mr. Mallet presents economic and political aspects of society before the Revolution; attempts to explain why the Revolution came; why the men who made it failed to attain the liberty they so ardently desired, or to found the new order which they hoped to see in France; by what arts and accidents, owing to what deeper causes, an inconspicuous minority gradually grew into a victorious party; how external circumstances kept the revolutionary fever up, and forced the Revolution forward. History offers no problem of more surpassing interest and none more perplexing or obscure.

GREECE IN THE AGE OF PERICLES

By Arthur J. Grant of King's College, Cambridge. 12mo, with Illustrations, $1.25 *net*.

Contents: I. The Essentials of Greek Civilization—II. The Religion of the Greeks—III. Sparta—IV. The Earlier History of Athens—V. The Rivalry of Athens and Sparta—VI. Civil Wars in Greece—VII. The Athenian Democracy—VIII. Pericles: His Policy and his Friends—IX. Society in Greece—X. The Peloponnesian War to the Death of Pericles—XI. The Peloponnesian War—XII. Thought and Art in Athens.

LOGIC, INDUCTIVE AND DEDUCTIVE

By WILLIAM MINTO, M.A., Hon. LL.D., St. Andrews, Late Professor of Logic in the University of Aberdeen. With Diagrams. 385 pages. 12mo, $1.25 *net.*

FROM THE PREFACE.—"*In this little treatise two things are attempted. One of them is to put the study of logical formulæ on a historical basis. The other, which might at first appear inconsistent with this, is to increase the power of Logic as a practical discipline. The main purpose of this practical science, or scientific art, is conceived to be the organization of reason against error, and error in its various kinds is made the basis of the division of the subject. To carry out this practical aim along with the historical one is not hopeless, because throughout its long history Logic has been a practical science; and, as I have tried to show at some length in introductory chapters, has concerned itself at different periods with the risks of error peculiar to each.*"

CHAPTERS IN MODERN BOTANY

By PATRICK GEDDES, Professor of Botany, University College, Dundee. 12mo, Illustrated, $1.25 *net.*

Beginning with some of the strangest forms and processes of the vegetable world [Pitcher Plants], it exhibits these, not merely as a vegetable menagerie, but to give, as speedily and interestingly as may be:

(a) Some general comprehension of the processes and forms of vegetable life, and, from the very first,

(b) Some intelligent grasp of the experimental methods and reasoning employed in their investigation.

Other Insectiverous Plants, with their Movements and Nervous Action, are discussed. The Web of Life, Relations between Plants and Animals, Spring and its Studies, Geographical Distribution, Landscapes, Leaves, etc., form the subject of other chapters, and handled in a way to open the general subject of systematic botany most invitingly.

THE EARTH'S HISTORY

An Introduction to Modern Geology. By R. D. ROBERTS, M.A., Camb., D.Sc. Lond. With colored Maps and Illustrations. 12mo, $1.50 *net.*

A sketch of the methods and the results of geological inquiry to help those who wish to take up the study in its most interesting features. The purpose is to answer such questions as readily suggest themselves to the student, among which may be mentioned the following : What is the nature of the crust movements to which the land-areas and mountain ranges are due? What was the distribution of land and water that obtained in the area when each group of rocks was formed? What was the condition of its surface, and what the forms of life inhabiting it? What were the oceanic conditions; the depths in different parts; the forms of life inhabiting the water; and the nature and extent of the materials brought down by the rivers that poured into the seas from the land-areas of that period?

THE ENGLISH NOVEL

Being a Short Sketch of its History from the Earliest Times to the Appearance of Waverley. By WALTER RALEIGH, Professor of Modern Literature at University College, Liverpool. 12mo, $1.25 *net*.

The book furnishes critical studies of the work of the chief English novelists before Scott, connected by certain general lines of reasoning and speculation on the nature and development of the novel. Most of the material has been given by the author in the form of lectures to his classes, and possesses the merit of being specially prepared for use in the classroom.

HISTORY OF RELIGION

A Sketch of Primitive Religious Beliefs and Practices and of the Original Character of the Great Systems. By ALLAN MENZIES, D.D., Professor of Biblical Criticism in the University of St. Andrews. 12mo, 438 pages, $1.50 *net*.

This book makes no pretence to be a guide to all the mythologies or to all the religious practices which have prevailed in the world. It is intended to aid the student who desires to obtain a general idea of comparative religion by exhibiting the subject as a connected and organic whole, and by indicating the leading points of view from which each of the great systems may be best understood.

LATIN LITERATURE

By J. W. MACKAIL. Sometime Fellow of Balliol College, Oxford. 12mo, 286 pages, $1.25 *net*.

Prof. TRACY PECK, *Yale University*.—"I know not where to find in such a convenient compass so clear a statement of the peculiar qualities of Rome's Literature, and such sympathetic and defensible judgment in the chief authors."

SHAKSPERE AND HIS PREDECESSORS

By FREDERICK S. BOAS. Formerly Exhibitioner at Balliol College, Oxford. 12mo, $1.50 *net*.

Shakspere's writings are treated in this work in their approximate chronological order. The relation of the writings to their sources, their technique and general import, and their points of contact with the literature of their own and earlier times, engage the author's attention. The Rise of the English Drama is clearly sketched, while Shakspere's kinship to his predecessors is given much greater prominence than is usual.

CHARLES SCRIBNER'S SONS

153–157 FIFTH AVENUE - - NEW YORK CITY